THE WOMEN LINCOLN LOVED

Mary Todd at Twenty

A painting from her first daguerreotype, by her niece, Katharine Helm.

The
WOMEN
☆ LINCOLN ☆
LOVED

By

WILLIAM E. BARTON

Author of

THE LIFE OF ABRAHAM LINCOLN

☆

Illustrated

☆

INDIANAPOLIS

THE BOBBS-MERRILL COMPANY

PUBLISHERS

In Memory of
The Woman I Loved

CONTENTS

CONTENTS—*Continued*

LIST OF ILLUSTRATIONS

LIST OF ILLUSTRATIONS—*Continued*

INTRODUCTION

Lord Byron is authority for the affirmation that—

> "Man's love is of man's life a thing apart;
> 'Tis woman's whole existence."

Byron had liberal opportunity to learn about the love of women, and experience enough of his own to discover something of the nature of love as men display it. The distinction which he makes is valid; his dictum is more than a half truth. But women are not motivated exclusively by the urge of sex, and no normal man passes through life without some experience of attraction or repulsion, or both, growing out of the love of women. Holy monks like Savonarola and Saint Anthony would have been foremost in admitting the influence of women in shaping their character, and there were and possibly are other monks, as for instance, Fra Lippo Lippi.

If any man lived, moved and had his being in a world of men, that man was Abraham Lincoln. His active life was spent principally in the court-room, the law-office, the tavern, the corner grocery and on the stump. The motives that mainly determined his choices were legal and political, and they were definitely masculine. Yet even to him love was not a thing apart. It was a rather constant factor in his development. His love affairs have been told mainly as if they had been detached incidents, leaves of superficial emotion that dropped without any special reason and floated on the surface of his life, neither floods that were part of its deeper current nor cargoes that registered anything of depth or displacement. If an exception has been acknowledged, it has usually been freighted with the ballast of imagination.

The present book proceeds on a different assumption, and as the author hopes, on knowledge more secure. It undertakes to sketch somewhat connectedly the life of Abraham Lincoln against the background of the women who were making an important part of his world in successive periods of his development from the cradle to the grave.

This book undertakes to be a contribution to history. While some of the more important dates appear in the narrative, it has appeared best not to load the pages unduly with them, but to append a Chronology which will keep in order the principal incidents recorded. For more detailed account of the life-story of the hero of this series of adventures, reference may be had to the author's *Life of Abraham Lincoln,* in two volumes.

The author has interviewed the nearest living relatives of the women mentioned in these pages, and thanks them sincerely. Among libraries he acknowledges his debt to the Library of Congress, whose courtesies are many and unfailing, the Huntington Library of San Gabriel, California, where he obtained important manuscripts, the John Hay Library of Brown University, Providence, the Library of the Chicago Historical Society and the State Historical Libraries of Virginia, Kentucky, Indiana and

Massachusetts. He must record his special gratitude to Miss Georgia L. Osborne, Librarian of the Illinois State Historical Society at Springfield, Illinois. Large, too, are his obligations to the Bureau of the Census at Washington, whose labors on his behalf have assisted in solving some of the most perplexing of his problems.

Among individual friends who have assisted him he holds in special gratitude the Misses Mary and Martha Stephenson, of Harrodsburg, Kentucky; Honorable William H. Townsend, of Lexington, Kentucky; Reverend Louis A. Warren, of Zionsville, Indiana; the late Honorable Albert J. Beveridge, of Indianapolis; Mr. Oliver R. Barrett and Mr. Carl Sandburg, of Chicago; Honorable North Todd Gentry, of Columbia, Missouri; Mr. Paul M. Angle, Secretary of the Lincoln Centennial Association of Springfield, Illinois, and Mr. E. Carter Delano, of Warsaw, Virginia.

Portions of this book have appeared in *The Ladies' Home Journal*, *The Dearborn Independent*, *Liberty* and the New York *Times*. The courtesy of the editors is acknowledged in permission to use the material in book form.

Not only in English, but in many, if not all languages, ancient as well as modern, the verb "to love" is one of the most elastic of all words. In this book it is employed to cover all degrees of interest which Abraham Lincoln, as boy and man, showed in particular women. If the list is not complete, it is as least comprehensive, and is truthfully representative.

The human race is so constituted that no individual stands complete. The division of humanity into two sexes is the most interesting and important fact in the social life of the globe. We can never understand in full the personality of Abraham Lincoln till we know in what manner his life was influenced by girls and women. That is what this book undertakes to relate.

W. E. B.

The Lincoln Room,
Pine Knoll, on Sunset Lake,
  Foxboro, Massachusetts.

THE WOMEN LINCOLN LOVED

The Women Lincoln Loved

CHAPTER I

LUCY HANKS

I. A NEIGHBOR OF THE WASHINGTONS

WHEN Lucy Hanks was ten years old she learned that
there had been a battle at Bunker Hill. Where Bunker
Hill was, she had very little idea, but all the strangers
who rode through North Farnham Parish brought news
and rumors concerning it, or asked if any further tidings
had been received about the battle. There had been two
earlier and smaller fights at Lexington and Concord, but
those had not seemed so significant. Still earlier there
had been a fight in North Carolina on Almanace Creek,
but Bunker Hill seemed more important to the older
people who talked about it in her hearing than any of
these.

A little later she learned that Colonel George Washington had been chosen commander-in-chief of an army
that was to fight the King and drive the British soldiers
out of the colonies. She understood better about George
Washington, for she had heard about him all her life. He
was born only thirty-three years earlier than herself, on
Bridges' Creek, near her own birthplace, which was on

1

the Indian Town Branch in North Farnham Parish. She had seen the Washington house very often; it was rather a low square house with two large stone chimneys. George Washington's father and mother moved from there to Fredericksburg while he was a little boy, but the birthplace still remained in the Washington family. George's older brother, Lawrence, having returned after completing his education in England, married and made his home there. George, having had some rudimentary lessons from a Fredericksburg sexton named Hobbey, came back to his birthplace in his early teens and studied under Reverend Mr. Williams, learning arithmetic and surveying, besides much that his brother taught him. Fredericksburg itself was only sixty miles away, and Bridges' Creek, where the Washingtons lived, was only a third that distance.

George Washington's mother, Mary Ball, lived not quite so far in the other direction. Her people still owned and occupied the old Ball homestead, which, for that matter, is standing at this day. In the lower half of the Northern Neck were four parishes: North Farnham, St. Mary's or the "Old White Chapel," Christ Church and Lunenburg. Most of the time the same minister served all four, conducting service one Sunday a month at each. The Balls belonged to St. Mary's, but successive generations of the Balls and of the Hankses were baptized by the same clergymen. Indeed, the same minister may have baptized George Washington and Lucy's father.

Lucy could remember having seen the gay young soldier, George Washington, and his mother, on one or more visits which they made to their relatives in the old Ball home. They had to pass through North Farnham Parish on their way from Fredericksburg or from Bridges' Creek.

George Washington had been a famous man since his fight with the French and Indians at Fort Duquesne. People said he was a greater general than Braddock who commanded the British and who was killed in that battle. True, there were some jealous people who said that George Washington would never have amounted to very much but for the favor of Lord Fairfax in the beginning and his marriage to the rich Widow Custis afterward. Yet, if prophets are without honor in their own country, successful military leaders were not held in low esteem in Virginia when Lucy Hanks was a girl. There were other soldierly leaders in the neighborhood: the Lee family had several men who aspired to martial honor, and even Patrick Henry had some ambition to fight. There were other men near by besides George Washington who were of a military temper, but Washington had been chosen commander-in-chief, and nearly everybody said there would be a war and a short one and that Washington would sweep out the Redcoats as once he had swept the Indians. This was the kind of talk that Lucy Hanks heard when she was ten years old.

Lucy Hanks was the eldest daughter in a large family of children. She had five brothers and three sisters. Her father was Joseph Hanks, who was born December 20, 1725. Her mother's name was Ann. While all the nine children were presumably baptized in the North Farnham or one of the adjacent parishes, the records are so fragmentary that at this date we have recovered only one; Elizabeth or "Betty," daughter of Joseph and Ann Hanks, was baptized March 4, 1771, and was six years younger than Lucy.

Joseph Hanks's father, whose name was John, died

when Joseph was between fourteen and fifteen years of age. His widow's name was Catherine. The County Court was in considerable distress over the prospect of her suffering want through the care of so large a family. Her husband had died while still a comparatively young man. He was under age on July 7, 1708, when, his own father, William, having died, John Hanks chose his older brother, the younger William, as his own guardian; but John at that time must have been quite a sturdy lad, for he himself was married about June, 1714, so he was born between 1687 and 1693. These dates are rather uninspiring, but they are our chief data for some of the essential facts concerning Lucy's family.

The County Court, on August 4, 1740, ordered that the sheriff summon to the next court Catherine Hanks "to show cause why her children should not be bound out by the church wardens as the law directs." Apparently she did not come into court; presumably she was able to satisfy the justices and the church wardens that she was competent to take care of her own children. This she did until they were of age. She was still living when George Washington took command of the armies, and could remember well the wars with the Indians when she was young.

Tidewater Virginia is made up of a series of three peninsulas formed by the inflow into Chesapeake Bay of four tidal rivers. The first settlements were on the southernmost of these rivers, then called the Charles but now the York. The next river was the James, and the first of the peninsulas settled was that between the York and the James. The next peninsula was that bounded on the south by the James and on the north by the Rappahannock. The third, called the Northern Neck, was bounded on the one side by the Rappahannock and on the other by the Potomac. The general course of all these streams was southeasterly.

The Northern Neck was at that time the most isolated of the three main sections of Virginia; even at this day it has no railroad. It is now reached by taking rail to Fredericksburg and traveling thence by wheeled vehicle; or access is had by ferry, from Tappahannock midway down the neck, and at certain other points. On this rather narrow strip of land, with the tidal waters of the Potomac on the northeast and those of the Rappahannock on the southeast, lived the Washingtons, the Lees, the Mountjoys, the Fontleroys, the Carters, the Balls, the Tayloes and other noted families. There, too, from before 1653 down to the present date the Hankses have had a home. For some of the family still reside there.

While the Hankses in Lucy's day were, as Abraham Lincoln said, "a second or undistinguished family," they were a reputable family, and the people whom they married were of good average social standing.

For the most part, the Revolutionary War did not come very near to Lucy and her home. Her brothers were not old enough to be soldiers and her father was too old. There was much talk of the war, however.

In 1781 the British were still holding New York, and Washington's attempt to dislodge them had ended in a series of defeats. Benedict Arnold was ravaging the coast of Connecticut and burning New London. The Colonial troops were both ravenous and rebellious. There had been mutterings before; there was actual mutiny now. The Colonial cause was in desperate straits. Washington learned in what situation the army of Cornwallis was, and also learned that the French Government was sending Count DeGrasse with a heavy fleet to the coast of Virginia. The fighting which DeGrasse was to do in Virginia was preliminary to what, for the French, seemed a more important undertaking in the relations between France and Spain. DeGrasse had fifty-two ships of the line, some of them with three and even four gun-decks, the largest armada of the period and quite the superior of the British fleet. Washington determined to join forces with Lafayette and crush the army of Cornwallis. Before Lord Clinton missed him from New York, Washington and his little army were far on their way toward Virginia.

Events happened rapidly. The British fleet was outnumbered and overpowered by the French ships, and Washington and Lafayette together completely hemmed in Cornwallis at the tip of the York peninsula. Cornwallis sent desperate appeals to Clinton for reinforcements, but the help that was sent arrived too late. On the nineteenth of October, 1781, Lord Cornwallis surrendered his entire army to the joint Colonial and French forces.

All this is a familiar page, torn out of American history, and reciting events that all intelligent readers are supposed to know, or at least to have known when they were in grammar school. What has all this to do with Lucy Hanks? It has much to do with Lucy Hanks, and Lucy Hanks has much to do with the subsequent history of the United States.

For the most part, we must reconstruct the girlhood of Lucy Hanks from our knowledge of the conditions under which she lived and the extremely meager but highly important data of fragmentary records. But one thing we know,—which is that she learned to read and write.

It was with difficulty that the most prosperous families in Virginia in that period educated their sons. Governor Berkeley had ample support when he publicly and officially thanked God that Virginia had no free schools and printing presses. The sons of such families as the Lees, and the older brothers of George Washington, were sent to England for their schooling. A majority of the young men whom Lucy Hanks knew could not sign their names, and few of her girl friends could read. The mother of George Washington could read and write a little, but not much, and she was exceptional. But Lucy Hanks could read and write, and she was the only member of her family who could do so. Of men who signed deeds, and these were the landed proprietors, only about forty per cent. could write their names; the others signed with a cross. Landless tenants were almost all illiterate, and nearly all women made their mark in signing early Virginia deeds.

What impelled Lucy to undertake this task of learning to read and write? What made her desire to gain education above that of her family? Who was her teacher? How we wish we knew the answers to these questions! We do not know, and it is idle to conjecture. But in some way she felt a superiority to her environment, an inward urge toward self-improvement, and a determination to know more than most young women of her acquaintance knew. She learned to read, and she wrote, not the cramped hand of the nearly illiterate, but like most of the Hankses who could write at all, she wrote with freedom and a flourish.

The surrender of Cornwallis drew to Williamsburg and

Yorktown great throngs of patriotic and curious people
from all that section of Virginia. We do not know that
Lucy Hanks went thither, but it is far from being impossible. It was a day's easy ride, and there were friends
along the way. It is not at all impossible that one or more
companies of young people from North Farnham Parish,
more or less adequately chaperoned, made use of the
pleasant autumn weather for a ride to the scene of the
surrender. Those who made this journey saw the Colonial
militia and the French soldiers in the one camp, and the
loosely guarded British, already fraternizing with the
Colonial troops whom many of the invaders had had no
heart in fighting. Not a few of the British were eagerly
inquiring about possible homes in the Colonies, and saying
that they would rather marry some pretty American girl
and live here than go back to England. Washington was
treating the captured Cornwallis with almost royal festivity, and was commending to the Colonial soldiers the
most considerate treatment of their prisoners, and the
soldiers were in the mood to obey.

If Lucy Hanks was, indeed, among the many Virginia
girls who at that time made the ride to the scene of the
surrender, she might possibly have met in some local celebration a young soldier named Henry Sparrow. He was
from Mecklenburg County, but his ancestors had lived
near Tidewater, and he possibly had relatives near Yorktown. Henry and Lucy were not so far apart as to have
made a meeting impossible or even improbable. They
were later to exercise an important influence upon each
other's lives.

When Cornwallis and his generals had been paroled
and had sailed to New York and thence to England, and

the captured British troops had been marched far inland
to Winchester or to Pennsylvania, and the French fleet,
after its timely but disappointingly brief aid, had sailed
away on other quests, the tidewater counties of Virginia
gave themselves up to a winter of gaiety such as they had
never known. Washington and Lafayette did not remain
long to share in the festivity, but while they were there,
they had their full part in it.

But after the principal actors in the drama had left the
stage, the curtain did not ring down on festivity. The
Colonial army, and those companies of the French troops
who remained, went into winter quarters. No fighting
was in prospect before spring. Discipline was easy. Leave
of absence was cheerfully granted and had generous limits. The soldiers scattered, some to their homes and others
to friends who lived nearer.

The corn crop had been gathered. The seven water
mills between Warsaw and Kilmarnock were busy grind-
ing portions of it, and there were at least seven stills
making use of generous portions of the grist. The soldier
boys came home, and brought other boys with them.
There was plenty to eat and more than enough to drink.
There were dances and games all winter long. There was
horse-racing and cock-fighting and not a little courting.
The girls of eastern Virginia had never seen so merry a
season. There were balls at Sabine Hall and at Mount
Airy, with Light Horse Harry Lee and his friends in uniform home on leave, and there were less brilliant but no
less jubilant affairs in less pretentious homes.

There still was such a thing as social distinction, both
as between officers and privates, and between the first
families and those of humbler lineage; but the war had

been a leveler, and Lucy Hanks may have attended balls
in homes where she had previously been a stranger, and
under the escort of young military men of some repute.
While the Hankses were certainly not of the aristocrats,
neither were they disreputable. Lucy was under no social
ban in that winter of gaiety. She was sweet sixteen,
plump, ruddy and vivacious, with a healthy and attractive
flush in her dark cheek. We are not at liberty to suppose
she lacked partners in the sports of that season.

Furthermore, there was at the close of the Revolution
a period of uncensored living. They had no jazz, but they
had the spirit that in a later generation was to express
itself in jazz. The war would have produced this result
even had there been no foreign influence; but the presence of so many French troops was not without its effect
on the thought and conduct of the young Virginians who
served with them. It was a period of infidelity in religion,
and of laxity in morals. The French Revolution was getting under way, and was not without its marked influence
in the life of the Colonies.

All organized church work suffered during the Revolution. No churches were affected more than those of
the Church of England. Most of the rectors were Loyal-
ists, and there was not only the religious indifference
which depressed all religious societies, but in the case of
the Episcopal churches, there was positive hostility.
Bishop Meade in his notable work has left a pathetic picture of the state of the churches in the Northern Neck
at the close of the war. He calls it "deplorable" and the
term seems to be properly applied.

One tradition we must not overlook, which is that after
the surrender, Washington and Lafayette attended a serv-

ice in Christ Church, the southernmost of the Northern Neck parishes. This may or may not be true, but it is not impossible. Washington's journal is fragmentary in the days following the surrender of Cornwallis, and tells practically nothing of his personal movements. The burden of his record was his effort to persuade DeGrasse to continue the use of his fleet in the Colonial cause, and his disappointment at that officer's aloofness, delay and ultimate refusal.

Washington ordered services of thanksgiving on the first Sunday, the second day following the capitulation, and that day he would almost certainly have spent in Yorktown or Williamsburg. There were two more Sundays before he left Yorktown, and there is no improbability in the tradition that he and Lafayette crossed over to Christ Church. He knew that church very well. There his mother had attended a school maintained by Robert Carter, the famous "King Carter." There he might expect to meet his friends, the Carters of Sabine Hall and the Tayloes of Mount Airy, and others whom he had not now time to visit. After November seventh there is a long gap in his diary. On that day he set out for Eltham, where John Parke Custis lay dying with camp fever contracted while in service as Washington's aide-de-camp. It is possible that on one of the two intervening Sundays, Washington, accompanied by Lafayette, crossed over and attended service in the old brick cruciform church. If so, we may be sure Lucy Hanks saw them—both those Generals. Lafayette had a habit of kissing every pretty girl who was introduced to him, and the girls so kissed showed the spot on their cheeks to their granddaughters many years afterward. Did Lucy Hanks tell her grandchildren that she had such an experience when she was a girl of sixteen? Probably not. That was an innocent enough adventure, but there were matters about which she did not talk freely.

If we knew the whole story of that winter, we might have some light which we now lack on the development of the character of Lucy Hanks. Perhaps it was then that for the first time her beauty lifted her above her social rank and gave her new and dangerous companionships.

Perhaps then for the first time she heard the challenge of the dogmas and repressions of her childhood faith. Perhaps it was then that she heard pleasant flattery joined to seductive suggestion. There is no rumor of misconduct on her part so long as she lived in that part of Virginia, and no reason to believe that she was at this time other than a virtuous young woman; but that this was a period of peril for many girls in that neighborhood is beyond question. It may be that that winter, if we knew its whole story, contained a part of the explanation of some things that occurred afterward. Perhaps her parents were disturbed by her frequent parties, late hours and boisterous associates. Let us hope and believe that for her that winter was one of innocent gaiety, in which she emerged from girlhood into womanhood, happy and radiant, admired and popular, and unconscious of the perils that were thick about her. With the coming of spring a new experience was in store for her.

2. THE PICTURESQUE POTOMAC

"The Right Honorable Thomas Lord Fairfax in that part of Great Britain known as Scotland, proprietor of

Patent of Land on Patterson's Creek with the Seal and Autograph of Lord Fairfax

Old Farnham Church

Court-House at Warsaw, Virginia

Record Office in Warsaw

Photographs by the Author

the Northern Neck" had inherited through his mother from Lord Culpeper enormous tracts of land lying between the Potomac and Rappahannock Rivers, and extending westward to a boundary to be drawn between the head waters of those two streams. Had he been happily married he might have been content to remain in Great Britain and let factors and agents look after his domain, but he loved a lassie who promised to marry him, and who then found and embraced an opportunity to marry a man with a higher title and a fortune more ready at hand. So he crossed to Virginia to heal his heart and see his lands. He never lacked for women to love, but he never married. He loved them and left them. He had a cousin in Virginia, William Fairfax by name, and William had a daughter who married Lawrence Washington. Lawrence was visited by his younger brother, George, at that time a tall, awkward and very love-sick youth.

Lord Fairfax took a great liking to George Washington, and when the latter was only sixteen years of age his Lordship employed this athletic, love-lorn fox hunter, with his own relative, George William Fairfax, and sent them across the Blue Ridge to survey certain of the lands which Lord Fairfax had inherited from Lord Culpeper. That was much better for Washington than pining over the girls who had refused him.

For three successive summers, beginning in 1748, George Washington and his associates lived in the open, surveying this vast domain. Portions of it were divided into enormous tracts called "manors." One of these, embracing many thousands of acres, has a special interest for us. It was known as the Patterson Creek Manor.

"The Right Honorable Thomas Lord Fairfax of Cam-

eron, in that part of Great Britain called Scotland, proprietor of the Northern Neck," was not without his share
of the canny frugality of that nation which gave him his
title. He planned to sell this land at a microscopic price,
two and one-half cents per acre, and in tracts each sufficient for a homestead, but to require thereafter in perpetuity the payment to him or his heirs or assigns a small
annual rental on the feast of St. Michael the archangel.
He computed the income he was to derive from this
source; it was to yield him and his heirs and assigns forever an annual payment of one hundred and fifty thousand dollars. That probably would have made him the
richest man in all the Colonies.

But Thomas Jefferson was laboring in the Virginia
legislature seeking to break up the habit of entailing land,
and demanding that deeds be given in perpetuity. This
proposal seriously hampered the plan of Lord Fairfax,
though many of his earlier patents, if not all of them,
were given in this form. Thomas Jefferson was also hard
at work on a bill providing for religious freedom, and the
success of that measure was to bring into Virginia a very
considerable new element. These Pennsylvania folk of
German descent were Christian people indeed within the
meaning of King Charles, whose patent declared this land
to be for Christian folk, and they certainly were not red
Indians, but they were not members of the Church of
England.

Still one other thing happened which Lord Fairfax had
not taken into account. That was the Revolutionary War.
Lord Fairfax was a quiet but determined Loyalist. He
was an old man and inoffensive, and he retained the
friendship of George Washington and other men who were

ardently fighting for independence. But when he died, his great estates were confiscated because he was a Tory. Not one acre of all the Fairfax land remained in the Fairfax family under the original title, and all the lands that had been entailed became the property in fee simple of those persons to whom they had been ceded under the Fairfax patents.

When Lord Cornwallis surrendered, Lord Fairfax lay down and died at the good old age of ninety. It was just as well he died when he did, for had he lived, his would have been the bitter experience of plunder and ineffective protest.

But Lord Fairfax was generous with George Washington. That young man received a daily stipend for his work ranging from about eight dollars to twelve dollars and fifty cents. Abraham Lincoln, a century later, was glad if a day's surveying yielded him three dollars. Furthermore, to George Washington and his brothers Lord Fairfax sold great tracts of land on very favorable terms. George Washington, quite apart from the land he acquired by his marriage to Martha Curtis, had thirty-five thousand acres of land in Virginia alone, and considerable areas outside that state. Nearly all this Virginia land had once been the property of Lord Thomas Fairfax.

Little did George Washington suppose when he was setting his compass on the western side of the Blue Ridge, and dragging his chain from the shore of Patterson's Creek across one of its smaller tributaries, that he was measuring one side of a farm where some years later was to be born the mother of another surveyor, who would be named Abraham Lincoln. After this land had passed from the Hanks family, and there was occasion to describe a

portion of it in a suit for division to secure dower rights
for the widow of a later owner, the recorded line began
"where Mike's Run of Patterson's Creek crosses the rode"
and thence continued "in a strate line to the Washington
line." It is interesting to find this reference to George
Washington's survey in one of the earlier records of the
farm where was born the mother of Abraham Lincoln.

The death of Lucy's grandmother, Catherine, widow of
John Hanks, was the signal for a breaking up of the
Hanks family. She died some time in January, 1779, and,
her eldest son William being dead, Joseph, the second son,
Lucy's father, became administrator of his mother's estate. The death of Grandmother Hanks may have been
the occasion of genuine sorrow, but she was a very old
woman, who had been a widow for thirty-nine years, and
there was no occasion for crushing grief. Moreover, her
death meant some improvement in the fortunes of her
children.

It took a long time to settle the estate. The final papers
were not presented and recorded until 1782. We have the
inventory, and we know that each of her children received
goods and chattels that made up a fairly good list. But
before the final papers had been filed, Joseph Hanks had
taken such portion of his mother's property as in equity
he might possess, and made a preliminary journey up the
Potomac River. This was some time in 1781, and the next
spring he moved his family. He came back and filed his
final accounts, but his home was already established, far
up the Potomac, on Patterson's Creek. On this journey
the family trod in the footsteps of George Washington,
who from 1748 till the French and Indian War had several times made this pilgrimage.

The Hankses became an extremely migratory family, but it is said that in England they stuck very closely to their ancestral home near Malmsbury, and certainly in the first generations in Virginia they were not rolling stones. They appear to have been clannish and to have held closely to the old home on Indian Town Branch in North Farnham Parish. That parish was successively in several different counties, which is one reason among others why records are not easy to find; but from before 1653 till after the Revolution the family was located in the southern half of the Northern Neck. For five generations before Lucy Hanks, her people had lived not very far from the spot where she was born. The earlier generations, as shown in the distribution of property after the decease of a parent, were not very large. The family became more prolific about the period of the Revolution.

We can conjecture with some degree of probable accuracy the route they traveled. It was hemmed in between the Rappahannock and the Potomac, and they had no occasion to cross either river, but in time they followed the Potomac. They moved northeasterly past the birthplace of George Washington at Bridges' Creek, and left Fredericksburg, where his mother was living, a few miles to the south. They may not have followed the windings of the Potomac River all the way, and if so they may have cut across the big bend, on whose shore was George Washington's home at Mount Vernon. If they did not go within sight of that establishment they were not far from it. Traveling, as they doubtless did, some of the family on horseback, and the younger and less rugged ones in a wagon drawn by oxen, and having their live stock with them, they probably did not journey more than fifteen miles a day in the springtime when the roads at best were not very good and there were frequent and heavy rains.

The valley of the Potomac grew more picturesque as they ascended. The hills were higher and stepped in nearer to the river on either side. The foliage was changing rapidly as their journey advanced. The southern end of the Northern Neck abounded in evergreens. There was wide diversity of pine and there were several varieties of mountain laurel which they called "the ivory plant." There was great wealth of trailing vines that kept their green all winter, and much of the red berried holly. The travelers observed somewhat less of this type of verdure as they ascended the river, but the blossoms and leaves were coming out, and the spring smiled on their daily journey even if the clouds sometimes dropped rain upon them and the road.

As they approached somewhat nearer to their destination, they came to the mouth of the Shenandoah, where it enters into the Potomac, and were ferried across the smaller stream by a young man named Robert Harper. He had a legal title to one hundred and twenty-five acres of land at the confluence of the Potomac and Shenandoah. Lord Fairfax granted him his patent, and the land remained in the Harper family until 1796, when it was bought by that discriminating judge of real estate values, George Washington.

It was probably a very primitive boat in which the Hankses were set across the Shenandoah. Lucy, nearly seventeen years old, must have looked with admiration on the varied beauty of that scene. Three states now corner there, Maryland, Virginia and West Virginia. Of this she knew nothing except that the Potomac divided Virginia from Maryland. Not till the Civil War did the western portion of Virginia become the separate state of West Virginia. Whatever emotions stirred her soul, she had no conception of how that spot was to influence the career of one of her descendants. It did not enter her thought that one day a man named John Brown would do incredible things at Harper's Ferry and be hanged for them, that hundreds and thousands of men would come in answer to her grandson's call, singing as they came, "John Brown's body lies a-mouldering in the grave, but his soul goes marching on."

There is, of course, no record of the details of this journey, but it can not have been an easy one for the oldest daughter of the Hanks family. She had to share her mother's responsibility for the younger children, and the days were weary and the nights broken. Wild beasts were in the forest close at hand, and the horses and live stock were a daily care. She had left behind her all the memories of her ancestral home on the Indian Town Branch in North Farnham Parish. All her girlhood friends, both men and maidens, were there. The wilderness they penetrated had grown daily more mysterious and ominous. Whatever enthusiasm her father and her brothers had about cheap land in a region more fertile than the tobacco-cropped farms at home, she can have found little to kindle her enthusiasm in the dreariness of her dark task or the solitude of her outlook.

Beyond Harper's Ferry, and the mouth of the Shenandoah, the South Fork flowed into the main channel of the Potomac. This stream, also, the Hankses must have ferried across. They passed the sawed-off ends of other

mountain ranges, and then came to where the valley of
the Potomac widened in an attractive half-moon. This
was the valley of Patterson's Creek. Here they built their
camp-fire, assured that two more nights would bring them
to their new home. They turned abruptly to the left and
moved up Patterson's Creek. The valley smiled its springtime welcome. It promised fertile soil and an attractive
home. The lower end of the stream was already possessed by occupants, some of whom had had Lord Fairfax's patents for a number of years. The Hankses had to
move farther up to the land which had remained in his
lordship's possession till 1779.

Their last day's march began and ended. The wild
honeysuckle was abloom. The rhododendrons made the
banks of smaller streams glorious with their wax-like
blossoms. Here and there the wild crab-apple scattered
its fragrance and drew the bees from afar. Beside the
rutted roadway where the wheels jolted over roots and
boulders, bluets, cranebills, lady-slippers and wild violets
grew in profusion. It was a scene of intoxicating beauty.

They forded Patterson's Creek about twelve or fifteen
miles from its mouth, and then crossed the little stream
that came in from the right. This had the unpoetic name
of "Mike's Run." They turned to the right, and ascended
to where this stream forked, and near a spring they found
the shack, whatever it may have been, which Joseph
Hanks on his earlier visit had erected as a rude shelter
preparatory to their coming. That night the Hankses
may be presumed to have slept under the roof of their
own rude home above the forks of Mike's Run of Patterson's Creek.

Lucy and her mother saw the last tired Hanks child **to**

bed, and Lucy perhaps stood for a few weary minutes in the door and looked out. The valley was beautiful, the blossoms were abundant and fragrant. Perhaps she saw on a near-by hillside, in the lingering twilight, a tree that burned its brilliant spot into the landscape—the red-bud or as some call it, the Judas tree. That was the tree, according to tradition, on which Judas hanged himself, and ever since that day it blushed to shame every spring-time. Could Lucy Hanks have seen anything ominous in its guilty blush?

3. ROSE AND THORN

The Hanks family established their home on Mike's Run of Patterson Creek in the spring of 1782 and re-mained a little less than two years. They arrived in time for the enumeration of inhabitants which was made that year. The list was incorporated in 1790 into the first official census of the United States. The family of Joseph Hanks, as reported in 1782, consisted of eleven persons, all white. There was not anywhere in the thirteen colo-nies, so far as that census discloses, another Joseph Hanks with a family that anywhere nearly duplicated this. At that time there were but thirty-two families in a very considerable district between the mountains west of South Fork and the main stream of the Potomac where flowing northerly it made its great bend toward the east. Of these thirty-two families in the Patterson Creek area only four owned slaves, and the total number of slaves was eight. It was a primitive region with most of the homes newly established, and these by immigrants without very much money.

Not every settler had waited for a patent from Lord Fairfax. Claims were established on what were known as "tomahawk rights." A few trees, gashed with a hatchet to mark a corner, designated a claim that usually was respected. We know, however, by what right Joseph Hanks acquired his land. It came first by patent from the Right Honorable Thomas Lord Fairfax to George Terry under date of February 6, 1779, and there were several subsequent grants of land to the Terry family. George Terry sold a contract for a tract of one hundred and eight acres to a Pennsylvania German named Peter Hartmann, who, however, found a farm he liked better and assigned his contract bond to Joseph Hanks. This was the Hanks title, and it gave Joseph undisputed possession with assurance of a good deed to come as soon as he completed his payments.

These Pennsylvania Germans were honest thrifty people, and most, if not all, were religious. They went at their work with a stolid patience which was in striking contrast with the easy-going habits of the native Virginians. They planted spacious orchards and had generous woodpiles. Ere long they were sitting under their own vines and peach trees, placidly smoking their long pipes. They practised a more varied crop culture than the Virginians, and built excellent stacks of hay, wheat and oats. They were not so restless as the Virginians, and did not move so often, but built permanent houses and better barns, and begat sons and daughters and proceeded to occupy the land.

The Buttmann family appear to have been the nearest neighbors of the Hankses. An interesting instance of Americanization is disclosed in the evolution of Peter

Buttmann's surname. He was able to write his name, and if his children had done the same the form of the name might have remained unchanged. His two capital letters "P" and "B" were elaborated with painstaking curves, but the small letters were written in a firm, slow, careful, perpendicular hand. But he doubtless pronounced his "B" like "P," and people called him Putman. His son Peter, when he had occasion later to sign his name, did not make a criss-cross mark, but used a capital "P" which answered for the initial of both names. There were four successive generations of Peters in that family; the first was Peter Buttmann, and the second was Peter Putman, which was also the name of the third. But by the time of the fourth Peter, the name had evolved into Putnam. By this time, Peter Buttmann's descendants may be seeking admission to membership among the Daughters of the American Revolution as lineal descendants of Israel Putnam of the Wolf Den and of Bunker Hill.

It is not likely the Hankses and Buttmanns had very much in common, nor have we reason to suppose that any of the near neighbors made up to Lucy for the friends she had left behind. The valley was attractive, the holly berries were red and the mistletoe was white in winter, and spring brought the wild honeysuckle and the dogwood and the ivory flower and the blossoms on the tulip tree and the fateful red-bud. But no change of season brought to her compensation for her severed friendships in North Farnham Parish.

Then there came to her a friend, or one whom she counted to be such. He can hardly have been one of the nearer neighbors. Presumably he rode from the South Fork Valley through the gap which Mill Creek made when it sawed the mountain in twain. What business brought him to Patterson's Creek we do not know, but the distance was not great, nor was the ride a hard one. He was a young planter of good family, and he met Lucy, and then came again. We know not on what pretext he came and continued to come—whether the sale of seed grain or the purchase of tobacco gave him excuse or whether he came without any excuse at all—but he came.

We can not help wondering if he was interested in the fact that this attractive girl, nearly eighteen years of age, could read, and whether he brought her books or otherwise encouraged her education. If so the case was not an isolated one; all the way from Eve to Heloise the woman has seen the fruit of the tree of knowledge as something to be desired to make one wise, and the teacher has become the tempter.

Perhaps he told her stories of earlier days in that region, for he was quite possibly of the second generation that had inhabited the South Fork Valley. He could tell of Indian fights, and of the time when they built houses out of walnut logs two feet in thickness and mitered them into one another with no chinking and so provided for better protection against the bullets of the savages.

Perhaps Lucy's lover told her the thrilling story of Jacob Kuykendall and Barbara Decker. They were married and lived for a brief and happy time together in the South Fork Valley, but he was carried away by Indians, and Barbara thought him dead. In due time came James Colvin who married her. When Jacob Kuykendall came back he found what Enoch Arden found on his return. His wife was married, and she had children by her marriage to James Colvin.

Jacob Kuykendall faced that situation like a brave man. There was no statute law that provided for just such a condition, nor did the English Common Law, as applied in the American colonies, provide means whereby one man might deed his wife to another; but Jacob Kuykendall entered upon the Deed Book of the County Court of Hampshire a quit-claim to his wife Barbara. In that strange document he certified that whereas his wife Barbara, formerly Barbara Decker, had intermarried with James Colvin, he, the said Jacob Kuykendall, did freely acquit and discharge the said James and Barbara from all trouble and damage by reason of their intermarriage, and did consent that they might cohabit and dwell together as husband and wife without interference from him, the said Jacob Kuykendall.

Now, the face of Barbara had been before Jacob in all the years of his life in Canada among the Indians, and the lure of it and the hope of having it pressed against his bronzed cheek had brought him back to the South Fork of the Potomac. But he performed the act of a brave man, and gave her freely to the man she had married in good faith, and who had become the father of her children. Jacob Kuykendall went back with the Indians. He married an Indian princess, so the story runs, and his blood flowed, and presumably still flows, in the veins of a race of blue-eyed Indians of great ability and phenomenal courage. For him is named a town in Wisconsin, Waukesha.

These were the stories that Lucy Hanks heard in her brief sojourn on Mike's Run, and it is more than possible that she heard them from the man she thought of as her lover.

The eastern rivers of Virginia bore either Indian names

or names of the royal family, but what shall we say of Patterson's Creek, and especially of Mike's Run? A more plebeian name could scarcely have been imagined, yet the stream itself is not unattractive, and it is the scene of Lucy Hanks's fateful romance. She did not know the poetry of Robert Burns, but this was her "Bonnie Doon." Of it she might have sung:

Oft ha'e I roved by bonnie Doon
　To see the rose and the woodbine twine,
An ilka bird sang o' its luve
　And fondly sae did I o' mine.

Wi' lightsome heart I pu'd a rose
　That grew upon its thorny tree,
But my fause lover stole my rose,
　But, ah! he left the thorn wi' me!

When Lucy knew that she had been betrayed; that she had loved not wisely but too well; when the time came that the ugly truth could no longer be concealed, and her lover refused to stand by her, and left her to bear the burden and pain and disgrace alone, did she repent in sackcloth, or did she become stubborn and defiant? When the virtuous children of the stolid neighbors yelled their spiteful taunts at Lucy's younger brothers and sisters, and the children came home and upbraided her, did she bear it in meekness, or did she give back hot and unwise answers, and say that she hated this place, and that it served her parents right that she should thus have disgraced them for having brought her thither?

It is so easy to ask questions which it is impossible to answer. But one thing we know, and that is that the man

The men stand on the site of the Hanks cabin

View of the valley from the cabin

The Valley of Mike's Run

Photographs by the Author

The Henry Sparrow House

Graves of Rev. Henry and Ailsy Sparrow   New Liberty Church

Photographs by the Author

who betrayed Lucy Hanks, and failed to make good the
vows he made to her, however much of success he attained
in life, and however much he profited socially and financially by any other possible marriage, lost his one chance
of immortality. We might be able, if we knew who he
was, to say of him with respect that he gave such and such
fine qualities to the complex personality of his grandson
Abraham Lincoln. Fine qualities Lucy's lover almost certainly had, and Lincoln was probably not in error in
thinking that he inherited some of them; but the man who
refused to give his name to the girl he betrayed obliter-
ated that same name from all possibility of fame that
otherwise would have opened to it.

There is no accurate record of the date of birth of Lucy
Hanks's baby. It occurred in the winter, either at the end
of 1783 or the very beginning of 1784. She was a little
girl. Lucy named her Nancy. Her other name had to be
Hanks, for her father did not claim her, and Lucy did not
prosecute him, and thus cause his identity to become a
matter of court record.

Of course everybody knew about it. The only good
thing about that was that there were not more of them to
know. Lucy could go nowhere without being conscious
that she was observed and talked about. The neighboring
Hausfraus withheld their greeting when she met them, and
solemnly warned their own daughters to beware of her sad
end. Against her tongues wagged; at her were pointed
accusing fingers. And Lucy held her head high, as we may
not doubt, and was called a brazen hussy and an impenitent strumpet, and when she got home she burst into passionate and self-accusing tears.

Doubtless she said and did all the rash and foolish

things which other girls have said and done in like case.
Doubtless she walked beside Patterson's Creek and
looked down into its deeper pools and said she would
drown herself and her baby, and cease to suffer the insults
of her neighbors and the reproaches of her own kindred.
And equally without doubt there were hours when she
hugged her little Nancy with maternal ecstasy, and said
they might talk all they liked, hers was the dearest baby
a mother ever had, and she was glad she had her.

What kind of talk there was about it in the Hanks home
we may only conjecture. Ann Hanks probably was as
unwise as many other mothers have been. Probably she
chided Lucy with reminders that Lucy had always chafed
under restraint, and had behaved shockingly during the
last winter of the family sojourn in the old home. Probably she said that this was the first, the very first time,
that such a thing had ever happened in the family, and
Lucy was the very first even of the Hanks girls, to say
nothing about those of her mother's family, to whom such
a thing had ever been possible. And now to think that a
daughter of her own should have brought them this disgrace. Most of us who have been called in counsel in
matters of this character could supply the dialogue without great strain upon the imagination.

And Lucy flashed hot answers, saying that she was not
a bad girl, and never had been. She had always loved life
and society and fun, but she never had been bad, and
even in this matter she had not deliberately sinned, but
had trusted the man she loved, and trusted him too far.
She was every bit and grain as good as the Dutch girls,
horrid things, any one of whom would have given their
eyes for the slightest attention from so fine a gentleman,

but who were so hideously ugly in their bovine unattractiveness, no one but a blind man or a stolid Pennsylvania Dutchman would ever look twice at them.

She said such things, probably; they are part of the vocabulary of young women under such conditions. And then, at times, she sat silent under all reproach and taunting, and was declared obstinate and impenitent. Perhaps she still took pains to look as well as she might when she went out, reflecting that after all, she was the best-looking girl in the neighborhood. And if so, then older women said she was a proud hussy, and a very wicked girl.

And then, at times, she broke down, and said to her mother that she was the very worst and wickedest girl who had ever lived, and that she hated herself and wished she was dead; and she would be good, good, good, and would never do such a thing again, never, never, never. But how she wished her parents would take her away somewhere out of this terrible place.

That argument, at least, had weight with all the family. The farm was satisfactory, and the valley was attractive and fertile, but the neighborhood had become intolerable. The Hanks family began to prepare to move.

To move would require money, and the Hankses had none. Moreover they must sell the farm, and that for ready cash. No new settler came just at that time, but Peter Buttmann was a man who might entertain hospitably the suggestion of adding a farm on Mike's Run to his larger fertile acreage. Peter was a man who kept a little money on hand to help a neighbor when he had to sell a piece of property at a very low price.

Joseph Hanks approached Peter, and Peter smoked his pipe and thoughtfully considered the matter. He agreed

at length to loan to Joseph a small sum and take a mortgage on Joseph's farm. He shrewdly guessed that there
would be no redemption of the land, and he set the time
limit at six months. What earlier and larger sums were
discussed we do not know, but the deal was closed on the
basis of a cash payment of twenty-one pounds, nine shillings, Virginia money. It was a pitiful sum. The Lincolns sold their Shenandoah Valley farm for five thousand
pounds. To be sure, Virginia currency was not quite so
badly depreciated in 1784 as in 1780, but by any possible
reckoning twenty-one pounds nine shillings of Colonial
script was a paltry price. But it was all that Peter would
pay, and the situation of the Hanks family was desperate.

The Hankses were not crowded out; the neighborhood
was still sparsely settled. There had been no flood or
famine, no pestilence in the neighborhood. No explanation is on record, and no explanation is needed, to account
for the sudden surrender of the Hanks holdings and the
removal of the family just when their farm was beginning
to be a home. The mute and unexplained mortgage is
eloquent of domestic tragedy. On November 9, 1784,
Peter foreclosed. The Hanks family had been gone six
months. The mortgage was dated March 9, 1784.

It must have been a sorrowful procession that departed
from Mike's Run in the early spring of 1784. The older
boys rode horseback, and Polly and Betsy may have ridden double on one horse. The boys herded the hogs and
cattle, and drove them ahead. Thomas and Joshua and
William were all old enough to share in this responsibility.
Charles and Joseph and Nancy, the youngest child of
Joseph and Ann, presumably rode in the wagon drawn by
oxen. In that wagon were the household goods, the skil-

lets and pots, the spinning-wheels and the loom and few
chairs and the bedding, the axes and tools. Joseph and
the boys carried the rifles and provided game along the
way. They had little occasion to look out for Indians,
but the fear of redskins was long in dying out in the heart
of the pioneer. In the wagon were Grandmother Ann
Hanks, Lucy and her baby Nancy with no other surname
than Hanks.

They headed up-stream though a country increasingly
mountainous, and over roads increasingly bad, till they
crossed over and reached the main road from the Shenandoah Valley to Cumberland Gap. Then the roads were
better and they had company along the way. But it was
a much longer, harder journey than that of two years before.

Spring had come again. The tulip-trees were bearing
high their floral crowns. The mountain laurel, with its
delicate blossoms justified the name of "ivory" by which
the Hankses called it. The wild honeysuckle perfumed
the air. The wild crab-apple blossoms brought the forest
bees from near and far. Squirrels scampered through the
woods and up the trees as the cavalcade wound its way
through the forest. The robins were building their nests.
The bluebirds, those belligerent optimists, were building
and chattering and fighting other birds. Here and there
the oriole hung his nest to a swinging limb and showed
his gay breast to the procession. At intervals the cardinal
cut a path of flame across the road as he flew through the
woods. And red as the breast of the cardinal bloomed the
Judas-tree in the sight of Lucy Hanks. It was springtime
everywhere except in her heart.

The weary procession jolted over roots, and the wagon

wheels sank deep in muddy ruts as the Hanks family
made their way from Mike's Run of Patterson's Creek
along the Wilderness Road through Cumberland Gap to
the new home in Kentucky. And Lucy, weary of body
and sick at heart, yet with something in her that was still
unconquered and that enabled her to hold her head rather
disgracefully high, clutched to her plump bosom her little
Nancy to whom a father's name had been denied, her own,
and hers only, Lucy Hanks's baby, Nancy Hanks, who
was to become the mother of a president.

4. LUCY FINDS A HOME

The Rolling Fork of Salt River flows near the base of
Muldraugh's Hill, that high escarpment which separates
the mountain country of Kentucky from the fertile blue-
grass region. On the side toward the blue-grass, but still
in a rough and heavily wooded section, Joseph Hanks and
his family made their new home in the spring of 1784. It
was not a very good farm and was held by a precarious
title. It was part of an entry of a thousand acres made
by Joseph Barnett, October 3, 1783, and it passed to John
Lee, who on February 28, 1787, made a contract to sell
one hundred and fifty acres of it to Joseph Hanks "as
soon as deed can be obtained from Joseph Barnett." Apparently the Hanks family had been living on the land by
verbal contract for three years prior to this legal agreement.

All the hard conditions of pioneer life which the family
had experienced on Patterson's Creek were repeated in
this new home beside the Rolling Fork. Some kind of
house had to be erected to shelter a large family, and Jo-

seph and his sons had to work hard to clear a little patch of the wilderness and plant the crops on which the family depended.

Inside the house was the daily round of preparing three meals, with milking, churning, washing and baking. Lucy had to bear her full share in this labor along with her younger sisters, and besides, she had the care of her baby Nancy.

We may not know what struggles she had in the wilderness of Kentucky. We do know that whatever hope she and her parents cherished that she would now be free from temptation proved futile. After a time she broke away from all restraint, and either left her father's house or found the door closed against her. Leaving her little girl with her parents and sisters, she departed from her father's home, and when we next hear of her, she is in the adjoining county of Mercer and not behaving any too well.

Ann McGinty was one of the most useful women in the history of early Kentucky. She came to Fort Harrod, later Harrodstown and now Harrodsburg, the oldest town in the state, being a few months older even than Boonesborough. A woman of active mind and forceful character, she set herself to invent a way of spinning and weaving cloth in a country where as yet sheep could not be kept on account of wolves, and cotton was not grown. She devised a method of spinning thread from buffalo wool and nettle lint, and all the women of Harrodstown and the region round about came to her to learn how to do it. Few women have served a community better than Ann McGinty, and she deserves all the honor which posterity has accorded her.

If, added to these responsibilities, Ann McGinty took

on a supererogatory burden of responsibility for public
morals, she is not to be unduly chided for that. All the
women came to her for instruction in spinning and weaving, and she heard all the gossip and knew who were the
offenders against good manners and sound morals. Moreover, she had the courage of her convictions. If any woman was leading a dissolute life, or had given birth to an
illegitimate child, and other people failed of their duty,
Ann McGinty rose to the emergency. Fornication was
then an indictable offense. Bastardy was not simply a
trespass for which the father could be sued, but a misde-
meanor for which the mother could be indicted. Several
young women, already suffering heavy burdens and harsh
judgment, were indicted by the Court of Quarter Sessions
"on information of Ann McGinty." We do not know that
it was she who told the Grand Jury about Lucy Hanks.
No name appears on record. Perhaps Ann requested that
her own name as informant be suppressed by reason of her
desire not to gain too great merit as the virtuous custodian
of the community's morals.

The courts of Kentucky in those days did not lack for
business. The township had no place in the political organization either of Virginia or Kentucky. The County
Court did almost everything, and court days brought large
numbers of people to the county-seat for business and social purposes, as well as to attend the sessions of the court,
but the criminal docket was usually not a long one. The
work of the Grand Jury was generally light, and at times
its service was perfunctory. There was one matter which
always gave them something to do. Every member of the
Grand Jury who had ridden on horseback to the county-
seat had ground for complaint against the surveyor, as

they called him, of the public road.   Hence, when they
had nothing else to do and were ashamed to send in a bill
for their *per diem*, they brought in indictments against the
road commissioners.   On November 24, 1789, the Mercer
Court of Quarter Sessions, having nothing else to do than
to record its disapproval of the negligence of the road sur-
veyors, had presented to them a complaint concerning the
misbehavior of Lucy Hanks.   Midway down in the list of
their presentments of the path-masters, between an indictment of the surveyor of the road from Harrodsburg to
George Buckhannon's and one against the overseer of the
road from the county line to Chaplin's Fork, are these four
words: "Lucy Hanks for fornication."   "And having
nothing further to present, the Grand Jury were discharged."

A summons was ordered to be issued against Lucy, but
it was not served.   Three months went by, and on March
23, 1790, an *alias* summons was ordered to be issued.
Still Lucy did not appear, and the sheriff had no liking for
the task that was thrust upon him.   The May Court was
about to convene, and Lucy would have had to appear in
public and answer to this charge, had there not occurred
an event of remarkable significance.

Henry Sparrow went to Lucy Hanks and offered to
marry her.

Henry Sparrow came of a good Virginia family.   There
were Sparrows in the House of Burgesses in early days,
and some were officers in the Colonial Militia.   It may be
remembered that Mary Johnston in that interesting novel
of a generation ago chose the name of Reverend Jeremy
Sparrow for one of her most interesting and virile characters—the fighting minister of that narrative.   Henry

Sparrow came of that stock. He was born in Mecklenburg County, Virginia, October 9, 1765, and was just
about the age of Lucy Hanks, that is between twenty-
three and twenty-four. He had been a soldier in the Revolutionary War; had served in the campaign at Yorktown
in Captain Thomas Shipp's Company of Colonel William
Mumford's Regiment, and as we have already taken occasion to remember, was present when Cornwallis surrendered, and doubtless saw both Washington and Lafayette.
He had come to Kentucky with his parents, James W. and
Mary Sparrow. His father died May 18, 1789, leaving a
large family, of whom Henry was the oldest. He became
the support of his mother, and the guardian of his younger
brothers and his sister Biddy. Women by this time were
not scarce in Kentucky, and we have no reason to suppose
that Henry was restricted in his choice. He did a rather
heroic thing in offering to marry Lucy Hanks who just at
that time was the talk of the county.

Lucy accepted his offer. Poor girl, she was not in position to do anything else, and she had every reason to feel
honored by Henry's proposal. So it came to pass, on April
26, 1790, that Henry Sparrow, accompanied by his brother-in-law, John Daniel, Biddy Sparrow's husband, rode to
the court-house at Harrodsburg, and gave bond for a license of marriage shortly to be celebrated between Henry
Sparrow and Lucy Hanks.

In that day it was the almost universal custom that he
who signed the bond with the prospective bridegroom
should be the father or guardian or older brother of the
bride, but Lucy Hanks was in no frame of mind to send
over to Rolling Fork and ask her angry father to come

and sign her marriage bond. John Daniel became her surety, but the county clerk might require evidence that Lucy herself consented and was of age and had right to consent. So Lucy Hanks took her pen in hand and with a rather bold flourish wrote out her own certificate that she was of age, and that she gave her approbation for Henry Sparrow to get out license for their marriage "this or enny other day." She misspelled some words, as Mary Ball Washington and even George Washington himself habitually did. For that matter, these things happened before the day when people held the notion that every word must always be spelled the same. There was some individuality in spelling in those days, and Lucy practised it. But the wonder is not that she made mistakes in spelling, but that she spelled so well and wrote with such freedom, and had a vocabulary which included such words as "approbation," a word, which, by the way, caused her a moment's hesitation, but which she finally spelled correctly.

The marriage license was issued. The May term of court convened. The indictment against Lucy Hanks came up, and the justice, "for reasons appearing to the court," dismissed the case. There can be no doubt what those reasons were. One reason was that the court did not want to prosecute Lucy unless it had to do so. The other reason was Henry Sparrow.

Henry Sparrow and Lucy Hanks were duly married by the Reverend John Bailey, a well-known Baptist preacher. Mr. Bailey was a man prominent in the life of early Kentucky. He was a member of Kentucky's first constitutional convention. In that convention he and every other minister who was a member of it, including some Methodists and Presbyterians, voted against slavery. John Bailey married a number of the Sparrow children. The Sparrows were Baptists, and the Hankses, whose early home was in the Church of England, had become Baptists.

Thus Lucy Hanks found shelter and protection in the home of an honest husband.

5. MRS. HENRY SPARROW

For many years, Henry and Lucy Sparrow lived together as husband and wife, and no husband in Mercer County had a wife more faithful than she. She was intelligent, industrious and capable; she was generous and sympathetic and kind. Our few descriptions of her personality come to us from her later years, and represent her as resolute, rather quiet, but forceful, gracious and helpful, and very religious. Dennis Hanks is to be believed when he says of her as he knew her in those days that she was "a fine Christian lady in every respect."

Knowing all that we know about her, we shall not question the accuracy of this characterization.

She did not run away from the scene of her reproach, but stayed and lived it down. She lived so worthily and well that her past was forgotten in the universal respect which she and her husband commanded. She brought up their eight children virtuously and religiously, and their record is one of good citizenship and integrity. Her grandchildren intermarried, and her great grandchildren and their children repeated the process until now there is scarcely a person living in the neighborhood who is not

descended by one, two, three or four lines, from Lucy
Hanks. They are honest, God-fearing people. In the
Civil War, while many went with the South, a majority
were for the Union. A righteous Kentucky legislature,
sorrowing that so many Sparrows sometimes caused the
county to go Republican, cut off the offending portion
where the Sparrows mainly nested, and attached it to another county where the Democratic majority was so over-
whelming that the Republican contingent could safely be
absorbed, and thus make two Democratic counties grow
where formerly there was one.

One cause of this perverseness was, that in the Civil
War, two of Lucy Hanks's sons, Reverend James Sparrow
and Reverend Henry Sparrow, were so outspoken in favor
of the Union as to turn great hosts of young Sparrows into
the Union Army, and they perversely voted the Republican ticket when they got out.

And these two preachers were sons of a woman no other
than Lucy Hanks!

Yes, she was "a fine Christian lady in every respect."
All her children were trained religiously, and these two
sons became effective preachers. They were Baptists till
they learned about the movement of Alexander Camp-
bell, and then became Disciples. They called themselves
"Union," politically and ecclesiastically.

We know more about Henry than James as a preacher.
He organized the "Sparrow Union Church" which now is
called "New Liberty." Its thick log walls are covered
with white clapboards, and it has a bell tower, and the
seats are more comfortable than in the old days. Henry
and his good wife, Ailsy Smith, are buried there. Henry

rode up and down the country, declaiming his sermons on horseback as he rode, and the congregations assembling could hear him coming while he was yet a mile away.

"Why, yes," said one of his many grandsons, "I remember grandfather. Everybody called him 'Uncle Henry,' and I do myself, mostly. They were Uncle Henry and Aunt Ailsy to everybody. He was a regular old-time preacher, and he hadn't much learning, but he was a terribly good man, and he rode up and down all around here, and civilized this whole wilderness."

It ought to be explained, perhaps, that in the "cut-off" where the Sparrows live, they do not say that a thing is "awfully nice," but that it is "terribly nice." Uncle Henry is conceded to have been a terribly good man.

The old log house in which he and Ailsy lived for many years is a barn now, and before its door Willow Creek widens and deepens into a pool where he baptized hundreds of converts. He dipped them deep. Most of them hit the bottom before he let them up, and they came up a-shouting.

He was a worthy and righteous man and a terribly efficient baptizer, and he civilized that whole wilderness.

We must attend a service at New Liberty and see how matters go there to-day. We shall find a great crowd assembled, on one Sunday a month, and a crowd of even larger dimensions on the Sunday which they observe as Decoration Day. Perhaps a thousand people are in the church-house or around the graves. Three-fourths of them are descendants of Henry and Lucy Sparrow.

And the preacher? A tall, vigorous young man—what is his name, and where is he from? He was "borned and raised right here on Willow Creek" and he is the great

great great grandson of Henry Sparrow and his wife Lucy
Hanks Sparrow. Yes, the preacher's name, also, is Sparrow.

6.   AS ABRAHAM LINCOLN REMEMBERED HER

Henry Sparrow and his wife were nearly fifty years old,
as Abraham remembered them. They had eight children
and the older ones were married and living near them.
There were grandchildren also. It was a large family,
held together by strong ties, of which the most potent was
the personality of the mother, Lucy Hanks Sparrow. She
was rather above medium height, self-possessed and matronly. She was quiet, industrious, intelligent and very
religious. She could read and write, and she spent much
time reading her Bible. Abraham Lincoln could remember one or two visits to the home of this couple, whom
his mother addressed as Uncle Henry and Aunt Lucy.

Uncle Henry had been a soldier and could tell stories of
General George Washington and General Lafayette and
Lord Cornwallis, for he had seen them all at Yorktown.
Abraham liked to hear his reminiscences, and Uncle
Henry had an old soldier's fondness for telling about his
adventures. But Abraham remembered especially concerning these visits the interest which his Great Aunt Lucy
showed in him. She was glad that he had been sent to
school, that he could spell, and had begun to read. She
had him read a little to her from the Bible, and com-
mended him for his proficiency. All that Abraham Lincoln saw of Henry and Lucy Sparrow occurred before he
was eight years old. Nothing that he saw and heard as
occurring between his mother and her Aunt Lucy seemed

strange to him at the time; but in later years he learned
some things that cast a new light on all that he remembered of what occurred, of deed and word, between these
two women. We know now virtually all that he ever
learned on this subject, and we have much knowledge also
that he never possessed about his lost grandmother.

7. WHEN LAFAYETTE CAME TO HIS OWN

General Lafayette visited America in 1824 and remained nine months. His was a triumphal pilgrimage.
He came by invitation of Congress and was welcomed by
the President. His tour from city to city and state to
state was one continuous ovation. Addresses of welcome,
banquets each with its thirteen toasts, receptions, balls
and fireworks everywhere awaited him.

Of course he visited Kentucky, and there was especial
significance in his visit to Lexington. That town had been
named for the battle fought in Massachusetts, of which
tidings reached the pioneers of Kentucky soon after their
arrival on the dark and bloody ground in 1775. And the
county of which Lexington is the capital was named for
him, and still bears the name, Fayette. Henry Clay,
who had been called from the chair of the Speaker of the
House of Representatives to be Secretary of State under
President John Quincy Adams, was in Washington, and
there had delivered the official address of welcome on behalf of the nation. Lafayette visited Clay's home in Lexington, and paid a formal visit to Mrs. Clay. Other ora-
tors, and many of them, welcomed Lafayette to Lexington.
In no town of its size in America was he more hospitably
or elaborately received.

It was springtime in Kentucky when Lafayette came, and nowhere is spring more beautiful. He landed from a steamer in Louisville, and by dignified and festive stages made his progress by way of Shelbyville, Frankfort and Versailles. He spent the night of May 15, 1825, in the home of his aide-de-camp, Major Keene, five miles from Lexington.

A pouring rain came with the morning, but if it diminished the crowd, no one was missed. The countryside, if we may believe the newspaper reports of the event, was alive with people. A military escort composed of three mounted troops from Fayette County, Georgetown and Woodford County marched to his lodging, and he heard and responded to the first of many speeches of welcome.

The procession moved along the Versailles road to High Street, from High to Broadway, and from Broadway to Main, and so to what is now the Phoenix Hotel, but then was Mrs. Keene's tavern, the oldest hotel west of the Alleghanies. There he was refreshed after the manner of the place and time, and learned at least one reason why Kentucky was justly famous. Also he heard more addresses of welcome, and was reminded again that Fayette County had been named for him, and he had come to his own.

Then the procession formed, and the cannon boomed, and the sun, ashamed to have been so long an unseen spectator of the glories of the day, began effective participation. Everybody forgot that there had been a rain.

The procession was in twenty-six divisions, and included all the institutions and organizations of Lexington and many from outside, including the Governors of Kentucky and Tennessee and their staffs. But next to the Marshal of the Day and his escort of Mounted Cavalrymen, and just ahead of General Lafayette in his open carriage, marched a pathetic group of elderly men, surviving soldiers of the Revolutionary War. And among them was Henry Sparrow, of the Virginia Militia, veteran of the Yorktown campaign!

In the afternoon, Major-General Lafayette "reviewed" the veterans of the Revolutionary War. They had been plowing corn for more than thirty years since their last military adventure, and their "hay-foot, straw-foot" marching lay far behind them. But they formed in line, and saluted the General, and he was proud of them and said so.

It was Lexington's greatest day. Lafayette was wined and dined for forty-eight hours, and how he ever lived to get away from it is a mystery. However, on the third morning, escorted by Governor Desha and staff of Kentucky and Governor Carroll and staff of Tennessee, he was conveyed to the county line, where a procession from Georgetown awaited him, to begin a round of festivities hardly less formidable.

In every city Lafayette kissed a long procession of pretty girls, as had been his former habit, and when he left America he took with him not only his richly jeweled presentation sword, but the gift of Congress of two hundred thousand dollars in cash and thirty-six square miles of land, and a great deal more honor than he ever got in France. Republics are said to be ungrateful, and Lafayette, in prison and in exile, and in danger of losing his head, had some reason to believe that concerning the French Republic; but few men have received more substantial tokens of any nation's gratitude than Lafayette received from America.

Abraham Lincoln's Lost Grandmother
Her one existing autograph. Discovered by the author

Know all men by these presents that we Henry
Sparrow and John Daniel are held and firmly
bound unto Beverly Randolph Esquire Governor
of Virginia in the just and full sum of Fifty pounds
Current Money to which payment well and truly to
be made the said Governor and his Successors we bind
ourselves our Heirs Extrs & Admors jointly and Severally
ly firmly by these presents Sealed with our seals and
dated this 26th day of April 1790

    The Condition of the above obligation is such
that whereas there is a Marriage shortly intended to
be solemnised between the above bound Henry Spar
row and Lucey Hanks for which a Licence has
Issued now if there be no lawful cause to obstruct the
said Marriage then the above obligation to be void
or else to remain in full force and virtue
                                                    Henry   his Sparrow
Test   mark
    J. H. Clark   John   his Daniel
                                                              mark

I hereby certify that Lucey Hanks is of full age
Given from under my hand this 26th day of April 1790
Test
                                                    John   his Daniel
                                                           mark

Marriage Bond of Henry Sparrow and Lucy Hanks
Discovered at Harrodsburg, Kentucky, by the Misses Mary A. and Martha Stephenson

And now on that day when Henry Sparrow marched ahead of General Lafayette, where was Lucy Sparrow when the procession went by?

Not in the front row of spectators, probably; those seats were crowded with pretty young girls in their new frocks, young and gay as Lucy had been at the end of the Revolutionary War, when she shared more or less in jubilant celebrations and saw Lafayette. She was back, but not very far back among elderly women, modest and decorously curious and keenly observant.

She saw Lafayette again. He rode by, not on horseback, as of yore, but in a carriage. He was an old man. His son George Washington Lafayette rode behind. This son was almost the age of Lucy's first child, but that was not a matter to be mentioned, even in her own memory, except in the quiet of the night when she lay awake and remembered. Yes, Lafayette was an old man, and she herself was no longer young. He was a hero, this gallant Frenchman, and Lucy joined in the cheering in whatever form it was counted proper for elderly women to share in it.

But there were other heroes in that procession. One of them marching there in his Kentucky jeans of homespun weave and cut was her own soldier husband, her knight without fear and without reproach, Henry Sparrow.

The man who withheld his name from Lucy Hanks when she needed it, and denied that name also to his child, saved his name and lost it. It has gone into eternal oblivion. If the present writer knew it, he would not now disclose it. Lincoln was sad because he did not know that name, but we will not seek to rescue it from its self-chosen and deserved oblivion. Nor can we substitute for the

name which Nancy Hanks ought to have had the name
of Sparrow which so worthily and so long she bore. But
this at least shall be done, that the names of Henry and
Lucy Hanks Sparrow shall not go altogether into forgetfulness nor be held up to scorn and contempt.

Henry Sparrow lived for fifteen years and more after
the visit of Lafayette to Lexington, and died at the age
of seventy-five or seventy-six. His last receipt for pension money as a soldier in the Revolution was signed in
Lexington, September 17, 1840. But Lucy died at sixty
or sixty-one, in the latter part of 1825 or the early months
of 1826. She did not live very long after the notable event
which we have described. It was the last great celebration which Henry and Lucy enjoyed together, and it must
have brought back to them many strange memories.

CHAPTER II

Betsy Sparrow

It was easy enough for Abraham Lincoln as a child to keep in mind the names and relationships of his kinsfolk on his father's side. He knew and remembered his father's mother, and his father's two brothers, Mordecai and Josiah; he stated in one of his letters that he distinctly recalled them both. He knew his father's two sisters, also; they were his Aunt Mary, who married Ralph Crume, and his Aunt Nancy, whose husband was William Brumfield. His Aunt Mary lived in Breckenridge County and his Aunt Nancy lived on Mill Creek in Hardin County. All these he knew and remembered, and it was easy to keep them in mind.

It was quite different with the Hankses. There were more of them, and they were much less easily sorted out and classified. But of one couple he felt very certain; this was Grandpa and Granny Sparrow, whom his mother addressed as father and mother.

There were several things he did not understand. He did not understand, for instance, how his mother's first cousin, and his own playmate, Dennis Hanks, was named Hanks, while the other sons of the same Aunt Nancy were Squire and Levi Hall. That has puzzled a good many people since. Abraham understood it perfectly after a while, and that was why he did not like to talk about it. We also

47

understand it, and will not discuss it. We know that Joseph Hanks's daughter Nancy, aunt of Abraham Lincoln's mother, was the mother of Dennis Hanks, and also the wife of Levi Hall, and the mother of his two sons. There were other perplexing matters in the Hanks relationships, none of which bothered Abraham Lincoln at the time, but which gave him some concern later. But it never occurred to him that he would have any trouble over Thomas and Betsy Sparrow.

When Abraham Lincoln was born, it was Betsy Sparrow who received him from his mother's womb, and washed him, and put on him the little yellow shirt which those who knew him in infancy remembered. It was Betsy Sparrow who rode over almost every day to see how his mother got along, and who looked him over with affectionate interest each time she came. It was she to whom his mother, Nancy, exhibited the lad with pride when he had learned to take his first step. Nancy called her mother, and he called her granny. A good while later he learned that Lucy Hanks Sparrow whom he thought of as his mother's aunt, was really his mother's mother, and that Elizabeth Hanks Sparrow, whom he thought of as his mother's mother, was really her aunt. But if in all this tangle of Hanks relationships there is anything about which he or his biographers should have felt sensitive, it is not a matter of the character of Thomas and Elizabeth Sparrow.

Thomas was the younger brother of Henry Sparrow, and Elizabeth was the younger sister of Lucy Hanks. The two brothers married the two sisters, and the relations which by birth existed between these two women and Abraham Lincoln's mother were completely exchanged.

Elizabeth, daughter of Joseph and Ann Hanks, was born in North Farnham Parish, Richmond County, (formerly a part of Lancaster and the old Tappahannock,) Virginia, and was baptized March 4, 1771. So much we learn from that very fragmentary record, the Register of North Farnham Parish. The bond of Thomas Sparrow, whose surety was his brother Henry, for the marriage of Thomas Sparrow to Elizabeth Hanks, was issued in Mercer County, Kentucky, October 17, 1796. A lawsuit after their death placed on record the fact that they died in Spencer County, Indiana, in October, 1818, and that they died childless.

Abraham Lincoln knew this couple from his birth to their death. They were best known to him of all his mother's relations. She addressed them as father and mother, and the Indiana neighbors who laid his mother and these two older people in their graves together never doubted that the relations they sustained were those which these names implied.

We have no description of either Thomas or Betsy Sparrow. Their appearance, if we had a description, would tell us little. What we know is that they, having no children of their own, mothered Dennis Friend Hanks, child of Betsy's sister Nancy, and gave him an education superior to that of any Hanks of his own, or so far as is known, of any preceding generation among the Hankses related to Abraham Lincoln; and that they took little Nancy Hanks, child of Betsy's sister Lucy, and reared her as their own, and did their share toward making her the worthy mother of a president.

This is very nearly all we know of this humble and unlettered couple, who must appear again for brief mention in connection with the life-story of their foster daughter, Nancy Hanks Lincoln. They gave her shelter, parental love, education and even a name. And they were faithful unto death.

Lucy — Henry Sparra

CHAPTER III

Bathsheba Lincoln

When, in 1829, a number of the descendants of Mordecai Lincoln, eldest brother of Abraham Lincoln's father, Thomas, were removing from Grayson County, Kentucky, to a point in Illinois within the present county of Hancock, and then designated as "the head of the rapids," they made what we have learned to call a detour, and spent a night with their Aunt Nancy Brumfield, their father's youngest sister. She was living on Mill Creek, close to where Thomas Lincoln owned his first Hardin County farm in 1803. Nancy and her husband, William Brumfield, were even then living there; for they had been married in 1801, and had established their home in that locality. In due time Nancy's mother gave up her home in Washington County, and moved over into Hardin and spent her last years with this youngest daughter.

Those last years were many. Her great grandson, Honorable J. R. Nall, who appears to have been wrong in nearly everything that he told to Nicolay and Hay, remembered her, and his recollection on this point is almost certainly accurate; but he thought she lived to the age of one hundred and ten, which would appear to have been from fifteen to twenty years too many. She was living, however, well along in the middle thirties. She then seemed a very old woman, and there appears to be no rec-

51

ord of her death or of her age when she died. Her daughter, who died not many years after her mother, and who is buried by her side in the old cemetery on Mill Creek, has a tombstone with this inscription: "Nancy Brumfield, wife of William Brumfield, departed this life October 9, 1845, at 7 o'clock, aged 65 years, 6 months, 14 days." But we do not know at what o'clock or in what month or year her mother died.

Her descendants who spent a night there on their way to Hancock County, Illinois, in 1829, remembered her, sitting in the chimney corner, an impressive figure even in her decrepitude. Even her great grandchildren remembered her. Great grandmother was too unwieldly a name; they remembered her as "Granny Basheby."

In the few legal documents and tax lists that we have bearing her name, the forms include Barbara, Bersheba and other less obvious variants. We have two of her own signatures, and they are no more consistent than those of William Shakespeare. But her name was Bathsheba. The tendency of the time to give Scripture names was not circumscribed too closely by the moral character of the persons bearing the names in the Biblical record. Bathsheba's conduct was such, unless we choose to blame King David for the whole of it, that Christian people might have been expected to avoid that name for their daughters; but they did not. And indeed, the Biblical Bathsheba was a woman of parts, as witness her success in placing hei son Solomon on the throne, and her traditional authorship of the thirty-first chapter of Proverbs. So Great Grandmother Lincoln's name was Bathsheba, or, as they called it, with strong emphasis on the first syllable, Basheby. We are not sure of her last name. There is some reason to think that it was Herring, and the Herring family in Virginia are proud of their belief that the pioneer Abraham Lincoln married into their family; but they take pains to explain that the Herrings stood socially above the Lincolns.

Captain Abraham Lincoln was born in Berks County, Pennsylvania, May 13, 1744, and removed to Virginia, where his father, John Lincoln, presented him a farm in the Shenandoah Valley. It was and is a fine farm. But for the hope of becoming ancestors of a president of the United States, the Lincolns would seem to have had very little excuse for leaving it. They left just when it was becoming valuable. This farm of two hundred and ten acres was presented to Abraham August 12, 1773. Abraham had then been married about three years. His marriage license, issued in Augusta County, Virginia, was dated June 9, 1770. Unfortunately, the name of the bride is not given, and that omission has resulted in a great deal of very foolish effort to present him with another wife, two ladies having been named as his consorts. One of these is an impossibility, and the other an absurdity. There is not the slightest reason to think that he was married twice.

The first time there was any known occasion to mention the name of his wife was when he sold that same farm, which fortunately for the world but unfortunately for him, he did in February, 1780. The wife of Abraham Lincoln then was Bathsheba. He still had a wife and her name still was Bathsheba in September, 1781; for she had not been able to ride seven miles and back to the court-house to relinquish her dower rights in the deed she had signed, and a commission was appointed by the court to visit her, separately, apart from and out of hearing of her husband, the said Abraham Lincoln, and learn and report to the court whether she did in fact acknowledge this instrument she had signed as her own free act and deed. She did so acknowledge her deed, and relinquish her dower rights. And for a long time it was declared in learned books that she never recovered her health, but died in Virginia, and that Abraham Lincoln married again. But all this was disproved in 1924 by the discovery of her name in the tax lists of Washington County, in the lists of 1792 and 1794, and again in her signed consent to the marriage of her daughter Nancy in February, 1801. Bathsheba was the name of Captain Abraham Lincoln's wife from the time his wife's name first appears of record, and it continued to be her name until his death, and for about fifty years afterward, when at a great age, probably about ninety, though inaccurately stated by her descendants as one hundred and ten, she died.

Children were born to Abraham and Bathsheba Lincoln there in the Shenandoah Valley, five of them in less than ten years; Mordecai was born in 1771; Josiah in 1773; Mary, who married Ralph Crume, was born about two years after Josiah; Thomas was born January 5, 1778; and Nancy, March 25, 1780. Bathsheba was not strong enough any time in the next eighteen months after the birth of her fifth child to ride seven miles and back, and she never bore any more children. But this wife and mother calmly consented to the sale of the farm, and gave her consent while in this condition of frail health, in full expectation that she might undertake with her husband and family a ride through all kinds of weather, and over every kind of road but a good one, up the Shenandoah to its head waters and across the ridge, down the slope into the tip of Virginia and across into Tennessee; up through Cumberland Gap and along the Wilderness Road, and then almost entirely across the state of Kentucky to a new home as yet unbuilded, and very near to the Ohio River. Verily, among the pioneers, the men had no monopoly of heroism!

Not one detail of that journey is of record. But we know that Bathsheba had the care of five children, the eldest eleven years of age, and the youngest little more than a babe in arms. And she was planning this journey during the whole period in which she was too feeble to ride to the county-seat! Somehow they made the journey, and the family lived for something like three winters in a block-house known as Hughes' Station, on Long Run of Floyd's Fork.

There, in May, 1786, Captain Abraham Lincoln was shot by an Indian. All three of his sons saw their father murdered. Little Thomas stood, petrified, beside the body. Josiah ran a quarter-mile to the station for help. Mordecai ran to the cabin and took down the rifle. Carefully aiming the gun between the cracks of the house, he drew a deadly bead on an Indian who stole out of the forest with intent to scalp the dead man and murder the boy. Mordecai fired. It was a good shot. There was one more good Indian, as the frontiersmen classified Indians. There was a widow weeping over the body of her dead husband, and five small children stood beside her and mingled their tears with her own. But one of them was already a hero; Mordecai had avenged his father's death.

That autumn there was an expedition against the Indians, led by George Rogers Clark. Expenses had to be

met by subscription, and subscriptions were in kind.
Horses, cows, blankets were subscribed, and there were
some guns. The one highest in appraisal was a rifle, gift of
"the Widow Lincoln." The gun with which Mordecai had
killed his father's murderer, we may believe, was the gun
she dedicated to that which she believed a holy war. I
remember to have heard something about the fortitude of
the Spartan mothers. Bathsheba Lincoln was like one of
them.

But within a very few months, as we know from the
papers of administration issued on her husband's estate,
she removed with her five children to Beech Fork, in
Washington County, a safer and a more settled neighborhood. There she lived till her youngest daughter married and went to Mill Creek.

Did Abraham Lincoln ever see her? He spent the first
seven years of his life in the same county where she was
living with his father's youngest sister; it is scarcely possible that he did not see her. It was something of a ride,
to be sure; for her home was in another part of the county
than that in which Thomas and Nancy lived. But Thomas
knew the way very well; there was where he had purchased his first Hardin County farm, the first farm he
has hitherto been known to own, though I think I now
know of one still earlier in Cumberland County. Thomas
knew the way, and there was every reason why he and
Nancy should ride over now and then and visit his sister
Nancy Brumfield and his aged mother. And most as-
suredly the family went that way as they were leaving
Kentucky, and spent a night, as Mordecai's children and
grandchildren did, with William and Nancy Brumfield,
and permitted Granny Basheby to see how many more

Site of Captain A. Lincoln's Spring and Cabin

Long Run Church on the Lincoln Farm, where the body of Captain A. Lincoln is probably buried

Photographs by Hon. R. C. Bullard-Thruston

Plowing corn on the Hanks Farm in Kentucky

The Site of the Lincoln Cabin on Knob Creek Farm

great grandchildren there were and how the older ones had grown.

We have no record of such a visit. No; most of the things which most surely happened are unrecorded, and a vast proportion of those recorded never occurred. But it would have been very strange if Thomas Lincoln should have lived seven years after the birth of his son Abraham in the same county with Abraham's aged grandmother, and never had ridden to see her. And if the little boy Abraham Lincoln saw her, he saw her as did his cousins who were moving to the head of the rapids, sitting calmly in the chimney-corner, greeting her grandchildren and great grandchildren as they came and blessing them as they departed. There she sat, with the patience which comes to the old, the patience which is the gift of God to those who have come up through great tribulations.

Two generations separated her from the joys of wife-hood and a sense of participation in the things of life. There was not much left that she could suffer. She had known and endured it all. There were no illusions for her in this pioneering matter; she had seen it, lived through it; she could have written a book about it, and would she had done so! Silently she sat, with little demonstration when her grandchildren brought their children for her to see. And yet, the great grandchildren did remember this, that she knew their names, and identified those who bore them; she had kept track and knew how many children were in each family. So far as I know they never named one of them Bathsheba; perhaps they had grown guiltily conscious of the possible implications of the name. But she knew their names, and said, "So this is Mordecai." "So this is little Mary Rowena!" For by that time it had become fashionable to find names in other books than the Old Testament. And she knew those names, the new names that mothers were getting out of story books and suchlike strange places. But it was not to a story book Thomas and Nancy had gone for a name for this tall, seven-year-old son of her youngest son. His was a name she knew and loved, the name of her own hero-husband.

She did not let this lad pass out of Kentucky and into the wilderness of Indiana and pay no heed to his appearance and character. He and his name meant too much to her. That name had been borne by one she remembered as a tall young ranger whom she married six years before they stopped praying for King George, and who, at the close of the Revolution, bore the title Captain. That name she had seen joined to her own in the marriage certificate. That name she had seen signed to the deed that conveyed away their land in the Shenandoah Valley, and she had signed her own beneath it. That name she had seen rudely scratched on some rough and perishable memorial above a grave on Long Run. She was proud of her children and grandchildren and great grandchildren, but for this lad she had especial affection. He it was whom her son Thomas had named for his father, her husband, Abraham Lincoln.

Numerous were her grandchildren and her great grandchildren. It would not have been surprising if she had been unable to keep all the names in mind. But she could not forget that name. For it she had exchanged her own, in the days when the tides of youth ran strong in her blood, and her lover's kiss was sweet upon her lips. The name, as she heard it addressed to this tall lad of seven, thrilled her with pregnant memories. It carried her back to her marriage, when the words, "I, Abraham, take thee, Bathsheba," fell solemnly upon her ear. It carried her back to the morning when she heard the rifle-shot, and knelt in her husband's blood. It carried her back to the long journey along the Wilderness Road, and the milestones were set all the way from the stile-blocks in the Shenandoah Valley to the unhewn gravestone on Long Run and the hearthstone of her widowhood on Beech Fork.

These grandchildren and great grandchildren of hers were following a track which she and her young husband had blazed when Kentucky itself was young. And now she had reached the ultimate oasis in her pilgrimage, and she sat where she could see her descendants moving across the line of vision into the newer unknown. She was impassive, unemotional. There were no children left in her loins and no tears left in her eyes. She was drained of emotion and of progeny. Yet out of her lacerated and now withered womb had been poured this flood of life! These four generations had all sprung from her! She sat as the sphinx sits at Gizeh, and with features as impassive. Backward without looking she could see ninety years. Forward she could look, and she saw that urge of life that was once herself moving in these younger generations, till generation by generation they disappeared across the horizon. But she sat silent in the chimney-corner. There was nothing more the wilderness could do to her.

CHAPTER IV

NANCY HANKS

1. GRANDFATHER HANKS

THE company that assembled around the grave of Grandfather Joseph Hanks was composed entirely of grown people, with one single exception. The neighbors were present, the Rineys, and the Hazels, and the Widow Hall and her son William and her daughter Betsy, and there were enough others to constitute a respectable assembly, for death had its solemn dignity on the Kentucky frontier. Besides, a burial was a social occasion of some importance, and afforded opportunity for no small amount of gossip, curious and impertinent, but not unfriendly, as to how the different members of the family "took it" and what was likely to happen to them now. The family of Joseph Hanks was a large one. There were five sons and three daughters at home, besides the married daughter Lucy and her husband over in Mercer. And there was the widow, Ann Hanks, who had never seemed happy and contented since the coming of the family to live on Rolling Fork. It was a large family, and all of the children were grown and able to take care of themselves and of one another. Old Joseph Hanks had left a rather well-stocked farm, capable of supporting them all till they scattered, as in the nature of the case they would and did before

many years. To each of the five sons, William and
Thomas and Joshua and Charles and Joseph, their father
left a horse, and as for the three daughters at home, Betsy
and Polly and Nancy, to each of them he left a heifer.
The rest of the live stock remained with the farm, which
the widow was to have during her lifetime.

Yes, the farm was well stocked, and the Hanks children
were all well grown and were not likely to be a burden.
The youngest boy, young Joe, and the youngest girl,
Nancy, were in their teens, and some of the older ones
were of age. William was soon to marry Elizabeth Hall,
and Polly was keeping company with one of Old Man
Friend's boys, the one they called Jesse.

In some such fashion the neighbors canvassed the situation, and agreed that, while the death of Old Man Hanks
was sad in its way, the situation was not without its elements of comfort. He was well on toward sixty-eight
years of age, and a man must die some time, and a man
was fortunate if he lived to see his family grow up and
able to look after themselves and one another.

And there was little Nancy; she would live right on with
her grandmother.

Yes, there was little Nancy, just nine years old when
her grandfather died. She had had an important place in
the history of the Hanks family since her first arrival,
but most of it the Kentucky neighbors did not know or
bother about. She was born back in Virginia and came to
Rolling Fork as a baby, and had been accepted as a member of the family without any necessity for much explanation. But she was undeniably there, and when the
group of relatives and neighbors assembled around the
open grave of Joseph Hanks that day in late winter of

1793, there was no other child present. It was a group of grown folk, or of folk nearly grown, and little Nancy.

Little Nancy was quite distinct from her young aunt Nancy, who was still in her early teens. The family had two Nancys and one Nannie; for by that pet name Old Man Joe Hanks called his aged wife Ann.

It did not surprise any one that Old Man Hanks's married daughter Lucy and her husband came to her father's burial. It would have been strange if she had not come. She had been gone from home a good while, working out, so it was said, over in Mercer. She had married in that county, and she and her husband, Henry Sparrow, came to the burial. The neighbors did not notice anything unusual in her attitude toward the family, or in the family's attitude toward her. Some of them doubtless knew that there had been some talk about her some years back, but that was over in Mercer, and she was married and behaving herself now. The fact that Old Man Hanks did not name her in his will was not a matter that can have passed by without comment, but whether that was because she was married and had a husband to care for her, or, as some thought, because her father disapproved some things in her earlier life, was nobody's business. Her mother and her brothers and sisters evidently received her as a member of the family. She and her husband rode back to Mercer, and did not return to Nelson County to file any protest when the will was presented for probate, and if the family accepted the situation, there was not much for other people to complain about.

So they buried Joseph Hanks, Sr., late of Nelson County, Kentucky, formerly of Virginia, deceased, and his widow and unmarried children took up the burden of life where he laid it down. The five horses and three heifers which his will disposed of continued to remain in the home herd until the children married, as they did, one by one. The Widow Hanks, while far from rich, was adequately provided for, and had her sons and daughters.

Also, she had little Nancy, her granddaughter, now nine years old.

Nancy was always to be remembered.

The death of her grandfather wrought no immediate change in the daily life of little Nancy Hanks. Spring came, and the flowers were fragrant up and down the shores of Rolling Fork, and they bloomed abundantly also along Pottinger's Creek which flowed in on the Hanks side, and up the steeper shores of Knob Creek, which flowed out of the "knobs" on the opposite side. Nancy's childhood life was not one of hardship. She had her daily tasks to perform, but the heavy work was cared for by her uncles and aunts. Her Uncle Joe and Aunt Nancy were not too old to play with her, and the others were considerate. Whatever the faults of the Hanks family, its members were loyal to one another. Except for one thing, the year that followed her grandfather's death might have been a rather cheerful one. Her grandmother became despondent, and very homesick for Virginia.

It was not the more recent Virginia home on Patterson's Creek she longed for; that had never seemed like home to her. She wanted to be back in the old North Farnham Parish where she had been born, and where her old friends still lived. Day by day for a whole year she moaned and sorrowed about it, and then the children held a council, and arranged to send her back, and young Joe was to go with her.

William and his wife, Elizabeth Hall, stood ready to buy the farm, which under the will of the deceased Joseph was to belong to the widow during her life, and then to the youngest son. Joseph and his mother, Ann, assigned their rights to William, and a suitable financial arrangement was reached. The old home was still to be home for the other members of the family until their separate plans should carry them away to homes of their own. This would not be long for some of them. Mary was about to marry Jesse Friend, and the older sons were approaching matrimonial arrangements with young women of the neighborhood. Elizabeth was old enough to earn her own way and look out for herself. The daughter Nancy would be cared for by her sisters and by William's wife.

Little Nancy was the only problem. William's wife, Elizabeth, was assuming as many motherly functions as a bride might fairly be asked to undertake. Grandmother Hanks did not think it wise to take so small a child as Nancy back across the mountains with her to Virginia where she, herself, might have so short a time to live and care for the little girl. It was decided that Nancy should go to her own mother, Lucy Hanks Sparrow.

If Grandmother Ann Hanks had insisted that she needed little Nancy as a staff for her old age, and the little girl had accompanied her back to Virginia, the history of the United States would have been seriously modified.

2. THE SPARROWS' NEST

The home of Henry and Lucy Sparrow was in Mercer County, a rather long day's ride on horseback from the

Rolling Fork home cf Grandfather Joseph Hanks, but it was a cheerful ride. The time was spring, a year and more after Nancy's grandfather's death, and the road had no rough hills or dangerous fords. The Sparrow home was a comfortable one, and little Nancy had a suitable place in it.

Yet there was something of constraint in the welcome, and Nancy did not wholly understand it. She did not quite belong there, and if the fault was hers, she did not know it.

Here she was no longer "Little Nancy." There was no big Nancy from whom she needed to be distinguished. There was no one else who was older than herself, except only her mother and her stepfather. On the other hand, there were two small children, and Nancy was their nursemaid. She had suddenly grown up.

Her very name was changed. The neighbors soon forgot the necessity of distinguishing between Mrs. Sparrow's younger and older children, and the little girl who had been Nancy Hanks became the big girl, Nancy Sparrow.

Another baby was coming, and did come, to Lucy Sparrow, and her sister Elizabeth Hanks came over from Nelson County to remain with her a few weeks. This sister attracted the attention of Thomas Sparrow, Henry's brother. Elizabeth did not return to the old Nelson County home, but married Thomas Sparrow and remained in Mercer.

This marriage brought another change to Nancy Hanks, and she went to live with her aunt and new uncle, Elizabeth and Thomas Sparrow. The only explanation made to her was that her aunt Elizabeth wanted company, but

Nancy understood in some vague way that her mother, though loving her, was glad to have her in the other home, and not in her own.

The name Hanks fell still further away from her. Whether with her mother or her aunt, she was called Nancy Sparrow. The neighbors fell easily into this habit, and her relatives were quite willing that it should be so.

And thus occurred this strange shifting of relationships. Gradually Nancy's mother became her aunt, and her aunt became her mother.

Lucy continued to bear children, till she and Henry had eight of their own, not counting Nancy. But to Thomas and Elizabeth, no children were born. Nancy was twelve years old when she went to live with them in 1796, and as the years passed, and they had no children of their own, she came to be to them as a veritable daughter. Nancy called Elizabeth mother and addressed Thomas as father. Within four years, during which time the two Sparrow families lived in the same neighborhood, and were constantly back and forth, this transposition of relationships became practically complete. Henry and Lucy Sparrow became Nancy's Uncle Henry and Aunt Lucy.

Late in 1800 Thomas moved to the South Fork of Nolin Creek in Hardin County. For four crop years the family of Thomas Sparrow lived on Nolin Creek, and then for some reason they moved back and from late in 1802 till the fall of 1805 Nancy Hanks lived again in Mercer County.

But by this time she was a grown woman. She had attended school and had gained the rudiments of a common education. Moreover she had skilled herself in some of the finer of the domestic arts. There was increasing call for fine needlework, and she was a skilled seamstress. Where there was to be a wedding she sometimes was engaged for a week or a fortnight; and where there was a funeral, she had employment also, for women were beginning to wear black in token of mourning. Working for wages in families that now were growing rich, she was not regarded as a servant, but sat at table with the family, and she left behind her in Mercer County a distinct and reliable tradition of her industry, neatness, cheerfulness, intelligence and high character.

So Nancy Hanks, or Nancy Sparrow, as they more frequently called her, blossomed into young womanhood, and she did not look back on her youth as a time either of poverty or disgrace. She knew, of course, long before she became of age, the whole story of her birth, and at times it cast a shadow over her mind. But her mother, Lucy, was held in increasing respect in Mercer County, and her foster mother, Elizabeth, was respected everywhere.

Nancy's services were in frequent demand, especially in Mercer and Washington Counties, which were older and richer than Hardin, and when she was not thus employed, she had a comfortable and cheerful home with her foster parents, Thomas and Elizabeth Sparrow.

But once in a long time, when Nancy and her own mother Lucy were alone together, they sought each other's arms. They shed few tears and spoke few words, but they both understood. One of these occasions was in the late summer of 1805. Thomas and Elizabeth had decided to move back to Nolin Creek, and buy the farm on which

they had formerly lived as tenants. This second residence in Hardin County meant much in the future of
Nancy Hanks.

3. COURTSHIP

The level afternoon sun was sifting its rays through
the golden shade of the beech trees, and lighting up the
shed-room where Betsy Sparrow had set up her loom.
Nancy was on the porch, spinning. The dogs barked, and
two men rode up to the fence and called. Betsy looked
out of the door and hurried to the fence. One of the men
was her brother Joseph Hanks. The other was introduced
as Joe's friend, Tom Lincoln.

Thomas Sparrow appeared, welcomed Joe and was introduced to Tom, and the three men went to the barn and
stabled the horses. Then they went to the house and
greeted Nancy.

Uncle Joe expressed amazement at the way little Nancy
had grown up to womanhood, and remembered that when
he left with his mother for Virginia she had not been more
than knee-high to a toad, which was not very accurate, for
she had been tall even as a little girl, but that was the ac-
credited measure for such cases. And in due time, Mr.
Tom Lincoln was properly presented to Joe Hanks's
niece, Miss Nancy Hanks. That evening, after little
Dennis had been put to bed, the five grown people sat
around the fire and told each other many things.

Joe had remained in Virginia till his mother died. She
was glad to be back, but not as glad as she expected to be.
Things had changed, even in old Virginia. Her old friends
had died off, and her relatives, while bidding her welcome,

had families of their own and thought her own children were the ones who should have cared for her.

Her own children did care for her. Joe stayed with her in Virginia as long as she lived, and then returned to Kentucky, still unmarried. No one could say he had failed to care for his mother. But Virginia was no such place as Kentucky for a man who had his own way to make. So Joe returned.

He had picked up carpentry as a trade, and was hewing timbers for mills, and doing such work as was called for in his vocation. It was that particularly which had brought him into friendly relations with Tom Lincoln. Tom owned a farm over on Mill Creek, and he had a mother and a married sister living there. But he had found, after trial, that farming was lonely business, so he was working as a carpenter in Elizabethtown, the county-seat. Now and then he earned a little money from the sheriff, serving as guard at the jail.

Joe also had become a land-owner. He had bought a farm near that of his brother William, near the falls of Rough Creek. William had sold the farm on Rolling Fork, as they all knew. The sale had brought Joe unexpected good luck. He had assigned his interest to William before his own departure for Virginia. He did this in good faith, but he was not then of legal age. The fact of his minority clouded the title, and he had been asked to execute a quit-claim deed in addition. For this he received "an old chunk of a horse, that would have traded for about fifteen dollars," as he said, but that horse was just so much more than he had ever expected to get.

While it had not been much of a horse, it had four legs and a place for a saddle, and had served till Joe traded for a better one. He was well mounted now, and so was Tom. Both men were unusually good judges of horse-flesh. Joe's judgment is attested in the record which exists of a suit in which he sought to secure payment of a note, the said note having been given in settlement of a bet which the defendant was unwise enough to make on a race in which Joe Hanks rode his own horse. Tom Lincoln, though a lover of horses, did not race nor bet on races.

But the most important words that were spoken by the fire that night were not those of Joe, relating his adventures to his sister and her husband, nor yet anything that Mr. and Mrs. Thomas Sparrow had to tell him, but in certain unrecorded words, and acts more eloquent than words, that passed between Tom Lincoln and Nancy Hanks.

They made no undue haste about their approach, but they took a good look at each other. He was twenty-six, of medium height, solidly built, with hair so darkly brown it was almost black, hair cut around straight on a level with the bottom of his ears and not shingled up the back, and gray eyes, which now and then kindled with a love of fun. She was nearly twenty-two, tall, well proportioned, with dark skin and eyes. She had a high forehead, and possessed a good command of language. Her hands were skilled, and she had a good voice and could sing the old ballads.

Tom and Nancy did not say much to each other, but they looked at each other, and neither was blind. Joe interrupted their observation now and then to ask Tom to confirm some statement about Joe's horse. But if any one had had money with which to gamble that night, there was a safer wager possible than any that depended even upon the horsemanship of Joe Hanks. Tom Lincoln was riding to win. And in due time he won.

4. MARRIAGE

Polly Ewing was a Mercer County girl, and when she married Dick Berry she moved over into Washington County, where the Berrys were well established, and Dick was the second in a long line of Richard Berrys. Nancy Hanks visited Polly Berry, and plied her vocation as seamstress in her home. Tom Lincoln had two brothers living in Washington County, near neighbors to the Berrys, and he thought it time for him to visit his kindred.

Nancy had more friends in that portion of Washington, and in that part of Mercer which was adjacent, than she had in Hardin where she and her foster-parents had gone to live. Thomas, also, had friends in Washington, for there he had grown up, and a number of his relations were in the vicinage. Tom and Nancy arranged that instead of going back to Hardin to be married, they would be married in Washington County and go back as husband and wife.

Richard Berry, the younger, but not the youngest, mounted his horse and rode with Tom to Springfield, the county-seat, and the customary bond was given for the issue of a license of marriage, Richard assuming for the purpose of the certificate, the place of "guardian." For, while the law did not specify that it must be so, it was the custom that the person signing the bond with the prospective bridegroom should be a relative or intimate friend of the bride. The title "guardian" had no legal significance; Dick Berry had never been so appointed by the court, and Nancy was of age and needed no guardian; but for him to call himself "guardian" was a customary courtesy, and it was so done.

No formal invitations were issued to the wedding of Thomas Lincoln and Nancy Hanks. Some one who was riding from Springfield to Elizabethtown conveyed a message to Joseph Hanks, and so to Thomas Sparrow and William Hanks, and Grandmother Bathsheba Lincoln, and there were ways enough of sending word to friends in Mercer and Nelson Counties. News passed along from neighbor to neighbor and from neighborhood to neighborhood with surprising rapidity. If a court day or a preaching appointment intervened between the announcement and the marriage, the news was scattered still more widely.

Spring planting was over. The corn had been plowed once and in some fields twice. Haying and harvest were not yet at hand. The spring freshets were past and the streams were fordable. The homes of the neighbors were open for entertainment of those who came from a distance and the weather was such as to promise outdoor enjoyment.

We do not know just who were present of the relatives of Thomas and Nancy. His brothers and their families lived hard by. It would have been a long ride for his mother and the daughter and son-in-law with whom she lived, but in that season it was not an impossible journey. Certainly Thomas and Betsy Sparrow and Jesse and Polly Friend, and Levi Hall and his wife, Nancy Hanks, the aunt of the bride, were within a comfortable day's ride. Weddings in the backwoods were more than weddings. They were great assemblies of sundered friends who hungered for social relationships.

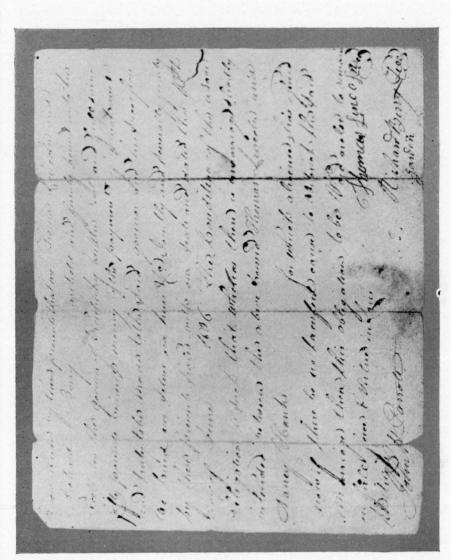

Marriage Bond for Marriage of Thomas Lincoln and Nancy Hanks

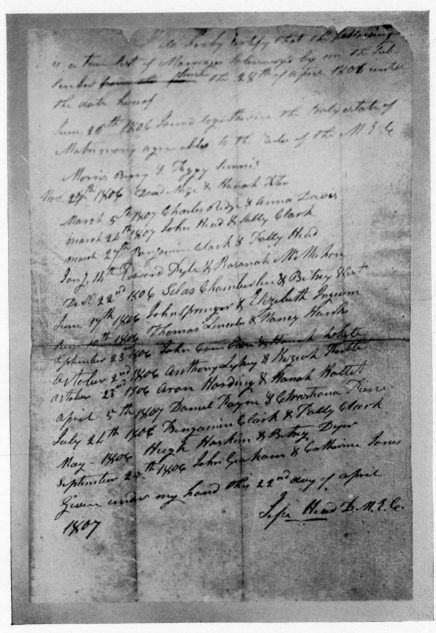

Marriage Return of Reverend Jesse Head
Certifying the Marriage of Thomas Lincoln and Nancy Hanks

We can picture the scene on the day of the wedding. The Berry house was a double, hewn-log structure that fronted the road a short distance from the ford of Beech Fork. A few houses were near, and the neighborhood was sometimes called Beechland and at other times Poortown. No reasonable explanation has been offered for the latter name, for the farmers were rather more than ordinarily prosperous. It may be that some of them were tenants of the Berrys, and that their cabins were small as compared with the two double log houses of Richard and Frank Berry. Below the Dick Berry House and near the road was, and still is, an excellent spring where each arrival refreshed himself, and the men made their outdoor toilet after their ride.

People were arriving nearly all day, and preparations were going forward on an extensive scale. The wedding feast was no matter of light refreshments, but a barbecue. Kettles were boiling and ovens were reeking the whole day long. A "snack" was provided for the guests who arrived before noon, and it did not diminish the provision for evening. The Berrys were well to do, and food was cheap. There was no market for surplus perishable food, and the actual cost of what people were to eat was scarcely a matter to be considered.

There was no lack of help. The Berrys owned slaves, as did the more prosperous of their neighbors, not even excepting the preacher, Jesse Head, whom modern authors have credited with the anti-slavery sentiments of the Lincoln family. There was help enough inside the house and out.

From the middle of the afternoon the guests arrived in considerable numbers. Those came earliest who had come farthest. The women went to the house and there refreshed themselves and prepared to look their best. The men, escorted by one of the Berrys, or a negro, led their horses to the stable, removed their saddles and turned the animals loose in the pasture lot. Those who arrived later, coming from no farther than Springfield, hitched their horses to swinging beech limbs. That method left the animals free to fight flies, and if a horse, in jerking his head, pulled too hard at the tether, the limb was flexible, and it was not likely that the horse would break his bridle rein. If a horse did break loose, he could be depended on not to stray far from the other horses. Moreover, the horses were never left long alone. Comparison and discussion of live stock, and even the swapping of horses, was likely to occur at a wedding. There was always a group of men hanging about the horses, ready to catch one that broke loose.

The yellow daffodils that grew in two parallel rows in almost every Kentucky dooryard had shed their bloom, and the roses were in full blossom. The little cuttings brought from Virginia a quarter-century before had multiplied, and roses were abundant. There was no great variety, but the bushes were numerous and they hung full. Their odor freighted the summer air as the guests walked from the stile-blocks to the front door.

At the back door were odors of another sort, and no less appropriate. A fat sheep or a young bull calf was roasting, and the larder and the smoke-house and the hen-roost had all contributed to the occasion.

Negroes were not numerous, but they were not negligible. The Berrys owned a half dozen, and several of the neighbors were loaning a darky or two for the occasion. A fat cook, with high-piled turban, stood with arms akimbo, holding in her right hand a basting spoon, her scepter of authority, her weapon of defense and offense, and incidentally the implement of her profession. In the cook-shed she reigned supreme. Outside, the fiddler, also a person of color, tuned and tested his violin, tried out his home-made cat-gut, and assured inquirers that he intended to keep sober, but could give no assurance as to whether the fiddle would do so. The sun shone bright on the old Kentucky home; 'twas summer; the darkies were gay. So also were the white folk, and there was every good reason why they should be so.

Not, certainly, because any of them were members of his church, but because he was a neighbor and friend, and because his work as cabinet-maker kept him within easy reach of the court-house, while preachers who rode circuits were not always to be depended on, the minister selected for the occasion was Reverend Jesse Head. Rather late in the afternoon, he rode up. We know the color of the mare on which he rode; she was gray. Later, by natural increase and some swapping, he owned at times as many as three horses, but at this time he paid taxes on one gray mare, and three slaves, these negroes being a mother and two children. He did not own the husband of Mrs. Jane Head's cook; that colored man belonged to a neighbor. Jesse Head was later custodian and guardian of certain free negro children, and so a trusted friend of their interests, but he was no abolitionist. He edited a paper which did not hesitate to advertise rewards for runaway slaves. On that subject he was neither ahead of his times nor behind them. But most of the preachers opposed slavery, and he did not.

He was recognized as he approached, for his gray mare and her rider were well known. Willing hands would have taken the bridle-rein from him as he dismounted, but he personally saw to the removal of the saddle. It was summer, and a horse's back might easily scald, and a sore-backed horse is no asset to a backwoods preacher.

Take a good look at this man, Jesse Head, not the fictitious creation of literature, but the man who is disclosed by patient research. He was thirty-eight years and two days old on the day he married Thomas Lincoln and Nancy Hanks, and he had no suspicion that this wedding was unlike any of the others to which he was accustomed. Yet it is that day which came to him unlabeled and un-named, to the end of his life undistinguishable from his other days, which gives him a place in history. He had been preaching ever since he became a man, and he con-tinued to preach throughout his long and useful life. After years of service at Springfield, he removed to Har-rodsburg, and there labored as carpenter, editor, politician and preacher. In 1806 there were no political parties, but when they arose he fought hard for Andrew Jackson, and against Henry Clay. He was a good, honest, hard-hitting Democrat.

Thanks to a ribald jingle then current, we know how he looked:

"His nose is long and his hair is red,
And he goes by the name of Jesse Head."

He was no saintly, mealy-mouthed man, this Jesse Head. He was a fighter of the devil and of desperadoes and of Calvinists and later of Whigs. He could eject a rowdy from a service, and thrash a bully till he cried for

mercy, and then kneel with him, and with tears streaming
from his eyes, pray that God would save the bully's miserable soul. He had a good library for his time, and he
was something of a lover of books. Not every one loved
him. He made many enemies. But wicked men feared
him, and every one respected him.

Well might that company assembled on Beech Fork rise
up and pay reverent regard to Jesse Head. Dogmatic,
controversial, censorious, he was; but mightily in earnest,
desperately sincere, and utterly without fear of Whigs,
Calvinists, Baptists, rowdies or the devil. He did his own
worthy share in saving the wilderness from Godlessness
and savagery.

The wedding was at sunset and the feast and the dance
followed. There were the good old tunes, *Vilikins and His
Dinah, The Girl I Left Behind Me, Turkey in the Straw,
The White Cockade, Sugar in the Gourd, The Money-
Musk*, and *Hey, Betty Martin, Tip-toe, Tip-toe*. The fiddler rosined his bow and drew it lovingly across the eager
cat-gut. There was enough to eat and more than enough
to drink. It was a gay and festive night.

It ought to be remarked, that, while all the groom's
relatives present were known to most of the company,
the bride's kin had never lived in Washington County,
and had to be introduced. It is not difficult to measure
the distances and conjecture which of those relatives
would probably have ridden over to share in the joy of
this occasion. But it may be well to mention one couple,
who, late in the afternoon, may have been seen splashing
through the ford, and pausing for their horses to drink.
Among the guests whom we must presume to have been
present was this couple whom we already know. The man

was a farmer, but had something of the bearing of a soldier, having indeed fought under Washington in the Yorktown campaign. He was forty-one and his wife was not much above forty. He was well built and capable; she was attractive and intelligent. They passed in the crowd and said their words of felicitation to the bride and groom, and there is every reason to believe that those words were sincere.

They were introduced to the company as another uncle and aunt of the bride, Mr. and Mrs. Henry Sparrow, from Mercer County.

In that high hour Lucy could not claim her daughter.

5. THE PLUM ORCHARD

The first home of Thomas and Nancy Lincoln after their marriage was in Elizabethtown, county-seat of Hardin County. Thither they rode from Washington County not long after the marriage service. There was no occasion for haste. They may have remained to an "infare" given by the Lincolns. While the bride's family or friends furnished the wedding, the groom's relatives often followed with that reception of the new couple into their clan by an "infare" which was often quite as noisy as the wedding. Dennis Hanks related that shortly after the wedding the bride and groom visited Thomas and Elizabeth Sparrow, and it would have been very strange if they had not done so. Their home was on the way to Elizabethtown, and there was every good reason why such a visit should have been made.

The cabin in Elizabethtown has no important place in

this narrative. After Abraham Lincoln had been elected president, what were said to have been its logs were shown in a shed then used as a stable, and its sorrowful condition called forth unnecessary pity for the inhabitants of 1806. It was never anything palatial, but there is no record that Thomas and Nancy found it unendurable. There the first baby was born, a girl. And because she was a girl, and they could not name her for her father's father, they called her Sarah. The name they wanted to use would keep, and did.

Thomas Lincoln had a good deal of work to do while he was living in the county-seat. He served on juries, he guarded prisoners, he worked at his trade as a carpenter. The year 1807 brought him into litigation concerning one of his largest contracts, and for several months he had lawsuits on hand. These suits related to his work in hewing out timbers for a mill erected by Denton Geohegan. In each of the suits Thomas Lincoln won his case, but Geohegan was a stubborn contestant, and the series of trials must have given rise to no little feeling and some anxiety.

Some time in 1808 Thomas and Nancy removed from Elizabethtown, and on December 12, 1808, he bought from Isaac Bush two hundred acres of land, including the Sinking Spring, and the cabin which later was to become famous. But when the purchasers of the Lincoln Farm a century later made their investigation prior to the transfer of that property to the United States Government, they discovered evidence, not wholly certain, but to them highly probable, that Thomas and Nancy were already living in the neighborhood some ten months before Abraham Lincoln was born. The home which, for one single crop season, they are believed to have occupied was located in "the Plum Orchard." This report was accepted by the attorneys representing the United States Government, and finds its place in the archives of the Lincoln Farm Association. If this be correct, it gives to the imagination a rather pleasant suggestion. The Plum Orchard was not accurately named. It was a natural grove of wild crab-apples. They bloomed so abundantly in spring that, according to the recollection of the oldest men now living near there, people used to come from a distance and load themselves down with the blossom-covered boughs. They profess to remember how it looked to see two or three horses moving off, with their riders almost hidden beneath the branches. These huge, moving bouquets they recall as no unusual sight in spring.

The cabin in the Plum Orchard was a temporary home. Tom Lincoln was tired of lawsuits, and of the kind of work that led to litigation, and Nancy wanted a home nearer to her foster-parents, Thomas and Elizabeth Sparrow.

And so, until possession of the home at Sinking Spring could be obtained, they lived for a few months in the Plum Orchard.

Thomas was not yet through with his lawsuits, and had to make rather frequent trips back to Elizabethtown, but usually he was gone only for the day, and Nancy awaited his return with glad anticipation.

Here, in May, 1808, while the wild crab-apples were in their glory, and the air was full of their fragrance, Nancy felt the thrill of a new expectancy. She whispered her secret to her husband, and to Elizabeth Sparrow, and they all were glad, and the crab-apples blushed happily. This time, Nancy hoped she would bear a son.

6. THE BIRTH OF A BOY

There was a neighborhood picnic in the woods of the Richard Creel place, in the summer of 1861, and the lunch baskets were assembled at the Sinking Spring. During the luncheon there was discussion concerning the cabin that had once stood there, and which had been removed, and whose logs some people present believed were still in the walls of a barn in the vicinage. The occupants of the cabin, Thomas Lincoln and his wife, had owned this very spring, and used its water; and it was here that their boy, Abraham Lincoln, was born. It seemed a very remarkable fact that the man who was at that minute sitting in the White House and directing the great war, in which Kentucky was likely to be involved on the one side or the other, should have been born on this very spot, in a cabin almost exactly where they were sitting, and that he and his parents should have drunk and bathed in the water of this very spring.

Some one present said he had heard that when the Lincolns lived in that place, they were a "no-'count" family, and perhaps not even married.

Aunt Peggy Walters answered the imputation with vigor.

"Mis' Lincoln was a fine woman," she said. "I knew her well. We lived just three-quarters of a mile over yonder, and I was here right often. She was a good woman, and nobody ever spoke a word against her while they lived here, nor against her husband, either."

Aunt Peggy Walters was a woman of character, related to half the people present, and her word had weight.

"Wasn't you here when he was born, Aunt Peggy?" asked one of the younger women.

"I most certainly was," replied Aunt Peggy, "and I remember it just as well as if it had been yesterday."

Plied with questions, Aunt Peggy rose and hobbled about for a few steps, for she had a broken hip, and had to use a crutch, and it wearied her to sit long in one position. If she was to tell a long story, she must make herself more nearly comfortable. She seated herself again, laid down her crutch, and told in her own language, which in the main was correct language, this story of the birth of Nancy Lincoln's baby:

"I was twenty years old, then, and helping to bring a baby into the world was more of an event to me than it became afterward. But I was married young, and had a baby of my own, and I had helped mother, who, as you know, was quite famous as a granny-woman, and I had gone several times to help when I was sent for. It was Saturday afternoon, I remember, when Tom Lincoln sent over and asked me to come, and I got up behind the boy that rode across to fetch me, and I rode across to the cabin that then stood here. It was a short ride, less than a mile. It was winter, but it was mild weather, and I don't think there was any snow. If there was any then, it wasn't much, and no snow fell that night. It was a clear night. I was here all night. They sent for me quite as soon as there was any need, for when I got here nothing much was happening. They sent for her two aunts, Mis' Betsy Sparrow and Mis' Polly Friend, and these both came, but they lived about two miles away, so I was there before them, and we all had quite a spell to wait, and we got everything ready that we could.

"They were poor folks, but so were most of their neighbors, and they didn't lack anything they needed. Nancy had a good feather-bed under her; it wasn't a goose-feather bed, hardly any one had that kind then, but good hen feathers. And she had blankets enough. There was a little girl there, two years old. Her name was Sarah. She went to sleep before much of anything happened.

"Well, there isn't much that a body can tell about things of that kind. Nancy had about as hard a time as most women, I reckon, easier than some and maybe harder than a few. It all came along kind of slow, but everything was regular and all right. The baby was born just about sunup, on Sunday morning. Nancy's two aunts took the baby and washed him and dressed him, and I looked after Nancy. That's about all there is to tell. I remember it better than I do some cases that came later, because I was young, and hadn't had so much experience as I had afterward. But I remember it all right well.

"Oh, yes, and I remember one other thing. After the baby was born, Tom came and stood beside the bed and looked down at Nancy, lying there, so pale and so tired, and he stood there with that sort of a hang-dog look that a man has, sort of guilty like, but mighty proud, and he says to me, 'Are you sure she's all right, Mis' Walters?' And Nancy kind of stuck out her hand and reached for his, and said, 'Yes, Tom, I'm all right.' And then she said, 'You're glad it's a boy, Tom, aren't you? So am I.'

"No, there isn't much you can tell anybody about things of that sort. But Tom Lincoln was mighty anxious

about his wife, while she was suffering, and mighty good
to her, too. And they were both proud and happy that it
was a boy. You can't tell much about the birth of a baby,
except that you were there, and that the baby was born.
But you can tell whether folks wants the baby or not, and
whether they love or hate each other on account of it.
I was young then, and I noticed and remembered everything. I remember it a heap better than I remember much
that happened afterward. I tell you I never saw a prouder
father than Tom Lincoln; and I never saw a mother more
glad than Nancy was to know that her baby was a boy.

"Yes, they was mighty proud it was a boy, both of
them; and Nancy says to Tom, says she, 'Now we can
use the name we couldn't use before.'

"And they sort of explained to me how they named
the little girl Sarah because the name Abraham didn't fit,
and Sarah was the next best. For Tom's father, that was
killed by the Indians when Tom was a little boy, his name
was the one they wanted the first baby to have. And so
Nancy says to Tom, 'Now we can use the name we
couldn't use before.'

"And Tom says, says he, 'Yes, Nancy, and it's a right
good name. This here baby boy,' says he, 'is named Abraham Lincoln.' "

That was the story as Aunt Peggy Walters told it to
her neighbors, and no one ever questioned her veracity.
It constitutes the only reliable narrative we have of the
birth of Abraham Lincoln.

Only two years did the Lincoln family live beside the
Sinking Spring. The title to the farm proved defective.
There was a lawsuit, and Thomas Lincoln won, but his
verdict and redress were against a man no longer in the

neighborhood. The Lincoln family moved to another farm, at the forks of Knob Creek, a short stream flowing out of the hollows of Muldraugh's Hill, and emptying into the Rolling Fork. As it happened, it was only two miles from where Nancy had spent her childhood in the home of her grandparents, Joseph and Ann Hanks.

7. LITTLE TOMMY

Abraham Lincoln liked to play in the shavings when his father made coffins. They were soft, nice, brown shavings of walnut, different in color and texture from those of pine or poplar. Abraham's sister Sarah also liked shavings, but, being older than Abraham, her use for them was different. Two large girls, riding by one day when they knew Thomas Lincoln to be working on a coffin, selected a long shaving ˀpiece, and holding it at arm's length, turned around three times with their eyes shut and each flung the shaving over her left shoulder. If the shaving made a letter where it fell, that was the initial of the girl's future husband. An apple peeling might be used for the same purpose, and so was often employed in autumn parties, but it was not so reliable as a shaving from a coffin. Sarah was not interested in husbands, but she knew a few of her letters, and liked to see if she could make them out of shavings.

The making of coffins was an irregular but still dependable part of the labor of Thomas Lincoln. Every one had to die sometime, and people were no longer content with home-made coffins if a carpenter could be had. They complained of the prices, as people in all lands complain of the rapacity of the undertaker and his readiness to traffic in the necessities of bereavement, but they bought the coffins, which cost a dollar a foot. A child's coffin cost three dollars, a woman's six and a man's seven. Not every day or week, but oftener than once a month, did he have this occupation; and at times when there was much sickness there were frequent visitors. Some one would ride to Thomas Lincoln's cabin on Knob Creek, bearing an alder rod that had been laid on the face and along the body of the dead person, and cut to show the required length. Thomas used that rod to cut off the boards for the bottom, allowing an inch or more of margin at head and foot. The top plank was both longer and wider than the bottom, for it was to be fastened down to the sides and ends. It was the top that was measured for the price.

Abraham and Sarah did not play in the shavings when little Tommy died. For the first time in their lives death had entered their own home. All the skill of Doctor Potter, who had ridden in the night from Elizabethtown, and that was a long way, had failed to save him. All the kindness of friends who gathered and filled the house and porch and spoke their words of sympathy and hope and advice proved unavailing. All the experience of Nancy's two aunts, Polly Friend and Betsy Sparrow, the latter her foster-mother, made no headway against the fatal malady. The doctor let go the pulseless little wrist and laid it with gentle sorrow on the breathless chest, and said, "I'm sorry, Nancy! Sorry, Tom; the little fellow is dead."

Nancy did not shriek, but she sobbed convulsively. The doctor closed the little eyes, and Thomas produced two great pennies and laid one on each eyelid. Then, after a word of thanks to the doctor for his long ride and his weary vigil, Thomas Lincoln stumbled, half-blind, out of the door, and began to pull down walnut planks from the beams above the shed.

His hands shook as he turned the planks to find those that were well seasoned and had good grain, and as he planed, there appeared wet spots on the board. Abraham and Sarah, who were crowded out of the house where the neighbor women with homely but tender art were "laying out" the little body, and trying to comfort Nancy, followed their father to the shed and stood in mute sorrow behind him. He stopped his work and for a moment gathered them in his arms and sobbed. They had never seen him shed tears before; they did not know that a great big man could cry. They cried when they were hurt, and mother cried once in a long time, but it was a new thing to see their stolid unemotional father in tears. He did not speak, but if that inarticulate man could have said anything, it would have been, "Thank God, I've got you left, you and your mother." But he released them without a word, wiped his own eyes and went back to work.

In the course of an hour or two, Nancy came out, glad to be away for a little time from the sorrowful kindness of her comforters. She brought two yards of flax-cloth of her own spinning, and a basket of cotton wool. These were extravagances, but she knew that some people provided white lining for the coffins of their loved ones, with a thin bed of cotton wool under the linen beneath the body. She and Thomas closed the door of the shed for a moment. They did not say much, but whatever they said in words, their hearts said, "Thank God, we still have each other and the other children, and one of them a son, our boy Abraham."

The neighbors assembled that night and "sat up" with the dead, singing at intervals through the night for the supposed comfort of the bereaved parents. Thomas and Nancy were in bed in the same room, and little Abraham and Sarah were asleep in the trundle bed. At intervals estimated at an hour, an experienced woman took the cloth that lay on the dead baby's face, wet it again in saltpeter water, and laid it back again upon the little white face. Thus, and for one night, were the dead preserved, but only for the space of about twenty-four hours, and never for a moment was the body left alone.

There was no religious service when little Tom was buried. It was not simply because ministers were scarce and hard to obtain when needed. The Kentucky Baptists had very definite convictions on that subject. As early as 1798 the Elkhorn Association of Baptist Churches had voted:

"That funeral processions, attended with singing, conform too much to the anti-christian customs, and ought to be omitted in the churches of Christ."

The funeral sermons were not strictly forbidden, and instead of a sermon preached at the burial, it became a common practise to hold such a service some months afterward.

We are at liberty, and indeed under some obligation, to believe that such a service was held, at some convenient time a few months after the interment, over the grave of little Tom Lincoln. The date probably coincided with the regular monthly appointment of the Reverend William Downs, who was pastor at the time of the Little Mount Church.

He would have "norated" that at the time of his next monthly appointment at Little Mount, he would preach the funeral of Tommy Lincoln, the infant son of Brother and Sister Lincoln of Knob Creek.

Of William Downs we have considerable information. He was a man of fair education and had been a school-teacher. He had oratorical ability, and possessed strong convictions. He was a strong opponent of slavery, and the Little Mount Church stood with him in his protest. It is no pleasure to add that he was a man of indolent and slovenly habits, and too much given to drink. He was the first minister whom Abraham Lincoln ever heard.

Thomas and Nancy Lincoln rode back down Muld-raugh's Hill after the service, their hearts heavy and sore, but with the comfort of knowing that they had done their best for little Tom while he lived, and had shown him now the utmost of respect which the principles of their church permitted.

They went back to their cabin in the forks of Knob Creek, and put up the horses and milked the cows and got supper and went to bed, weary and sorrowful, but with deep satisfaction that they still had children. There was the daughter, Sarah, a good girl, and much like her father. Thomas was especially fond of her, and he had dearly loved his little namesake. But Nancy, loving all of them, cherished a special affection for her surviving son, her man-child, Abraham.

8. A BACKWOODS MADONNA

It is a blessing that we are not permitted to sit down in our sorrow and to think of nothing else; that way mad-ness lies. There are things that must be done, and blessed are the mourners who have no lack of those compelling necessities. Thomas and Nancy Lincoln had their daily duties that must be performed. He had his farm and his shop; she had the cow to milk and the butter to churn and three meals a day to cook, and a spinning-wheel to be kept at work, and two children to be found in food and raiment. Time and labor are great healers, and little Tommy became a tender memory and no longer an agonized grief.

Much of the life of the wilderness passed to and fro through the road along Knob Creek, a creek whose forks divided the Lincoln farm, as Cæsar divided all Gaul, into three parts. It was a comfortable little farm, and well located, but Thomas Lincoln had a precarious title and was sued under eviction proceedings as a trespasser. Although he won the suit, the litigation was continued, and the result appeared uncertain. Passing travelers told of the glories of the new land of Indiana. Thomas had a brother Josiah living there and was eager to move. Nancy, also, came of a migratory race and accepted removal as part of the established order of nature. Her brother Joe had gone to Indiana. Thomas and Nancy had lived but two years in Nolin, and five years on Knob Creek, but these were fairly long periods for a family of their restless blood. In the autumn of 1816 they packed up their belongings and went to Indiana. Their decision to move involved the leaving of a home well established in a picturesque and convenient locality, within easy reach of Nancy's several groups of old friends in Hardin, Nelson, Mercer and Washington Counties; it involved leaving the church of which she and her husband were members; it involved the breaking of many ties. But it was the sort of experience to which she and her people and her husband and her husband's people had long been accustomed. And so they went to Indiana.

The experimental journey of Thomas Lincoln from his Knob Creek home to Spencer County, Indiana, had been made by flatboat, but the family migration was on horseback. It was accomplished in the autumn, and was probably not an experience of hardship. Nancy took one child with her on her horse, and Thomas took the other with him. At times they walked for their own comfort and that of their horses. They probably spent the first night with Thomas and Betsy Sparrow on Nolin Creek, and the next with Thomas Lincoln's mother, Bathsheba Lincoln, then and for many years afterward living with her daughter and her husband, Nancy and William Brumfield, on Mill Creek. Two or three more nights brought them to the ferry across the Ohio River at the mouth of Anderson Creek, where they stayed with a settler named Posey, with whom Thomas Lincoln had left the goods which he floated down the river on his flatboat. Then they moved on to the claim that was to provide their home in Indiana.

The golden autumn did not last, and it was followed by a winter of unusual severity. In all parts of the country that was remembered as the winter of "eighteen-hundred-and-froze-to-death." The home of the Lincoln family through the "pretty pinching times" of that winter, as Abraham long afterward described them, was a "half-faced camp." It was a pole structure, with the perpendicular bank of an excavated hillside as its back, and a bearskin or blanket for a door in front. It was a forlorn place compared with the cabin on Knob Creek, but the family accepted it with that stolid fortitude that was part of the character of the pioneer.

In the following summer they erected a new house, eighteen feet square, and with a loft high enough to provide room for beds, one of which was occupied by Abraham, now a lad of eight years. In that cabin he was to spend the remaining years of his boyhood. The half-faced camp did not remain unoccupied. Thomas and Betsy Sparrow came on to be near their foster-daughter, and made their home near the Lincolns. Scarcely had this couple moved out of the hillside place than Levi and Nancy Hanks Hall came on, and they in turn occupied the camp until they had provided themselves a permanent home. The rude shack sheltered in succession three families known to us, and quite possibly several others afterward.

Southern Indiana was then a wild region, and the settlements back of the Ohio River were few and sparse. There were at first no regular church services, no physicians, no schools. Perhaps Thomas Lincoln did not regret the absence of schools so much as Nancy did. There is no reason to believe that he opposed such education as his children were able to secure, but apparently the mother was more intent on the securing of an education for her children than was the father. Abraham and Sarah had attended school portions of two terms in Kentucky. They had learned to spell and had begun to read. But there were no schools in their neighborhood in Indiana during Nancy's lifetime. If Abraham and Sarah learned anything more, they learned it from Nancy, or from Dennis Hanks, whom the Sparrows had sent to school in the old Baptist meeting-house on Nolin, and who claimed, with some apparent reason, to have grounded Abraham Lincoln in the elements of his education. There were very few books in the home of Thomas Lincoln and Nancy Hanks, and the same condition prevailed in all other homes in the neighborhood.

For two years Nancy Hanks Lincoln dwelt in Indiana, and saw some approach to comfort in the conditions of her home. Gradually the cleared area of land and "deadening" around the cabin widened, and the acreage of corn increased. The stock of poultry and of bacon grew, and the "pinching times," while not far pushed back into the woods, were not at the door as they were at the beginning. Conditions appeared to promise a reasonably comfortable future for the family.

Abraham Lincoln was old enough now to look with more possibility of appreciation on this mother of his, and to estimate somewhat her qualities. She was now approaching the age of thirty-five. She was above medium height and had a slight stoop as though predisposed to consumption. She weighed about a hundred and thirty pounds. Her complexion was dark, and her face was thin and sallow. Her forehead was unusually high, and all her relatives commented on this feature of her appearance as belonging to and exhibiting her intellectual nature. She was usually cheerful, but her face in repose was sad. At times she displayed a marked tendency to mirth, but she had moods of melancholy.

Abraham had a boy's limitation of judgment; perhaps he did not appreciate these qualities so fully in his youth as he did later, but we have no reason to suppose that he was wholly blind to them. She was a good mother to him, and he knew it. She was ambitious for him, and desired that he should have the opportunities which both she and her husband had almost wholly missed.

The autumn of 1818 brought to southern Indiana a terrible sickness, afflicting both man and beast. The cattle were first to suffer from it, contracting the disease from eating the foliage of snake-root, and as it was found to have been their milk that carried the illness to their human owners, it was called "the milk-sickness." A number of the people in the neighborhood where the Lincolns lived contracted the disease and died. Levi and Nancy Hall died, and so did Thomas and Betsy Sparrow. Two uncles and aunts, one couple being her foster-parents, were swept away as with a flood. Then Nancy herself contracted the disease. There was no physician within thirty-five miles. We have the testimony of a neighbor who was an eye-witness, that Abraham and his sister were faithful in waiting on their mother, and doing what they could for her. "She struggled on," says this neighbor, "a good Christian woman, and died on the seventh day after she was taken sick. The mother knew that she was going to die. She was very weak, and the children leaned over her while she gave her last messages. Placing her feeble hand on Abe's head, she told him to be kind and good to his father and sister. To both she said, 'Be good to one another,' expressing a hope that they might live, as they had been taught by her, to love their kindred and worship God." Thus, at the age of thirty-five, on October 5, 1818, died this madonna of the backwoods, the mother of Abraham Lincoln.

Whatever seasoned lumber Thomas Lincoln had in stock had been used in making the coffins of those neighbors who had already died. The whip-saw was called into

Photograph by the Author

The Cabin in which Nancy Hanks brought to the World the Gift of a Noble Life

Grave of Nancy Hanks Lincoln

requisition, and with Abraham's assistance, Thomas Lincoln sawed out the planks from which he made the coffin wherein was buried his worthy wife, Nancy Hanks. The Halls and the Sparrows had been buried, two and two, and somewhat apart from the other interments in the little cemetery. On a lovely hill in the vicinage, Nancy Hanks was laid to rest beside her foster-parents, Thomas and Elizabeth Sparrow. Their dust mingles with hers inside the iron railing that encloses her monument.

The question which had earlier agitated the churches in Kentucky, whether funeral sermons were to be preached at the time of burial of the dead, had now moved on northwestward, and was mooted in the new settlements in Indiana. So when Nancy Hanks Lincoln was laid to rest on a sightly knoll in southern Indiana, it probably did not occur to any one that it would be fitting to have a funeral sermon. And if it had occurred to any one, and no objections had been raised, there were too many sick people in the settlement for an attendance of the living, and too many dead for any one of them to be honored by an individual funeral sermon.

A few months later, Reverend David Elkins came that way. He was an almost unlettered son of the forest, a man of unusual ability and of strong sympathy. He was asked to preach a funeral sermon above the grave of Nancy Hanks, and he doubtless included in his sermon her relatives and probably also the neighbors buried near. The interval of some months between the death and funeral was quite in accord with the custom of the people, and the funeral was not in this regard at all unusual. The sermon seemed to those who heard it appropriate, and we may be sure it was comforting and sympathetic. We can imagine David Elkins standing amid the graves near Gentryville, and lining out, two lines at a time, his opening hymn:

"Death has been here and borne away
    A sister from our side;
Just in the morning of her day,
    As young as we she died.

"Not long ago she filled her place
    And sat with us to learn;
And now she's run her mortal race,
    And never can return."

We can imagine the sermon, with its warning and its comfort, its simple and heart-felt eulogy of the dead and its stern admonition to the living. It is good to know that thus adequately, as it seemed to the family and friends, the simple virtues of Nancy Hanks were recognized, and that her life was interpreted to the little backwoods neighborhood in terms of her religious hope and aspiration. Humble lives need such interpretation, and every life deserves to be remembered by that which it aspires by faith to be. We can imagine the closing hymn:

"You may bury me in the East,
You may bury me in the West,
And we'll all rise together in that morning."

The word "rise" had a strange and mighty syncopation, carrying its accent to a new beat, and with it rose the courage and faith of those who sang.

Then came the word of blessing, and Thomas Lincoln took the hands of his two weeping children and led them back to his desolate home. The feet of millions of pilgrims have walked and will walk that path. They will stand within the granite temple that now enshrines the log walls within which, at Hodgenville, the maternal pain of Nancy Hanks gave to the world her son Abraham; and they will tread reverently through the leafy aisles of the State Park at Gentryville, where a massive granite stone now marks the spot which Abraham Lincoln in his boyhood watered with his tears.

He loved his mother while she lived, and he loved her memory afterward. It was a pathetic memory, and had in it elements concerning which he was properly reticent; but as to his inheritance through her of the qualities which he deemed to be some of the best within him, he spoke with deep feeling, "God bless my mother. All that I am or hope to be I owe to her." Although in this utterance, her son spoke of the mental traits he thought himself to have inherited from her, rather than of her direct influence over him, it was of her mind and character he spoke when he said that however unpromising her early surroundings might have been "she was highly intellectual by nature, had a strong memory, accurate judgment, and was cool and heroic."

To him, as he looked back upon it from the standpoint of later experience, it seemed her life had been a tragedy. But we are not sure that she so regarded it. She had sad experiences, and times of depression, but she had lived and learned and loved. She had known the joys of wifehood and motherhood. She had never suffered hunger or neglect. Always there were those who cared for her and for whom she cared. To her it may not have seemed that hers had been a sad life; and she left that which permanently brightened the life of humanity.

CHAPTER V

SARAH BUSH LINCOLN

A HORSEMAN could approach the clearing unproclaimed, but a wagon heralded its approach a long time before its arrival. What with the chuck-holes and the rocks and roots that varied the surface of the road, and the strips of corduroy that partly bridged the more nearly bottomless mud-holes, the way of a wagon through the woods was an adventurous one, and the chucking of the hubs upon the shoulders of the axles, the protest of the various obstacles encountered by the wheels, to say nothing of the shouts of the driver, gave audible announcement of the coming of a wheeled vehicle. When the Lincoln children, Sarah and Abraham, knew that a wagon was approaching, they were at the front of the house, waiting for it. With them was their cousin, Dennis Hanks, who since the death of Thomas and Elizabeth Sparrow lived with the Lincolns, and there also, though temporarily, were Squire and William, the two sons of Levi and Nancy Hall.

Whatever might have been their expectation when they heard the wagon wheels, their imagination afforded them no approach to the reality of their vision as the vehicle drew near. It drove straight up to the door, and disclosed as the driver of the four horses no other than Thomas Lincoln. He had ridden away to Kentucky on a saddle horse, and here he was back again with that horse

98

and three others hitched to a wagon. The children could not have fancied such a change. But that was not all that gave them occasion for amazement. Beside him, on the front seat, was a woman whom they did not know, and behind these were two girls and a boy, distributed around among the various articles of a wagon-load of household furniture.

Thomas Lincoln shouted out a salutation which the children responded to with embarrassed wonder. Then Thomas climbed down on the "off-side" and the woman climbed down over the wheel on the "nigh-side."

"Children, this is your new ma," said Thomas Lincoln.

Individual introductions were unnecessary. The new ma knew the names of her own new children and also those of their cousins. She had no difficulty in recognizing Sarah, for there was only one girl in the group. She knew which one was Dennis, for he was several years older than the other boys. The Hall boys she readily identified. There was one more, and she quickly recognized him, her own boy, whose maternity she had inherited by right of succession of Nancy Hanks, her own boy henceforth, Abraham Lincoln.

"These are my children," she said. "This is John, and these are my two girls, Betsy and Matilda."

The children may have been shy toward one another at the first; the wilderness makes children shy; but they were not long in becoming acquainted, and in reckoning themselves members of one family.

Sally Bush Lincoln stood among these representatives of the Lincoln and Hanks and Hall and Johnston homes, all broken by death, and it would not have been strange if she felt some sinking of heart as she comprehended in

the accurate definition of her present vision the task she
had undertaken. Her own children were clad as the children of a poor widow might have been attired, and besides this they were travel-stained; but they looked im-
maculate in comparison with the unkempt condition of
the forlorn group in Thomas Lincoln's cabin.

It would be interesting to know just how definitely
Thomas Lincoln had charted his course before he said
good-by to the children in his Indiana home in the end of
November, 1819, and bestrode his horse for a visit to his
old home in Kentucky. It was safe for him to leave the
children; they were old enough to take care of themselves
for a fortnight. He left them and went back to Elizabethtown. Tradition has it that he had courted Sally Bush before her marriage to Daniel Johnston, and his wooing of
Nancy Hanks. He knew that she was now a widow. It
was to woo and marry her he went back. And yet he may
have had no such assurance of her acceptance as to focus
his purpose wholly upon her. He was in sore need of a
wife, and his children of a mother. It would be interesting
to know what he planned to do, and whether he had any
plan, in case of her refusal.

If he had in the back of his mind any second matrimonial possibility, he found no occasion to refer to it. He
went straight to the house of the Widow Johnston, and his
courtship was direct and manly. He told her in so many
words that he was a widower and she a widow, and that
they were in position to be a comfort to each other, and to
make together a home for each other's children. He proposed to marry her, and whether he did it for the first
time, or renewed a proposal that he had made before the

first marriage of either, he was no stranger to her, and she recognized the advantages of his offer.

She confided to him an embarrassment. She was in debt. Her first husband had left her thus hindered. Concerning the dead she probably spoke good only, but Daniel Johnston ought not to have left her in that condition. Her first husband was not by any means a better one than Thomas Lincoln. He had been the county jailor, and his political companionship had not conduced to his leaving his widow and children well provided for. She worked hard while he lived, and now she was in debt, and she could not marry and move away leaving unpaid obligations behind her.

The author holds no brief for Thomas Lincoln. He was an easy-going and unambitious man from whom all qualities of greatness would seem to have been absent. But he is still remembered with respect by the old people who as children knew him in Illinois, and he was a man capable of meeting an emergency such as Daniel Johnston's widow presented to him. He asked from her a list of her creditors and the amounts which she owed to each of them. Having obtained this information, he withdrew.

While he was gone, she sent for her brothers and asked advice of them. They had known Tom Lincoln when he lived as a carpenter in Elizabethtown, and one of them had been with him in a journey down the Mississippi to New Orleans. If there is any place where two men come to know each other intimately in their conduct and their conversation, in their courage and ability to meet emergencies and to endure the strain of monotonous toil, it is on a flatboat. It is much to Thomas Lincoln's credit that the male relatives of Sally or Sarah Bush encouraged her to accept the proposal of Thomas Lincoln.

In due time Thomas returned to the home of the Widow Johnston, and brought with him receipts for all her debts. He offered these as evidence of his ability to care for her, and as credentials of her right of removal from the community. Her answer was ready. Thomas Lincoln and Sarah, daughter of Christopher Bush and widow of Daniel Johnston, were married at Elizabethtown, December 8, 1819.

Although she was widowed and in debt, she was not without dowry. She had a very respectable lot of household furniture. Thomas had moved and moved and had almost nothing in the way of furniture except what he had made since his last pilgrimage, and that was not much. But the Bush family had lived long in Elizabethtown, and Sally had spent the whole of her short married life there in the official circles of Elizabethtown's central group of inhabitants. She had bedsteads, and with them featherbeds and blankets and homespun coverlets and pillows. She had one or more chests of drawers and some tables and chairs. She had more knives and forks and spoons than Nancy Hanks had ever possessed, though Nancy was not destitute in this regard. She had two spinning-wheels, one for wool and one for flax, and also a reel and a loom. She had one or two chests filled with clothing and other conveniences. It was not the furniture of a rich woman, by any means, but it was the respectable outfit of a woman who had lived her married life in the town in which she had been born, and had carried with her some belongings from her childhood home and accumulated a few others. Nothing that Thomas Lincoln possessed or

ever had possessed compared with her outfit in extent
or value.

Thomas Lincoln acquired with his second wife an embarrassment of riches. He could not transport Sally
Bush and her three children and her household furniture
on horseback. Two horses, even, when hitched to a
wagon, were hardly equal to such a load over rough winter
roads. He went to his brother-in-law, Ralph Crume, and
borrowed a wagon and three horses, making with his own
steed a four-horse team, loaded in his bride and her belongings, and after three or four days of travel through
the winter woods, he arrived, and they arrived with him,
cold and hungry, and ready for a blazing fire and a hot
supper. The fire, if not already blazing, was a ready possibility. The supper of corn-pone and bacon was not far
away. The horses were unharnessed. The furniture was
unloaded and distributed in the several corners and available positions in the cabin. The supper was eaten and
the dishes were washed. John Johnston joined Abraham
and Dennis in climbing up the corner-pegs to the loft. The
two Johnston girls and Sarah went to bed and were soon
asleep. Thomas Lincoln and Sally Bush sat down before
the open fire and looked each other over.

He was forty-one years of age, and his heavy black hair
had no streak of gray in it. His round beardless face was
gentle and kindly but rather lacking in expression. He
was a powerful, slow-moving man with latent energy only
occasionally called into action, and he had beneath his
good-natured imperturbability a mighty temper that seldom was aroused. There was nothing of the hero or saint
in his appearance, but he was honest, sober, kind-hearted,
of good judgment, religious and not quite illiterate, being

able to read stumblingly the Bible and, as his son Abraham long after said, able also "bunglingly to sign his own name."

Sally had not made a brilliant match, but she might have done worse; indeed, she had done worse in her first marriage and was consequently worse off in her widowhood.   There was no bed of roses for her in the poor cabin of Thomas Lincoln, but there were shelter, protection, food and fuel, a home for her children, and an honest name.   And there was another daughter Sarah, and a new son, yes a son, her new son Abraham.   Biographers since her day have pitied her, but we have no reason to suppose that she pitied herself.   The place was rude and primitive enough in itself, and was more uninviting in the conditions that had followed Nancy's death, but Sally looked around with assurance that she could bring comfort out of the disorder and neglect.

Thomas looked at her.   She was very tall, straight as an Indian, as her granddaughter described her, "very handsome, sprightly, talkative and proud."   She had black hair, and she curled it and was conscious that she increased her attractiveness in that fashion.   She was industrious, charitable and kind-hearted.   And she knew how to manage Thomas Lincoln, who was not reluctant to be managed.

Her mild tyranny began the very next morning.   Here he was, a carpenter by trade, with the whole forest for a lumber-yard, and all his saws and planes within reach, living in a cabin without a floor.   She told him she wanted a floor, and no puncheon floor, either.   The floor was to be made of sawed plank, and the plank must be planed. The whipsaw and the planes came into use.   The floor was sawed out and planed and laid, and the house had thenceforth a solid basis of comfort underfoot.

The boys had to assist in the sawing, but that was not all they had to do. She assembled them at the horse-trough, and provided a gourdful of soft soap. They had such a scrubbing as they had not endured in months, and their changed raiment, albeit patched, was clean.

She learned of a place where men were burning lime, and she sent Thomas Lincoln thither for some of it. The whitewash brush came into use, and its results were apparent inside the cabin and out. The place became cleaner, more sanitary and more attractive.

"She certainly had faculty," said Dennis Hanks, remembering years afterward the vigor of the scrubbing which he underwent and the general renovation of the place under her direction.

She had faculty in other relations. She established the children of the broken households in a unified home life. There was need of discipline and good judgment to fit and make the household happy and productive. This she used, and there comes to us out of the reminiscences and traditions of those years of adjustment no echo of strife or disagreement, but united testimony of affection and content.

Sally Bush was not slow to discover in her new son qualities which were not present in the son who was of her own flesh and blood. With no word of disparagement of her own boy, she never failed to praise and encourage Abraham. The time had come when Thomas Lincoln and his son did not understand each other any too well. The boy had shot up marvelously in stature, and the changes of adolescence wrought in him unaccountable transformations. He became dreamy, and at times unsociable. There were within him the stirrings of strange ambitions which did not please his father.

Thomas Lincoln did not hate or ruthlessly hinder his son. There is no evidence that he opposed Abraham's desire for an education; such evidence as exists is rather to the contrary; but he did not highly appreciate the need of education, and that is not strange. Abraham was lazy; so for that matter was Thomas, if by laziness one means that he was disinclined to exertion for which there was no apparent necessity. But the precise form of Abraham's indolence was one which Thomas could not well comprehend. It was not simply that he was disinclined to work, but that he was inclined to other activities which lay beyond Thomas Lincoln's vision. Abraham was a forward lad, if we are to believe Dennis Hanks, quick to start conversation when a traveler passed by, when he ought to have permitted his slower-moving father to begin and pursue the interview. Abraham was given to field oratory, which pleased his companions, but was not conducive to labor. Adolescense imposes a strain on the relation of parent and child, and such a strain came in the relations of Thomas and Abraham. Dennis Hanks records that Thomas knocked Abraham off the fence for his forwardness on at least one occasion. It has been inferred that Thomas was cruel or tyrannical, but that is too much of a deduction from a premise of this character. The boy was reading and cultivating an ambition to which his father was a stranger, and Thomas Lincoln now and then became angry about his boy's perverseness.

In this situation the mother often understands the boy when the father does not. This fact is the basis of much

Portrait of Sarah Bush (Johnston) Lincoln
Her only photograph

Courtesy of Eugene J. Hall, Oak Park, Illinois

Thomas Lincoln's Indiana Home

silly sentimentality, and has become the occasion of a most unjust disparagement of fatherhood and a flabby and half-hypocritical adulation of motherhood. But the experience of the Lincoln household is not unique. Blessed is the boy who at such a time has a mother who understands him and is able to express a sympathy which the father perhaps does not know how to define or perhaps even to think necessary.

Such sympathy Abraham Lincoln found in his new mother. She encouraged his reading, and persuaded Thomas Lincoln to look upon it with favor. Sally Lincoln saw this raw-boned lad outstrip her own son, and was not jealous, but encouraged Abraham to persevere. So far as we have any data to serve as the basis of correct judgment, her influence on him was wholly good.

Year in and year out, through the period of his late boyhood and young manhood, Abraham Lincoln saw and admired and loved this handsome, curly-haired new mother of his, and he carried into life a finer ideal of womanhood for what he discovered in her. He made such provision that she and his father continued to have a roof above their heads when John Johnston would willingly have cashed in on their modest investment and let the future take care of itself. To the end of their lives they were sheltered and protected by Abraham's gratitude.

Only twice after his election to the presidency did Abraham Lincoln leave Springfield before his final departure for Washington. One of these visits was to Chicago, where he met his associate, Honorable Hannibal Hamlin, and was tendered a great reception. The other time was when he went to Charleston, Illinois, and from there to Goose Nest Prairie and Shiloh Cemetery. At the latter place he viewed the grave of his father, Thomas Lincoln. At the former place he saw his stepmother, in the home he had provided for her.

Of this visit the old lady cherished the most vivid and pathetic memories. She had a premonition, so she declared, that it was the last time she was to see this well-loved son of hers, and she clung to him in the tenacity of maternal affection. That he had been elected president did not seem strange to her; she believed him great enough and good enough for that or any position. But she was proudly sorrowful that he had been so elected, for she felt sure that some tragedy lay ahead of him. "I can say," she was accustomed to relate, "what not one mother in a thousand can say. Abraham gave me never one hard word."

She long outlived her husband, who died January 17, 1851. She lived until after the death of Abraham, dying December 10, 1869. To the end of her life she loved to talk of him, and to say that in all the years of his boyhood and manhood he never gave her a cross word. No mother, she said, ever had a better son.

No, and few sons have ever had better mothers.

CHAPTER VI

Sarah Lincoln Grigsby

WHEN Thomas and Sarah Lincoln were preparing to depart from Indiana to some unknown locality in Illinois, they applied for their church letters from the Little Pigeon Primitive Baptist Church, and the letters were ordered to be issued. The vote to this effect was recorded November 12, 1829. Two months later, on January 10, 1830, this entry appeared:

"Inquired for fellowship and Sister Nancy Grigsby informed the church that she is not satisfied with Brother and Sister Lincoln. The church agreed and called back their letters until satisfaction could be obtained. The parties convened at Wm. Hoskins and agreed and settled the difficulty."

So the Lincolns left Pigeon Creek in good and regular standing in the church, Mrs. Nancy Grigsby to the contrary notwithstanding. Before the Lincolns got away, March first, Thomas Lincoln, still being a member of the church until departure and the acceptance of his letter elsewhere, was chosen as Moderator in "a difficulty" in which Sister Grigsby brought a charge against Sister Crawford. The report of the Moderator and his associates states that:

"We the Under Signed Refereas being Convened at the meeting house on the 20th of February in 1830, the Ref-

ereas agrees that the Charge is in legal therefore agrees
that the defendant is aquited. T. Lincoln, mod."

If Thomas Lincoln had wanted any revenge upon Sister
Grigsby for her demand that he and Sister Lincoln be required to hand back their church letters, he had it in this
opportunity to preside as one of five "Refereas" in a case
where the meddlesome Sister Grigsby brought a charge
against another member, and could not prove it to the
satisfaction of the referees. The Lincolns and the Grigs-
bys were not on the best of terms. Against the Grigsby
family Abraham Lincoln wrote his coarse and satirical
"Chronicles" and his story of the double wedding of
Reuben Grigsby to Betsy Ray and Charles Grigsby to
Matilda Hawkins, April 16, 1829, less than a year before
the Lincolns left Indiana. It is said that Abraham Lincoln's stepbrother, John T. Johnston, had a fight with
William Grigsby growing out of the same unpleasantness.
The occasion of this hostility of two families in the same
little settlement and the same church, goes back to the
marriage of Aaron Grigsby to Sarah Lincoln, August 21,
1826, and to her death January 20, 1828. She died in
childbed, the child also dying. Her husband, born in
1801, was six years her senior, and did not long survive
her. He died in 1831. Whether the Lincoln family had
any ground for the belief that Sarah had been overworked
or neglected, is not now possible to state. But the death
of Sarah is alleged, and with apparent reason, to have
been the occasion of a long standing bitterness between
the two families.

That might not matter now, were it not that the painful circumstances of the death of this young woman made
the whole family reticent in conversation concerning her.

As they removed from Indiana two years after her death to a region where she had never lived, there was not much occasion to mention her, and such occasion as arose was met with very little information. Abraham Lincoln's partner, William H. Herndon, noticed that Lincoln was never very communicative regarding his sister. This was not because of any lack of affection between them, but because the thought of her was associated with a painful memory. Our lack of knowledge concerning Abraham Lincoln's only sister is to be regretted, for what little we know is attractive rather than otherwise. She was Lincoln's companion, schoolmate and playmate for nearly twenty years. The little that we do know, ought, with greater reason, to be collected and preserved.

Sarah, daughter and first child of Thomas and Nancy Lincoln, was born in Elizabethtown, Kentucky, February 10, 1807, almost exactly two years before her brother Abraham, whose birth occurred February 12, 1809. Of her childhood we know almost nothing, except that Abraham Lincoln has told us that:

"Before leaving Kentucky, I and my sister were sent, for short periods, to A. B. C. schools, the first kept by Zachariah Riney, the second by Caleb Hazel." This is meager information, but it is important. Thomas and Nancy Lincoln desired that their daughter as well as their son should have educational advantages. Not every family among their neighbors felt an equally strong solicitude for book-learning on the part of their daughters. Nancy Hanks and her mother were both "educated" and Nancy's daughter had as good opportunity for instruction as Nancy's son.

The life of this girl following the next year and more

after her mother's death is unwritten. Though only a child of thirteen she was the one woman of the household, and upon her fell the full weight of its domestic responsibilities. However much she was assisted by her brother Abraham and by her cousin Dennis Hanks and by her father, she had to bear a heavy load. Let us hope that they assisted her with the outdoor work, taking off her shoulders the milking and a part of the care of the poultry; still her task was not an easy one.

It is highly to the credit of this little mother that she performed her tasks so well. There is no record of the way she did it, but we know how it had to be done. Whatever help she had, she deserves high praise for the work of her hands. When the new mother came, and it was possible for the children to go to school, and there was a school to go to, she attended with her brother, as she had done in Kentucky. She was less brilliant than he, we are told by those who knew them both, but she was more industrious. She also seemed to the family more religious and she was immersed and joined the Little Pigeon Church. "She had a good mind," said Aaron Grigsby, and he had opportunity to know, though he said he knew Abraham better than his sister.

Elizabeth Crawford described her to Herndon in 1865 as being slow and lacking in initiative and spirit, and being more like her father than her mother; just as Abraham in these respects appears to have resembled his mother rather more than his father. She was rather short of stature, solid and plump in build, and had dark brown hair, straight and rather coarse, and gray eyes. Dennis Hanks knew her all her life, and his description agrees, as does that of her stepmother.

John Hanks said of her:

"I knew Abraham's own sister Sarah. She was a short-built woman, eyes dark gray, hair dark brown. She was a good woman, kind, tender and good-natured. She is said to have been a sweet woman. That is my opinion."

It is unfortunate that Nicolay and Hay called her Nancy, and that other biographers of Lincoln have said that her real name was Nancy but that she took her step-mother's name of Sarah. Her name was Sarah, and never Nancy. We have no details of her marriage, except the date, already given, and none of her death, except that she died in the futile hope of bringing new life to earth. The staggering sorrow of her death, and the feeling, rightly or wrongly held that it might possibly have been averted, left their mark on Abraham Lincoln and on his father and stepmother.

She is buried in Little Pigeon Churchyard, and an impressive stone rises above her grave. She would be bewildered if she were to come back to earth and find that monument, the most conspicuous in the little cemetery. So would be her mother if she could return to earth and know that the Nancy Hanks State Park is named for her. Each of these two women would cast about helplessly for a reason. They might not wholly understand when told that it was because Nancy was the mother and Sarah the sister of Abraham Lincoln. But each of them would think that if the honor was on his account, it was not wholly strange.

CHAPTER VII

The Johnston Girls

GEORGE WASHINGTON was a lover in his very early youth. In his young teens he was bewailing in his letters his unrequited love for divers and sundry young women of Westmoreland and adjacent Virginia counties. Considering that he was a tall and handsome young man, that he rode well, and had a courtly manner, it is surprising that he had such frequent occasion to lament the hard-heartedness of the young women whom he loved.

It was not so with Abraham Lincoln. From the very beginning he let opportunities for love escape him. There were in his very home two girls, either one of whom might have been approached. Abraham's stepmother, Sally Bush Johnston, brought her one son and two daughters to the Lincoln home. Both the Johnston girls liked Abe, but Dennis Hanks married Elizabeth, the older one, and Squire Hall married Matilda, the younger. Abraham appears to have liked these girls, but to have had no other thought of them than as sisters. Abraham saw Dennis Hanks courting one of the Johnston girls, and Squire Hall making love to the other, and so far as we know, made no effort to thwart their love by any claim of his own.

These girls did not go to school as regularly as Abraham's sister Sarah did. The Johnstons and Halls had meager education. It was not at school Abraham met these girls; but they were under the same roof with his family for a number of years, and he did not woo them. Almost the only incident we have of Abraham's relations with these stepsisters is one which Matilda related. She liked to go with him when he was chopping at such a distance from the house that he had to take his lunch and spend the day, but this she was forbidden to do. One day she followed him, and desiring to make her presence known in a clever feat, she sprang upon him, Indian fashion, from behind, and brought him to the ground, and in process of doing so, cut her bare ankle on his sharp ax. He bound up the cut, and then had to assist her in an explanation to be made to her mother. "I'll say I cut it with the ax; that will be true, won't it?" "Yes, Tildy," was the advice of this big honest brother, "but that would not be the whole truth. Tell her the whole truth."

The Johnston girls admired and loved him; probably he could have married either of them if he had chosen. But he was not a precocious lover. In youth and later he saw a long procession of girls go by at close range, and they did not greatly disturb him.

If Abraham Lincoln had any love for these two girls or either of them, it was such love as belonged to the normal life of children of different families thrust together by the vicissitudes of death and the uniting of sundered households. Sally Bush was a good mother to all her children, and they were affectionate and faithful to one another.

Elizabeth Johnston married Dennis Hanks in 1821. Her sister Matilda married Squire Hall in 1826.

This, then, would seem to be all there is to say about the Johnston girls, that Abraham Lincoln was a good stepbrother to them, and they were sure of his protection and brotherly care.   There is no occasion to make a long chapter about them, or to record in detail the uneventful narrative of their subsequent lives.   They both removed, with their husbands, to Illinois, and lived near their mother, and Lincoln saw them from time to time in later years. His relations to them, if not affectionate. were considerate, and they held his memory in honor.

CHAPTER VIII

The Girl in the Covered Wagon

EVERY man is an author, and, however varied his list of literary productions, his favorite book is a bulky volume of fiction in which he himself is the hero. If he reads other fiction, or even reads history or biography, his purpose, in no small degree, is to obtain material for his own life-story, shaped to the heart's desire. Indeed, it may be said that we understand history or biography only in proportion as we are able to project ourselves into the situations and even into the personalities described. That this work of fiction is seldom written is little to the point; the *lex non scripta* is vaster and more truly law that the *lex scripta;* and the written books we make or read are the bits of broken mirror that fashion forth some aspects of our own imaginary heroism in our large and mostly fictitious *liber non scripta.*

Abraham Lincoln in his adolescence dreamed out his own romance and "wrote out in his mind" the narrative of an adventure in which he was the hero.

Now, this great book of fiction which we make and do not write, or write in bits and fragments and not very truthfully, is never all imaginary. The picture-making power of the human intellect is not capable of working without some materials to work upon. The wildest of our imaginary autobiographies, though they outdo Gulliver in

117

their latitude with respect of veracity, still have a basis in fact. The historical basis which afforded Abraham Lincoln material for his unwritten romance, with himself as hero, was the breaking down of a settler's wagon not very far from the Lincoln cabin in the woods of the Pigeon Creek settlement. That wagon contained, among other characters of his novel, the heroine of his romance. She was his first sweetheart, and he himself has told the story of their adventure, both as to the fact and the work of imagination which he built upon it.

This episode in the evolution of Abraham's relations with women is based on the following incident, as it was related by Lincoln to T. W. S. Kidd, editor of the *Springfield Morning Monitor:*

"Did you ever write out a story in your mind? I did when I was a little codger. One day a wagon with a lady and two girls and a man broke down near us, and while they were fixing up, they cooked in our kitchen. The woman had books and read us stories, and they were the first I had ever heard. I took a great fancy to one of the girls; and when they were gone, I thought about her a great deal, and one day when I was sitting out in the sun by the house, I wrote out a story in my mind. I thought I took my father's horse and followed the wagon, and finally found it, and they were surprised to see me. I talked with the girl and persuaded her to elope with me, and that night I put her on my horse, and we started off across the prairie. After several hours we came to a camp; and when we rode up we found it was the one we had left a few hours before, and we went in. The next night we tried again, and the same thing happened—the horse came back to the same place; and then we concluded that we ought not to elope. I stayed until I had persuaded her father to give her to me. I always meant to write that story out and publish it, and I began once; but I concluded it was not much of a story. But I think it was the beginning of love with me."

The incident comes to us undated, save that it happened when Lincoln was "a little codger." If, for the purposes of a little inquiry into the nature and extent of the juvenile literature of the period, or for some study of Lincoln's psychology of adolescence, we suppose it to have occurred when he was fourteen or fifteen, we shall have a conjectural date of 1823 or 1824 which is sufficiently definite for any purpose the story is likely to occasion.

Charles Dickens, traveling thirty miles eastward from St. Louis in 1842 for a view of "Looking Glass Prairie" thus described what he saw in the way of wrecks of these heavily laden and fiercely buffeted vessels:

"Here and there, and frequently, too, we encountered a solitary broken down wagon, full of some new settler's goods. It was a pitiful sight to see one of these vehicles deep in the mire; the axle-tree broken; a wheel lying idly by its side; the man gone miles away to look for assistance; the woman seated among their wandering household goods with a baby at her breast, a picture of forlorn, dejected patience; the team of oxen crouching down mournfully in the mud, and breathing forth such clouds of vapor from their mouths and nostrils that all the damp mist and fog around seemed to have come direct from them."

If a settler's wagon had to break down, it was fortunate if it broke somewhere within reach of the cabin of Thomas Lincoln; for he was skilled in the repairs of such vehicles; and the woman and her child or children did not need to sit long amid their household goods. There was a place for them in the well-filled but still hospitable home of the Lincolns. Lamenting, as such a family must needs lament, the misfortune of their break-down, such a household could but congratulate itself that if such a thing must needs be, it happened where a roof like that of the Lincoln cabin could afford shelter, and the strength and skill of the backwoods carpenter could make the necessary repairs. The family carried its own food, but even this was a minor matter. After the first season the settlers usually had plenty of corn and meat, and what they had they shared freely. Whatever sins the frontier had, it did not lack hospitality.

Who was this family, and whence did it come, that had books, and story books at that? It might have been a family from the eastern end of Pennsylvania, moving westward to New Harmony, and thus traveling on a road well to the south in the state but still north of the Ohio River. It might have been a Massachusetts family that had moved west and thus far south to Marietta, and finding that region well settled, was continuing on to one of the new settlements in Illinois. It was quite certainly not a family from across the river, whence the Lincolns and their neighbors had come.

The mother and the stories she read made a deep impression upon the boyish mind of Abraham Lincoln, and one of the daughters impressed him yet more deeply, and afforded him material for a story of his own. The family moved on, but the tall boy could not keep the girl out of his mind, and indeed made no attempt to do so.

The mind plays strange tricks with us. We think we are flying with it on gilded wings, and find we have been plodding on leaden feet, round and round the same limited area. It is curious what walls and fences the imagination builds for itself, saying to us, Thus far shalt thou go and no farther. The inhibitions of our own minds, chastening and restraining them and fencing them when within unbidden areas, is a phenomenon which no psychologist had fathomed. The boy Abraham Lincoln met that limitation in this home-made novel of his own composition, not in the girl's refusal, or her father's opposition, or her mother's scorn of his rude attire, but in the sheer inability of his imagination to break out of the circle of its incapacity to go further. Most people have had similar experiences when neither whip nor spur will force the picture-making power of the mind to work beyond its own fixed limit.

This innocent little day-dream of Abraham Lincoln's adolescence was clean and honest. In it was no reckless abandonment of mind to the debauchery of juvenile lust; there was no prurient element or abandonment of moral principle. "We concluded that we ought not to elope," he said as he related his dream, and the imagination was loyal to his sense of right.

The most erotic devotee of a perverted Freudian psychology, seeking to reduce all human motivation to a single desire and that a nasty one, will find no material in support of his grosser theories in the adolescent imagination of Abraham Lincoln.

A professional novelist could have done far more with the material than Abraham Lincoln was able to do. He could have located this family in New Harmony, and sent Abraham Lincoln thither a few years later in a quest of the knowledge and altruism of Robert Owen, and have caused the young couple to meet and marry. He could have sent the family on to Illinois and arranged to have the girl present on a day when Abraham Lincoln was stumping his legislative district as a candidate, and they could have recognized, each the other, the soul-mate of reciprocal dreams. For it is wholly possible that the girl dreamed as much about Abraham Lincoln as he dreamed about her. Such are the ways of the novel and the drama, but while they sometimes occur in life, they are exceptional. The covered wagon with the girl that stirred the heart of the boy Lincoln was as a ship that passed in the night and turned not again in its course. As Lincoln decided, it was not much of a story, for the incident had no sequel in the lives of the two persons concerned. They never met again, or if they met they did not know each other. But it was the beginning of love for him.

CHAPTER IX

KATIE ROBY

It is interesting to recall that of the dim and meager traditions of Abraham Lincoln's boyhood in Indiana there is none that records his presence at a play-party. It is not by any means to be inferred that he did not attend play-parties; had he not done so we surely should have been informed of it, for that would have been something so distinctive as to have marked him in the memory of his associates as a strange and unaccountable boy. We should have been told that, either because he was shy, or because he was wrapped up in his books, or because of this or that or the other eccentricity, he could never be induced to attend play-parties. We have no such distinctive recollection of him in his conduct with regard to this form of enjoyment.

The play-party was a marked feature of social life at the time when the Lincolns were in Indiana. Dances were not held in high esteem by the sober-minded religious people of the frontier, but there was no such interdict upon play-parties.

And now lest some reader, ignorant in this regard though intelligent in ordinary subjects that are talked about in books, inquires what a play-party was, and whether it was the same as some other kind of party, the answer is that a play-party was a play-party, and that is all there is to be said about it. There are card-parties and

tea-parties and other kinds of parties, the general character of each of which is supposed to be described in its title,
and there are, or were, play-parties, in which the play (not
the stage-play, but the game accompanied by music and
movement) was the chief feature. It might accompany a
corn-husking with its attendant search for red ears, or an
apple-peeling, with its by-product of a keg or crock of
apple-butter, but it did not need those occasions to justify
its existence. A play-party had standing in its own right.

Imagine Abraham Lincoln at a play-party. The boys
and girls are formed in two parallel lines facing inward
toward each other, and their first play may be that of the
sheep-stealer. In real life no man was held in more ab-
horrence than the sheep-thief, though the horse-thief was
by common consent a worse and more dangerous criminal.
To steal a horse was an invitation to be hung, while a
sheep-thief received imprisonment and contempt. But in
the play-party the sheep-stealer was not in so bad a case.
Let us suppose that Abraham Lincoln stands at the head
of the line, and opposite him, either by accident or design,
stands Katie Roby.

It is a relatively new play, and is the first time Abraham
has participated in it. There is an effort to begin on some
one to whom the play is a surprise. The boys and girls
begin by pointing accusing fingers at Abraham:

> There's the man that stole the sheep!
> There's the man that stole the sheep!
> There's the man that stole the sheep!
>   He stole it while we was all asleep.
> He helt the salt in his right hand;
> He helt the salt in his right hand;
> He helt the salt in his right hand;
>   And bid the sheep, "C'Nan! C'Nan!"

Abraham was certainly embarrassed by this accusation, and not less surprised when the company turned upon Katie the similar accusation as an accessory. Simplifying the threefold repetition, they sang:

> There's the lady that fried the meat,
> She fried it while we was all asleep;
> She helt the knife in her right hand
> And turned it over in the frying-pan!

Having established her guilt as *particeps criminis,* they turned again on Abraham:

> Irish potatoes, tops and all,
> Irish potatoes, tops and all,
> Irish potatoes, tops and all,
> Kiss her now or not at all.

Now under those circumstances, what was Abraham to do? We have no record of his actual conduct, but presumably he did what other young men were accustomed to do.

One swallow does not make a summer, nor does one play make a play-party. Perhaps the next play is about the young lady who sits down to sleep. Two chairs are placed side by side but facing in opposite directions. In one of them a girl is seated. The company circle round her and sing:

> There was a young lady sat down to sleep,
> Sat down to sleep, sat down to sleep,
> There was a young lady sat down to sleep,
>   So earlye in the morning.
> She wants a young man to keep her awake,
> To keep her awake, to keep her awake,

She wants a young man to keep her awake,
  So earlye in the morning.
Oh, write his name down and send it by me,
And send it by me, and send it by me,
Write his name down and send it by me,
  So earlye in the morning.

You are not to say "early" but "earlye," just as you are
to pronounce April "Aprile."

As these lines are sung, the young lady who is supposed
to have sat down to sleep, but who was never more awake
in her life to all the possibilities of her opportunity, selects
her confidante and whispers a name in her ear. That confidante possesses, and is supposed to be the only one who
could possibly guess, the name with which the next stanza
must begin:

Mr. Abe Lincoln his name shall be,
His name shall be, his name shall be,
Mr. Abe Lincoln his name shall be,
  So earlye in the morning.

Mr. Abe Lincoln, thus chosen, sits beside the young
lady, but has scant time or need to keep her awake.
She has made her choice, there is no kiss or other token
of affection. They sit together for a brief musical measure, and then she leaves him. The song goes on. There
is now a young man, seated in the expectation of slumber,
and needing a young lady to keep him awake, and he
whispers her name and has her by his side for a moment,
and leaves her to select another young man to keep her
awake, so earlye in the morning.

There is another play, or was, during the boyhood of
Lincoln and within the memory of at least one living man,

concerning "Weavilly Wheat." Weavilly wheat ain't fit
to eat, according to this play, or at least is not fit for the
hero, whose name descended possibly from the old Scotch
times with Charlie over the water, when there was not a
maid in all the land but vowed baith late and early, she'd
to no man give heart and hand who would not fight for
Charlie, the times when the highlanders came o'er the
heather, came all together, for wha'd be king but Charlie,
survived in several frontier songs, as:

> I won't have none of your weavilly wheat,
>   And I won't have none of your barley,
> Won't have none of your weavilly wheat,
>   To bake a cake for Charlie.

There was one that told of the joy of the miller when
he lived in the mill, the wheel turned around and it
couldn't stand still. There was another about the farmer
sowing his seed, standing and taking his ease, stamping
his feet, and clapping his hands, and turning around to
view the lands—the lands being a partner chosen by the
hand of fate in the revolution of the play. And there was
"Skip t'm'loo." It was probably "Skip to my love," but
the pronunciation was "Skip t'm'loo." This was a play
to delight a disciple of Hegel, for it was modeled on a
thesis, an antithesis and a synthesis. It started off, every
boy having a partner, with one single exception; one boy
was "it." And it was his care to descend like the Ben-
jamites at Bethel and steal a bride. The moment at which
he had opportunity to do this was the moment when all
partners dropped each other's arms, and each man robbed
became at once a robber, leaving another "it." For he
was little less than a booby who, having the whole com-

pany to select from and nothing else to occupy his mind, failed and was "it" for a second time in succession. The distribution being effected, the newly mated partners moved on, avowedly happier for the change. It would seem necessary only to resolve the whole of human life into one game of "Skip t'm'loo" to have a solution of all the problems of the universe, with every one happy in each synthesis, and the millennium coming progressively on the heels of every change. With this explanation, and a reference to the philosophy of Hegel for any further comment, the text of the play may be given:

> Pretty as a red-bird, Skip t'm'loo,
> Pretty as a red-bird, Skip t'm'loo,
> Pretty as a red-bird, Skip t'm'loo,
>   Skip t'm'loo, my darling.
>
> Gone again, Skip t'm'loo,
> Gone again, Skip t'm'loo,
> Gone again, Skip t'm'loo,
>   Skip t'm'loo, my darling.
>
> I'll get another one, Skip t'm'loo,
> I'll get another one, Skip t'm'loo,
> I'll get another one, Skip t'm'loo,
>   Skip t'm'loo, my darling.

It is fashionable to turn up the modern nose at those old plays, and snuff them out contemptuously as "kissing-games." Not all, nor even many of them were kissing games, and whether the kissing-games were more horrible and disgusting and whatever else you care to call them than the modern dances there is room for an honest difference of opinion. But there were kisses in the games in which forfeits were paid, as, for instance, that play that

called for agility and much besides, "Roll the platter."
When the forfeits were sold, they were held by one girl
over the head of another, the latter blindfolded, and possessed of a most elaborate knowledge of penalties:

"Heavy, heavy hangs over your head," said the girl
who held the forfeit, let us say Abraham Lincoln's pocket-
knife, in full view of all but the blindfolded image of
Justice:

"Fine or superfine!" inquired that lady.

"Fine," was the answer. If the forfeit had been Katie
Roby's back comb, and if she had been going about with
her lovely hair all down ever since she failed to catch the
platter, the answer would have been, "Superfine." But
a man's forfeit is "Fine."

"What shall the owner do to redeem it?" is demanded.

Then the oracle utters the bloodcurdling penalty, too
terrible for description here, though the legal language
may be employed:

"He must make a double-shovel plow with Katie Roby."

"He must make a sugar-bowl with Katie Roby and put
three lumps in it."

"He must bow to the wittiest, kneel to the prettiest and
kiss the one he loves best."

Making a double-shovel plow, or a sugar-bowl, or pick-
ing cherries, and putting four of them in the bucket, were
extreme penalties, as they involved no grace but courage
to go straight at the matter and have it done with; but
what a trial was before him who had to bow to the wittiest,
kneel to the prettiest and kiss the one he loved best! For,
even though the one he loved the best was grateful for
his choice of her, what was he to say in excuse for having
declared others to be prettier or wittier than she!

Did Abraham Lincoln attend these play-parties? Certainly he did, and he participated in all these various games and endured, we know not with what grace and submission, penalties such as these that have been named but whose cruelty has not been here described.

And let it be here shamelessly recorded by one who has witnessed not a few of these affairs that they were not attended by terrifying results. They were rude and frank and promiscuous, but they were part and parcel of the social life of a pretty well stratified society, and while modern folk may affect to be shocked by them, they are not so badly shocked as patrons of the play-party would be by the bunny-hug and the cheek-to-cheek indecency.

Abraham Lincoln attended two schools in Kentucky, and left that state when he was seven years of age. The terms were brief, and his attendance was irregular. In Indiana he attended three schools. The first was taught by Azel Dorsey, whose school convened only a mile and a half from the Lincoln farm. The schoolhouse was built of round logs, and was just high enough under the loft for the teacher to stand erect. The floor was of split puncheons. The windows were made by cutting out part of two logs, one on each side of the building. It is said that greased paper was placed over these apertures, but the author has known such buildings with no pretense of any paper, much less of glass, to keep out the weather. The chimney was made of poles and clay. The farmers furnished the firewood in rather long logs, which the older boys cut into four-foot lengths for the fireplace. The school-room probably had no broom, but was swept semi-occasionally by the older girls, who used a bunch of papaw or hazel bushes to raise and redistribute the dust.

Abraham was ten years old when he attended this school. He evinced qualities of leadership that his schoolmates remembered. One of his companions wrote in after years that he always appeared quiet during play-time, never was rude, and seemed to have a liking for solitude. He was often chosen to assist in the adjustment of difficulties between his schoolmates, and when he was appealed to his decision ended the dispute. He was known as a lad of courage, but had few if any difficulties with his companions. He won their respect for his character, and later for what they deemed his scholarly attainments. For from the first he was an apt student.

It was four years after the close of Azel Dorsey's school before Abraham Lincoln was privileged to attend school again. The second Indiana school was kept by Andrew Crawford, a neighbor. Two years later when Abraham was in his seventeenth year he attended his third school in Indiana—his fifth in all—kept by a man named Swazey. This last school was held four miles away. The distance being so great, his attendance was irregular and brief. Crawford's school would seem to have done more for him than either of his other periods of attendance upon book-education.

Lincoln's text-books were *Webster's Speller,* the *American Speller, Pike's Arithmetic,* and *Murray's English Reader.* It was customary to teach a boy to spell the entire spelling book through before he was taught to put words together. The author has known a girl who attended school for two school-years, spelling the book through three or four times without getting any definite idea of what the process was for, and who read with great delight a sentence that caused the significance of the educational process to dawn suddenly upon her—"Ann can spin flax." Spelling was one branch of learning that was not neglected in the backwoods schools.

The Bible was used as a reading-book in many of the district schools. We know this in many ways; among others, we know it from a story of Lincoln told by him to Senator Henderson, of Missouri, and by Henderson to Vice-President Adlai E. Stevenson, concerning the small boy who stumbled over the names of the three Hebrew children who were cast into the fiery furnace.

Crawford did more than teach the contents of books. He conducted a school of good manners. He would send one student out of the room, and bid him or her reenter as a lady or gentleman should enter a drawing-room or parlor. The other pupils were taught what Crawford deemed the proper forms of salutation. One pupil was detailed to greet the entering guest, and conduct him from seat to seat, introducing him properly to each member of the school, and those to whom he was introduced were taught their duty in situations of that character. We do not know how Lincoln acquitted himself in these exercises. He was very tall and awkward. He had shot up almost overnight, and he reached his full stature, six feet, three and one-half inches, before he attained his seventeenth year. He weighed about a hundred and sixty pounds, was strong and vigorous, but slow.

We owe to one of his schoolmates a description of him as he appeared in school:

"His skin was shriveled and yellow," said Katie Roby. "His shoes, when he had any, were low. He wore buckskin breeches, linsey-woolsey shirt, and a cap made of the skin of a squirrel or coon. His breeches were baggy, and lacked by several inches meeting the tops of his shoes, thereby exposing his shin-bone, sharp, blue and narrow."

Katie Roby was an observant girl of fifteen. The description she gave was not flattering as to personal appearance, but she was interested in something more than Lincoln's looks. She knew he was not handsome, but he was worth a careful looking-over. She observed him with sufficient care to remember for thirty-five years these convincing details of his personal appearance. Such a careful observation was not wholly disinterested. She and Abraham Lincoln liked each other. She remembered a spelling-match in which Abraham, though on the opposing side, helped her out. In those days, "spelling-down" was not only a regular weekly exercise in school but a frequent evening recreation which took in as participants the whole neighborhood. Two captains were selected in advance, and these determined by the tossing of a stick and the piling of hand upon hand above the hand of the catcher, who should have the first choice. Abraham was the almost invariable first choice; for he was recognized as the best speller in the community. That is saying much, for in the backwoods settlements were people who had an almost uncanny gift of accurate spelling.

The words were pronounced by the teacher, and spelled first on one side and then on the other. The process began with easy words, and sometimes it was several minutes before any one sat down. Almost any one can spell through the first page of "Words of two syllables, accented on the first,"—"baker, shady, lady, tidy" and so on. The second group containing "Words of two syllables accented on the second" is harder—"abase, translate, embroil" and so on. The next group of "Words of two syllables accented on the first" is still harder, containing, among others, "banquet, coupon, curfew, clergy" and others.

But the opposing lines of spellers begin their serious thinning in the sections beginning with "amity," "abasement," "blandish," "sirocco" and "luminary." From there on through "sycophant," "superfluity," "antipode," and "juridical" the mortality is heavy even in a contest between experienced spellers. The author has held the speller and given out these fatal words in contests that left few survivors beyond the middle of the book.

In a contest in Crawford's school, Abraham and Katie stood opposite each other, and the word "defied" came down the double line. It ricocheted from side to side, knocking over one contestant after another.

"Abe stood on the opposite side of the room," said Katie in 1865, "and he was watching me. I began d-e-f— and then I stopped, hesitating whether to proceed with an 'i' or a 'y'! Looking up, I beheld Abe, a grin covering his face, and pointing with his index finger to his eye. I took the hint, spelled the word with an 'i' and it went through all right."

It was safe enough for Lincoln to be magnanimous to any one who was in danger of misspelling "defied," for he was at home with "antiscorbutic" and other "words of five syllables, accented on the fourth," and with "words of four or five syllables, retaining the accent of their primitives" of which the top word was "alcholize," and with those very difficult words toward the end of the book in which some letters assume the sound of other letters. But still there was a reason for his willingness to see Katie Roby standing across from him a little longer, and not retreating toward her seat until the best spellers were on their way to the rear. So he grinned, and pointed his index finger to his eye, and Katie gave over all thought of spelling "defied" with a 'y.' She knew she could trust him. He was helping her, not trapping her, though she was on the opposing side.

Katie found occasion to admire Abraham for his literary genius. On Friday afternoons Crawford had rhetorical exercises. Boys and girls "spoke pieces" or read essays. Abraham wrote a number of essays. One of these was a protest against the habit of putting live coals on the backs of terrapin to compel them to thrust their heads and legs out of the shell. This and other examples of cruelty to animals Abraham resented. In these days he shot a wild turkey, but was able to recall in later years that he never afterward shot at any larger game. He was not greatly given to hunting, and seems always to have been a merciful boy and man. Another of his essays was on Temperance, as later was one of his first printed addresses. He had another essay against War.

In those days Abraham was a regular reader of a Louisville paper, and kept abreast with current events with rather remarkable facility, considering his antecedents and environment. William Wood, whom Lincoln called "Uncle Wood," was a subscriber to two papers, and Lincoln was an industrious borrower and reader.

At this time his books consisted of The Bible, *Æsop's Fables, Pilgrim's Progress, Robinson Crusoe,* a *History of the United States,* whose author has not been identified, and *Weems's Life of Washington.* The last of these books he earned by three days' hard work. He had borrowed the book from Josiah Crawford—not Andrew the

teacher, but one whom the boys called "Blue Nose." The
book was damaged while in Abraham's possession, and he
worked three days to pay for it.

Lincoln became a good penman. His early handwriting is exhibited in certain of his books. Perhaps the earliest of these are the following often quoted lines:

> Abraham Lincoln
> his hand and pen.
> He will be good but
> God knows when.

Some sentimental writers have professed to find in this
doggerel some foreground of the mind and character of
Lincoln; but these lines were already decades old before
Lincoln ever employed them. His use of these lines means
merely that he caught up a current jingle and copied it.

Two other lines he wrote:

> Good boys who to their books apply
> Will all be great men bye and bye.

He wrote some more serious verse. The following un-
grammatical stanza has been thought original with him;
but though the present writer has not identified, or attempted to identify, its author, he does not think these to
be the thoughts of a boy:

> "Time, what an empty vapor 'tis,
>   And days, how swift they are:
> Swift as an Indian arrow—
>   Fly on like a shooting star.
> The present moment just is here,
>   Then slides away in haste,
> That we can never say they're ours
>   But only say they're past."

Lincoln later wrote some stanzas of his own, and he exercised his gifts in other forms of composition, including some rude backwoods burlesques, which have been taken more seriously than they deserved. In all these matters, he was testing his powers, and showing the beginnings, but only the beginnings, of that strength which later he displayed. But he learned to write a good hand, and to use clear and forcible English.

In manual labor, Abraham Lincoln was not regarded as an industrious boy. "He was no hand to work like killing snakes," said a neighbor woman. "He worked for me," said John Romaine, "but he was always reading and thinking. I used to get mad at him for it. I say he was awfully lazy. He would laugh and talk, crack jokes and tell stories all the time; didn't love work half as much as his pay. He said to me one day that his father taught him to work, but he never taught him to love it."

He loved to read more than he loved to plow corn. He liked to lie down in the shade of a tree and study, moving around with the sun. He did his sums on "boards" riven or whip-sawed, odds and ends of lumber of split shingle, reserved for kindling. Sometimes he figured on the wooden shovel which served as one of the fireplace utensils. When the shovel had been covered so many times that erasure was no longer feasible, he would shave off the shovel, and begin anew with charcoal to cypher over the fresh wood.

Except at the Swazey school, which was so far away that Lincoln's presence was irregular and very brief, his attendance was prompt, and he was a general favorite on the playground and a good scholar in the schoolroom. He was the best speller, the best penman, and perhaps the best all-round scholar among the boys of the neighbor-hood. His attainments were meager, but substantial; and they exerted a marked and permanent influence upon his future. Poor as were his facilities for an education, and scant as were the qualifications of his instructors, Abra-ham Lincoln learned a great many valuable things in the days of his schooling in the woods of Indiana.

In March, 1828, Abraham went to work for James Gentry, the proprietor of Gentryville. Early in April, Mr. Gentry furnished his son Allan a flatboat, on which the latter made a voyage to New Orleans, accompanied by Abraham, who served as "bow-hand" at a stipend of eight dollars a month. This was Abraham's first emergence into the great world, and it meant much to him. While the boat was loading at Gentry's Landing, near Rockport, on the Ohio, Abraham saw a great deal of Katie Roby, whose family appear to have removed for a time from Gentryville to the village on the Ohio. In the evening, they would stroll together by the great river, and talk of many things. She had grown older since the day when Lincoln helped her spell "defied," and he had learned more than he knew three years before. He was now nine-teen years of age, and she was sixteen.

"One evening," she related, "Abe and I were sitting on the banks of the Ohio, or rather on the boat spoken of. I said to Abe that the sun was going down. He said to me, 'That's not so: it don't really go down; it seems so. The earth turns from west to .east, and the revolution of the earth carries us under, as it were; we do the sinking, as you call it. The sun, as to us, is comparatively still; the sun's sinking is only in appearance.

"I replied, 'Abe, what a fool you are!' I know now

that I was the fool, not Lincoln. I am now thoroughly sat-isfied that Abe knew the general laws of astronomy and the movements of the heavenly bodies. He was better read then than the world knows, or is likely to know exactly. No man could talk to me as he did that night unless he had known something of geography as well as astronomy. He often and often commented or talked to me of what he had been reading—seemed to read it out of the book as he went along—did so to others. He was the learned boy among us unlearned folks. He took great pains to ex-plain; could do so simply. He was diffident, then, too."

So far as is known, Abraham talked to Katie only of science and not of love. She married, later, not Abraham Lincoln, but Abraham's partner on the voyage, Allan Gentry. She took pains to say in after years that she and Abe just liked each other, and were never really in love. It was simply a boy and girl attachment, begun in school when Lincoln was young, continued in occasional meetings afterward, as Lincoln was emerging into manhood and she into womanhood. Lincoln was diffident, even then, she remarked. Perhaps he did not think of love at all; perhaps he thought of it, but saw no prospect before him that could justify him in making love to a girl. Perhaps Katie saw a more hopeful outlook in a match with Allan Gentry, son of the foremost man in Gentryville, and part owner of the boat, than in the raw deck-hand, Lincoln, with all his learning.

She was able to tell with pride in after years of her and Abraham's friendship for each other, and of the time he helped her spell the word, and of the evenings when they wandered by the Ohio and dipped their bare feet in the stream and saw the sun go down and the moon rise. But

they were not lovers; just good friends. She admired the
tall, awkward, diffident lad, in spite of his grotesque attire
and his lack of grace. He admired her, and liked to be
with her. Such relationships belong to the expanding life
of young people. It is well when they are as wholesome
and mutually helpful as was the case with Abraham Lincoln and Katie Roby.

CHAPTER X

CAROLINE MEEKER

THE case of Kentucky versus Abraham Lincoln was duly
called, and the defendant answered to his name, and
pleaded "not guilty." Both he and the complaining witness announced themselves as ready for trial, and the
issue was joined. Abraham Lincoln was defendant in a
number of lawsuits, in one of which he lost his horse and
surveying instruments, but only once in all his life was
he arrested, charged with a penal offense, and this was
the time.

The magistrate, Samuel Pate, Esquire, justice of the
peace in and for the County of Hancock and Commonwealth of Kentucky, took his office seriously. He had
erected a large, double log house, somewhat recently completed before this trial, and he had built the east room of
quite unusual size for the express purpose of holding court
therein. In any reasonable weather, court might be held
on the ample porch, and as a matter of fact was often held
there; but the hewn log walls of Squire Pate's temple of
justice suited his idea of the dignity of the law, and he
preferred the trials to be held inside.

No sheriff or constable had dragged Abraham Lincoln
into court; he had come voluntarily, but was guarded by
the two complaining witnesses, or perhaps more accurately, by the complaining witness, John T. Dill, and his
brother Lin.

141

It had not been the original intention of the Dill brothers that there should be a legal trial. They had intended to settle the issue out of court, and according to a method of their own. Lin Dill had stood on the bank of the Ohio River and hallooed across to Abraham Lincoln, and by repeated calls had induced him to row across the stream. The implication of the call was that some one wanted to cross the river and could not find the ferryman. That was a welcome message to Abraham Lincoln, and he got into his boat and crossed over. When he arrived, Lin Dill invited him to step out upon the bank, and Lincoln did so. Thereupon John Dill rushed out of the bushes where he had been hiding, and the two brothers seized the boatman with intent to duck him in the waters of the Ohio.

Although they had taken him at a disadvantage, and he was a prisoner in their hands, they held him in no such control as to assure them of success in ducking him. He was a tough, tall, athletic fellow, and his muscles were like rawhide from chopping and rowing. If he was not a full match for two men, he was far more than a match for either one of his antagonists, and not helpless in the hands of the two. Under these conditions a parley seemed logical, and with some heat on the part of the Dills, and good nature on the part of Abraham, it ensued.

John Dill declared that Lincoln had been taking away his customers, by running a ferry of his own across the Ohio River, Dill having a license from the Commonwealth of Kentucky, and being the only person legally authorized to convey passengers across. This, he declared, was contrary to law, and Lincoln was subject to arrest and fine; and he was due to receive a fine or a thrashing before he recrossed the river.

This suggestion Lincoln immediately acted upon. He told the Dills they might take their choice between the fine and the thrashing, but that if he stood trial, the worst that could happen to the Dills would be the losing of their case; whereas, if they attempted to thrash or duck him, something more serious might happen to them.

They told him that the house of Squire Pate was near; indeed, the ferry was operated from land owned by him. If Lincoln would go with them peaceably to the house of Squire Pate, and there submit to trial, they would not insist upon taking the law into their own hands. Abraham cheerfully agreed, and the three men climbed the bank together, and walked through the fringe of timber and the orchard, and past the little cemetery, to the big new house of Squire Samuel Pate.

Squire Pate was thirty-two years of age, and had a fertile and well-tilled farm. He owned slaves, and treated them well, and buried them, when they died, in a corner of his own little family graveyard. He was a man who had inherited some property, and had added to it, and now, still in the vigor of his early maturity, was giving much attention to his duties as an officer of Kentucky. Some local magistrates make little of the honor or the office, but Squire Pate was not one of these.

Court opened without much ceremony, but not without a quiet dignity. The defendant waived service of a warrant, and the trial began.

John T. Dill, complainant, testified that he operated a ferry across the Ohio River, having license so to do under the laws of the Commonwealth of Kentucky; that he was the sole person who had legal right to set passengers across the river at that point for hire; that Abraham Lincoln, the defendant, had at divers times interfered with his business, notably in one case when he took a passenger from the Indiana side, and delivered him aboard a steamer that stopped midstream, to the financial loss of Dill.

Lin Dill was sworn, and his testimony corroborated that of his brother.

Squire Pate heard this evidence with strong predisposition to find for the plaintiff. He knew the essential facts. The Dill brothers operated the ferry from land owned by him, and paid him rental. The Act of Congress under which Kentucky became a state gave that commonwealth jurisdiction of the Ohio River to high-water mark on the Indiana side. No Indiana license would have been valid. The Dill boys were neighbors, and the squire would prefer to please them; but he would not pronounce judgment till he had heard what the defendant had to offer.

Just then Squire Pate became conscious that others were present. A number of neighbors or strollers had heard of the trouble on the river bank, and had come over to see how matters were coming out. They were shown in by Squire Pate's negro servant, George, who was a year older than the squire, and outlived both the squire and his wife, serving the family till the war made him free, and still serving them and dying on the farm where he had spent his life, and being buried near his old master in the family cemetery. The little stone is there: George Pate, Colored, born April 23, 1794, died, May 29, 1867. That, and a hand pointing upward to the place where George had gone, tell the story of George.

But besides the neighbors and George, the squire was conscious of another presence, that of his niece, Caroline Meeker. She was an orphan, daughter of his older sister, and the squire was her guardian. She was seventeen, and had brown eyes, soft and winsome, eyes that sometimes lighted up with sudden fire. She had brown hair. It curled, and some of the curls fell over her forehead in rebellious fashion. Caroline was standing at the side of the room, and she was looking at the defendant, Abraham Lincoln. Her look caused Squire Pate to look again at Abraham Lincoln. And he was really deserving of the second look. The squire softened a little the judicial tone in which he addressed the defendant:

"Are there any witnesses for the defense? Does the defendant desire to testify?"

Abraham Lincoln rose to his full height. He almost knocked the floor beams above the court room, so tall was he. He answered that he had no witnesses, and that the facts were as had been stated. But he would like to ask a question.

Squire Pate did not see what question there could well be, if the facts were beyond dispute; but he permitted the question.

"The question I want to ask is, Do the rights of John T. Dill, under his license, forbid any other person to operate a ferry from the Indiana bank to the middle of the river?"

The squire replied that the entire width of the river belonged to Kentucky; but the defendant still pressed his point.

"It is not the right of the State of Kentucky to the whole width of the river that I question," he said, "but the extent to which the license of Mr. Dill applies to forbid traffic from the Indiana shore to vessels in the middle of the stream."

The squire began to be interested. And Caroline was interested. She did not like the Dill boys, and it seemed to her that a very unmanly thing had been done in their setting upon Lincoln as they did.

"I did what these men say I did," said Lincoln. "A man came to the bank of the river to catch a passing boat. The boat could not land because of low water, but stopped in the middle of the river. John Dill was not in sight, and his boat was on the other side of the river. Somebody had to take that man from the Indiana shore to the boat, or the man had to miss the boat. The steamer would not wait. I was there, and the man offered to pay me to take him out to the steamboat, and I did. Now, it seems to me that it was not fair to expect me to sit there in my boat, and let that man miss his steamer, just because the Dill boys were not attending to their business. And I did not set the man across the river, as Dill claims the exclusive right to do; I only set him half-way across. And I'd like to know whether his license says that no one else must help a stranger to get on his boat, when the boat is there and there is no other way."

Was the defendant quibbling, or was this a valid legal distinction?

Squire Pate looked at Caroline; she had no doubt that the defendant had expounded good law. Squire Pate began to think so also.

He looked into his book of statutes, read the license, and said:

"I find that John T. Dill has the exclusive right to operate a ferry at this point from the Kentucky shore of the Ohio River, and to set passengers across the river in either direction; but I do not find that the defendant is forbidden to convey a passenger from the Indiana bank to the deck of a passing steamer. The case is dismissed, and the defendant is discharged."

At least three persons present heartily approved the verdict. These were Abraham Lincoln, defendant; George Pate, of color; and Caroline Meeker, niece and ward of the magistrate.

The Dills returned to their ferry, ruefully grumbling over their defeat. The few neighbors scattered. Abraham Lincoln lingered, and the squire invited him to sit for a little while on the porch.

"That was rather a nice point of law you raised," said he. "You seem to me to have a legal mind. Have you ever thought of studying law?"

Then Lincoln told him about his life. He had a very meager education, obtained under great difficulties, with little prospect of being able to use it. He was not yet of age, was helping his father, and he had little incentive to study. But he liked to read, and had an ambition to be something more than an ordinary laborer.

He told Squire Pate that he was a Kentuckian by birth, but had lived in Indiana since he was seven years old, and he was now nearly nineteen. His father's home was sixteen miles from the river, but Abraham had come to work for Green Taylor, at Troy, nearly opposite where Squire Pate lived. His work was partly in Taylor's store, and partly on the flatboat which Taylor operated as a ferry across the mouth of Anderson's Creek. Abraham was getting six dollars a month and board, and was taking most of the money to his father.

He told the squire that he had inherited from his father some liking for the water; Thomas Lincoln had constructed a flatboat and on it made his first journey from the mouth of Knob Creek to that of Anderson's Creek, and so from Kentucky to Indiana. From him also Abraham had inherited some skill in the use of tools, and he had built for himself a flat-bottomed rowboat of his own. It was this offending craft that had got him into trouble with the Dills.   Indeed, as he afterward told William H. Seward, it was with this clumsy little boat he had earned his first whole dollar in a single day, conveying two men and their luggage to a passing steamer. The sums he gathered in this way were infrequent, for usually Dill was alert to his own interests; still, Abraham had earned an occasional fee in that manner, and it was the easiest money he had ever pocketed.

But this did not satisfy him. He wished he knew enough to do something else. His father had taught him to work, but not to love work. He wished he had education enough to be a clerk on a river boat, or something other than a farmer and splitter of rails.

He picked up the volume of Statutes of Kentucky, and Squire Pate suggested that if he would like to read the book, he might do so any time he cared to cross the river for that purpose. The squire could not lend it, as he needed it in his judicial business.

Abraham thanked him, and promised to return. He bade the squire good day, and walked past the little cemetery and down through the orchard toward the river.

Now it chanced that Caroline Meeker was in the orchard just at that time, gathering some apples for her uncle and for the family use. She met Abraham Lincoln, and offered him an apple.

That was the way the trouble began, a long time ago, back in the Garden of Eden. And it might almost be said that there is no prettier way for trouble of that kind to start.

"I'm glad you beat them," she said. "It was mighty mean of them to call you over the river in the lying way they did, and then both jump on you, two to one."

"It was sort of double-teaming it on me," laughed Abraham, "but they did not duck me, and they did not fine me."

"I think it was right clever," said she, "the way you showed that setting folks out from the shore on to a boat was not the same as setting them across the river."

"It seemed to save me from a fine," observed Abraham.

"If Uncle Sam had fined you, I would have scolded him," said Caroline.

Oh, Caroline, with your hand in the basket, filling Abraham Lincoln's pocket with apples, and your rebellious brown curls behaving just the way they ought not, why did you contrive to tell him about the cornhusking that was to occur the very next week in Eli Thrasher's big barn? Did you not know that he would offer to cross the river and escort you there? And I, even while I am scolding you, don't you know I am wishing I had been there in his stead?

No wonder Abraham Lincoln became interested in reading out of Squire Pate's big book of Statutes of Kentucky. And no wonder people said that he was not so much inter-

ested in law as he was in Caroline! I, too, studied law in
my youth, and I would have crossed the Ohio River several times for the sake of reading law on Squire Pate's
broad porch and drinking a glass of buttermilk as Caroline brought it sweet from the churn.

As for the husking—I can not say I ever enjoyed it. It
is hard on the hands, and it is wearisome for the back, but
I would husk till my finger-tips bled for the joy of walking to the party and back with a girl with brown eyes and
curly brown hair like Caroline, or another I once knew.
I verily believe Eve had hair and eyes like that. They
stir deep memories in me, and they stirred the rather sluggish spirit of Abraham Lincoln. On the night of the corn-
husking, he was there. He had rowed across the river,
hiding his boat where the Dills were not likely to discover
it and play any tricks upon him, and he walked up to the
front door of Squire Pate's home, and walked away with
Caroline to the husking party.

The Thrashers were kinsfolk of the Pates. Squire
Samuel Pate's wife's name was Arretta Thrasher. She was
a sister of Eli Thrasher; that is, she was a sister of one of
the long procession of Eli Thrashers; there was always an
Eli Thrasher, and sometimes there were as many as three,
all in a row. They crowd their corner of the little old
cemetery below Squire Pate's house. But the Eli Thrasher
who was a brother of Squire Pate's wife was very much
alive, and would inherit a large farm, and a number of
slaves, and a good family name. And he looked a little
surprised and not wholly pleased when he saw Caroline
Meeker enter the barn under the competent escort of
Abraham Lincoln.

The corn had been pulled from the stalks, and lay in a

long, oval pile in the middle of the barn floor. Two judges, skilled and experienced and supposed to be impartial, walked several times around it, and agreed that "the end to-*wards* the river was a leetle mite the biggest, but the other end had a heap the most nubbins in it," and the rail was laid accordingly.

Then they chose sides, two captains selecting in alternation, both men and women joining in the husking. Caroline was soon selected, not, presumably, so much for the corn she would husk as for her popularity, and Abraham happened to be chosen on the same side, which did not offend either of them.

Then there was a drawing of lots for choice of the two ends of the pile, and the captains, after much advice from the men of their respective sides, looked the pile over, and the fortunate one chose.

At a given signal they set to work, each side determining to be first to the rail, and each admonishing the other not to hide too much unhusked corn in the husks, and each one boisterously declaring that the pile was not divided fairly, and each young man surreptitiously hunting for red ears. For the young man who found a red ear was permitted to kiss a girl, and to make his own selection. If it chanced to be a girl who found the red ear—but that is part of this very story. And besides, girls were not so bold then as they are alleged to be now.

After the husking had made some progress, George Pate, a person of color, accompanied by Moses Thrasher, a gentleman a trifle darker, produced their musical instruments, a violin, then known as a fiddle, and a banjo. Some of the time they sang, and one of the songs had to do with the time-honored denunciation of the man who laid the rail, and of dire threats against his security and peace of mind:

> Hit's a mighty dry year when de crab-grass fail;
> Oh, rho, rho, rho, who laid dat rail?
> Hit's a mighty dark night when de nigger turn pale,
> De big-foot nigger dat laid dat rail!
>
> CHORUS:
>
> Oh, rho, rho, rho, who laid dat rail?
> Show me de nigger dat laid dat rail!
> I'll hit him wid de hoe and I'll hit him wid de flail—
> De big-foot nigger dat laid dat rail!
>
> Hit's a mighty pore crap when de red ear fail,
> Oh rho, rho, rho, who laid dat rail?
> An' I'se gwine to get de ear an' I'se gwine to kiss de gal,
> An' I'll find hit dar right under de rail!

Thus with maledictions on the man who laid the rail, and with keen search for the red ear, the husking proceeded. If too much corn was not pushed back into the shucks, the more fast and furious the husking went, the better. No man there husked more rapidly or threw more bushels of yellow ears into the pile than Abraham Lincoln. And he did not find one red ear the whole evening, except——

I do not want you to think Caroline bold, but what was a girl to do? She found a red ear, and she quickly hid it under her apron. She was not bold enough to display it and select a man and kiss him before that crowd. But she waited till she had opportunity to pass the ear to Abraham Lincoln, unobserved, as she hoped, and he knew a red ear when he saw it, and he did his duty. So far as I am aware that was as well as she could have managed the matter. And it is too late to make any complaint about it now. For it would indeed be a poor crop of corn that produced no red ears: no one more fully shared that opinion than Abraham Lincoln. He had an unmusical voice, but he had a good ear for rhythm, and the song that George and Moses sang was joined in by many of the huskers, including Abraham. Perhaps you would like to know that "rail" and "gal" in the pronunciation of these choristers made a nearly perfect rhyme, and that they gave to the word "ear" the present fashionable and aristocratic pronunciation, as they sang:

Hit's a mighty pore crap when de red yaw fail,
An' I'se gwine to find de yaw an' I'se gwine to kiss de gail.

Abraham Lincoln did both those things. He had help about the finding of the ear, as I have told you, and possibly some also with the remainder of the undertaking.

But, when Abraham Lincoln walked home with Caroline Meeker, and bade her good night on her uncle's wide porch, did he repeat the performance?

He did not.

It had been a part of the play, before, but this would have been something more serious.

Not but that he wanted to.

But what right had he to kiss this beautiful young woman, a member of one of the most aristocratic and prosperous families along the Kentucky bank of the Ohio? What had he to offer her? He lacked two years of being of age. And when he became of age, he would be landless and penniless. And her people had their land and their slaves and their pride. Nonsense! He was a fool for thinking of such a thing!

Moreover, if you must know the whole truth, Mrs. Pate

did not wholly approve of Abraham Lincoln. She wanted Caroline to marry her brother, Eli Thrasher. Then Caroline would have a good home, with land and servants, and a good, prosperous, steady husband. To be sure, Eli was eight years older than Caroline, but what of that? Why should a man of twenty-five be thought too old to marry a nice girl of seventeen, going on eighteen? Arretta Thrasher Pate did not like to see Abraham Lincoln coming to study law on her husband's porch, and Caroline taking him buttermilk fresh from the churn. Why should he be studying law and if he had to study it why should he come there to study it? For Caroline ought to marry Eli Thrasher, and not be bothered by landless young men from the backwoods of Indiana.

That was the way Mrs. Pate felt about it.

Abraham Lincoln quickly felt this opposition to his coming, and was ready to assent to the justice of it. He had no right, he said to himself, to thrust his attentions on this lovely girl. And he did not.

After his return from New Orleans he was not at the river for any long periods, and he saw less and less of the lovely girl with the brown eyes and the curly brown hair. In the spring of 1830, when he was barely twenty-one, he removed with his father and stepmother to Illinois, and he never saw her again.

But she did not forget him. She heard that he had served as a captain in an Indian war, and she was sure he was the bravest of them all. And after a while she heard from people who visited the Illinois country that Abraham Lincoln was a member of the legislature. She often wondered if he would not come back some day; and she put off her near-at-hand lover, Eli Thrasher, till Abra-

Old Pigeon Church

The Grave of Lincoln's Sister Sarah

Photographs by the Author

The Mouth of Anderson's Creek

The Home of Judge Samuel Pate

Photographs by Hon. William H. Townsend

ham Lincoln had been gone more than three years. Then
she married Eli Thrasher, just as every one had always
expected that she would.

Now, please do not ask me whether this is all true that I
am telling you, or whether I am making it up. And yet,
if you must know, I will tell you. I am not making it up;
I may be adding a touch of color here and there to fill in
the scant and faint outline of tradition, but my part in the
creation is a very modest one. Why, I can not even end it
as I want to do. Don't you know that if I were making it
up, there would be a happy ending? And that is just impossible.

Come, then, to where I learned this tradition, and we
will finish the story with the most solemn and indisputable
documentary facts. We will go to the solid old log house
of Squire Pate on the Kentucky shore of the Ohio, and
push our way through the tangle to where Caroline gave
Abraham the apple, and we will find the crowded and
overgrown little cemetery, and get some of the living Pates
and Thrashers to help us identify the names we do not
know.

Here is John Beauchamp, his grave marked by a stone
of unusual size, and he had no relation to this group of
families. He was a passenger on a river steamer, and
was taken off, desperately ill of pneumonia, down there at
the landing where Abraham Lincoln used to tie up his
boat. John Beauchamp died in his twenty-ninth year,
died in the hospitable home of Squire Pate, died a stranger
but not friendless, and they buried him here with their
own kin. That was the kind of hospitality Squire Pate
believed in.

And I have told you about George Pate, colored, who

refused to be set free, and was buried here with the family after the war had closed, with an upward pointing hand to tell that the Pate family believed he had to gone to heaven just like white folk. And the long line of Eli Thrashers; and Samuel Pate, Esq., and his wife, Arretta Thrasher Pate. They are all there.

But what about Caroline, wife of Eli Thrasher?

She is there, too. She died December 25, 1835, aged twenty-five years, five months and fourteen days, which makes her a year and a half younger than Abraham Lincoln. And her husband did not live many years. He died June 6, 1842, aged thirty-nine years, six months and twenty-six days. He never recovered from the tragic death of Caroline. The memory of that sorrowful Christmas shadowed him till he lay down beside his wife, whom he had loved for many years and possessed for less than two.

There is one other stone we must read. Caroline, daughter of Eli and Caroline Thrasher, did not live to repeat her mother's romance, but died June 2, 1851; and when we set down the fifteen years, five months and nine days that were reckoned as belonging to her earthly life, we know how her mother died. Little Caroline was born on Christmas Eve, and her mother died next day.

I wonder if Abraham Lincoln ever knew about this. I wonder if, in the winter following the death of Ann Rutledge, some one who had come from near his old home in Indiana brought word that Squire Pate's niece, the one who married Eli Thrasher, died giving birth to her first child.

But I do not know. I have told you all I know about it, and a very little besides. But not very much.

CHAPTER XI

POLLY WARNICK

CORN-PLOWING was over, and the wheat was in stacks. Oats had been cut and were in shock, and prairie hay, which was to be had for the cutting, was in stacks or cocks. There came a little respite between summer harvesting and fall plowing, and the farmers knew how to make the most of such interludes in their strenuous toil. If the signs of spring in Chaucer's day set folk longing to go on pilgrimages, the midsummer respite suggested to the frontiersman the exhilaration of politics. It was too early for camp-meeting, which belonged by divine right to the later days of summer; but elections were held in August, and the latter days of July were hot with the double fervor of the sun and of the American citizen's devotion to politics.

In the summer of 1830, Decatur and vicinity turned out to hear a candidate for office, of whom, unfortunately, we know practically nothing. His name was Posey, the same as the name of the man who had stored Thomas Lincoln's goods at Troy, Indiana, after the flatboat voyage and before the removal of the family. Of these two men named Posey, we know nothing but the name. The story of this one we have in the narrative of John Hanks, who said:

"After Abe got to Decatur, or rather to Macon County,

157

a man by the name of Posey came into our neighborhood
and made a speech. It was a bad one, and I said Abe
could beat it. I turned down a box and Abe made his
speech. The other man was a candidate—Abe wasn't.
Abe beat him to death, his subject being the navigation
of the Sangamon River. The man, after Abe's speech
was through, took him aside and asked him where he had
learned so much and how he could do so well. Abe replied, stating his manner and method of reading, and
what he had read. The man encouraged him to persevere."

In the opinion of John Hanks, the speech of Abraham
Lincoln on that day was far superior to that of Posey, and
that appears to have been the general impression. I have
talked with several men whose fathers profess to have
heard Abraham Lincoln on that occasion, and all of them
agree that it was a remarkable effort, or so seemed to
them, and the more so because it was delivered by a field
hand, a day worker in the harvest of a farmer near Decatur. Inquiry as to his personality elicited the information that he was Abraham Lincoln, son of a settler recently arrived from Kentucky, and living about ten miles
west.

What concerns us now is the fact that among those who
heard the speech and concurred in this favorable opinion,
was Polly Warnick, daughter of the sheriff of Macon
County.

But before we go on to tell about her, we must go back
to Indiana and relate how Abraham Lincoln happened to
be in Illinois in the summer of 1830.

About the middle of March, 1830, after fifteen days of
heavy travel, the family of Thomas and Sarah Lincoln

drew up at the home of John Hanks, four and one-half miles northwest of Decatur, in Macon County, Illinois. The family had camped the night before in the public square of Decatur. Lincoln was able twenty-eight years afterward to indicate the route by which the heavy wagon, drawn by two yoke of oxen, entered the town, and the precise spot where the company camped; and that spot indicated by him is now marked by a tablet.

John Hanks and his family had migrated to Illinois two years earlier. From his descriptions, and those of his cousin Dennis who made him a visit in 1829, it seemed to the Lincolns that Illinois was a more promising state than Indiana. Especially did it appear to be a location in which the family might escape the "milk-sick" which had earlier taken such heavy toll of the little colony at Gentryville, and which had never recently reappeared in that vicinity.

The occupants of the wagon of Thomas Lincoln, which, we are assured, was the very first he had ever owned, were thirteen in number, and included not only Thomas and Sarah Lincoln and Abraham, but Mrs. Lincoln's son, John D. Johnston, and her daughters, Sarah and Matilda and their husbands, Dennis Hanks and Squire Hall.

Weather was propitious, and the Lincolns quickly established themselves in a cabin of their own, which was erected by the joint labor of all the men and boys, including John Hanks. Its building did not require many days.

The early settlers of Illinois held the fertile prairie land in low esteem. They knew no way of establishing a new home without the chopping down of trees. They believed that land that did not grow trees would not grow grain. So they invariably made their homes in the timber, near the streams.   The Lincolns drove over five or six miles of excellent and unoccupied prairie and found a home-site in the timber, nine miles west of Decatur on the north bank of the Sangamon River.   To this day it is not an easily accessible spot.*

John Hanks had already cut logs for the home; and the available force was adequate for the erection of the cabin in short order.   The removal and the new location appear to have given a thrill of hope to all members of the colony.   Even Thomas Lincoln worked hard; and the Lincoln household was soon housed under its own roof.

Then Abraham, assisted by John Hanks, took the oxen and broke up ten acres of land.   Thomas had Dennis Hanks and Squire Hall and John D. Johnston to assist him, so he could afford to sow and harrow in a large field of sod-corn.   John Hanks and Abraham split out rails, doubtless while the others were dragging in the corn, and fenced the whole ten acres.   Those rails, and certain others in the neighborhood, were destined to become famous.

It was a good spring's work.   Had Thomas Lincoln and his assistants always been as industrious, there had been no good reason why they should not have prospered. The house was built, the land was broken, the crop was planted, and the field was fenced, all while the year 1830 was young.

This was the last important work which Abraham Lincoln did at home.   In the month preceding the arrival of the family in Illinois, he reached his twenty-first birth-

---

* A tablet marks the site of "Abraham Lincoln's First Home in Illinois" just beside the farm-house now standing.   The house is a frame building, and contains nothing that was in the original home.   There is a dispute as to whether the original house occupied that precise spot; some authorities holding that it stood very nearly where a wind-mill now stands, about a quarter of a mile nearer the river.

day. He remained at home long enough to see his father and stepmother housed and settled, and their crop planted, and then he left home.

He did not go far away. For a full year he remained in Macon County, and very near his father's home. He hired himself out to farmers, concerning one of whom, and his family, there is a story of interest to which we shall come presently.

For a full year, therefore, from March, 1830, until the deep snow of the following winter went off, leaving the ground so flooded that when he left to join Denton Offutt for his second trip to New Orleans, he was compelled to go down the river in a canoe instead of by land, Abraham Lincoln lived in Macon County, and worked at odd jobs. For the first time in his life he was a free man, living out from under his father's roof.

The names of the residents of that period in Macon County are well known, and there are few farmers, then resident in that vicinity, for whom Lincoln is not alleged to have worked. Also there were several girls who afterward married other men, to whom Lincoln is alleged to have paid some trifling attention in that period. One may gather in and about Decatur names of several young women on whom Lincoln is alleged to have called. But there was one to whom his attentions were more marked: and we know her name, and something about her. She was Mary Dillard Warnick, daughter of the Major Warnick for whom Lincoln made the thousand rails.

The Warnick family lived on the south side of the Sangamon River, eight miles west from Decatur, on the old Springfield and Paris state road. The house is still standing. It is probably the oldest house in Macon

County in continuous use as a dwelling. It dates back to and perhaps antedates the organization of the county. After it had been sold by William Warnick, it became the Ekel Tavern, or Eight Mile Tavern.

Social lines were not strongly drawn in those days, but Sheriff Warnick did not count the Lincoln family as of the same grade as his own. There is a rumor that Abraham Lincoln paid some attention to a girl of another family, and that Warnick influenced her father against Lincoln, as belonging to a family of little distinction, and giving small promise of amounting to anything himself. But he came somewhat near to having Lincoln as his own son-in-law, if we are to believe the rather well-authenticated story which comes down to us.

Sheriff William Warnick had eleven children, six daughters and five sons. Mary Dillard Warnick was the eldest daughter. Lincoln and his stepbrother, John D. Johnston, had a contract to split a thousand rails for Sheriff Warnick.*

It need not disturb us to find that in the brief period of Abraham's residence near Decatur a number of names emerge from the mist of semi-oblivion as those of girls to whom he paid some attention. A diligent author could compile a sizable card-catalogue of people who have assured him that Abraham Lincoln made love to their grandmothers. Nor is such a tradition wholly to be scorned. That was the first winter Abraham Lincoln lived away from home. Decatur was a rather gay place, and there

---

* Popular tradition says three thousand, and makes John D. Johnston Lincoln's partner in the enterprise. But John Hanks, who is the best authority on this subject, said: "Abraham, during the winter of 1830-31, walked three miles and made 1000 rails for Major Warnick." The precise number is unimportant, but as the narrative here is not wholly in accord with either well-known story, it may be well thus to cite the authority.

were play-parties and such-like performances at which he must surely have been present. If he saw Jemimah Hill home from a party, some time in the winter of 1830-31, and she remembered it pleasantly after Abraham Lincoln became famous and told her children and grandchildren about it, she probably told the truth, and if the story grew a little as the years went by, that was only natural and a thing to be expected. The writer, who has heard many such stories, is glad to say that there is none that any friend of Lincoln could care to deny. He was interested in girls, and he paid some little attention to several of them. But if he had anything approaching a love affair while he was at Decatur, the girl was Polly Warnick, and it did not last long.

Robert Warnick, through whom chiefly, though not exclusively, the story of Lincoln's relations with his family have come down to us, died in 1914, aged about ninety. Eleven years before his death, while he was in excellent physical and mental health, he told the story of Lincoln's first year in Illinois. It was written down at the time, and the notes of his conversation are our best connected narrative of the events described.

The liking of the two young people for each other did not develop to the stage of matrimonial proposals. Abraham realized that he was poor and that he had before him an uncertain future. He was trying to discover what he was good for. Young men as poor as he were making love and establishing homes; but he was too poor. He must have realized that Major Warnick had some ground for his objection to any such match as he could have proposed to Polly. The daughter of a county official could choose among the foremost men of the county; she had no necessity of accepting a poor young fellow who had just arrived in the state and who had no prospects.

So Abraham Lincoln split rails for Major Warnick, but did not propose to his daughter. And Polly looked the young man over, and decided that she could do better. Such matters were quickly adjusted in frontier days, and Polly had suitors enough among whom to choose. There was, among others, Joseph Stevens. He was a son of Leonard Stevens, who came in 1821, the first settler of Macon County, ten years before it became a county. Joseph was born in New York State, and was thirteen years of age when his father migrated to the prairies. He was twenty-one in 1830, and ready for a wife.

Thus two of the most prominent families in Macon County joined in the noisy festivities of a great wedding in 1830, and whether Abraham Lincoln was invited we do not know. The marriage license of Joseph Stevens and Mary D. Warnick was recently discovered with nine others in the old records of Macon County.* Of the ten brides one was named Delia, two were Elizabeth, two were Mary, and five were named Nancy. There is much of fleeting fashion in the choice of names for girls. But Mary is a good name, and has been for nineteen hundred years, while Nancy, which was a very popular name one hundred years ago is now considered old-fashioned.

After the marriage of Mary Warnick, Abraham paid some little attention to other girls about Decatur, one of the Green girls being named as one whom he escorted to a party. But he did not make love to any of them, and the Green girl is only a tradition, though the family is well

---

* The marriage license of Joseph Stevens and Mary D. Warnick is dated June 17, 1830.

known and reputable, while of Mary Warnick we have reasonably certain information.

The year sped on, Abraham working at odd jobs in harvest-field and at rail-splitting, and doing his share of the hard work at hog-killing time. He had been paid six dollars a month for butchering in Indiana; what his wages were in Illinois we do not know.

Winter came. It was the terrible "winter of the deep snow." Lincoln was crossing the Sangamon one day, when his canoe upset. The accident did not occur in midstream, but near the Warnick shore. It would have required a deep stream to wet the full length of Abraham Lincoln; and the Sangamon, while deep enough in midstream at that season was only knee-deep where he was thrown from his round-bottomed craft into the icy water near the shore. His feet were soaked, and before he could reach the Warnick house, they were frozen.

Frozen feet require heroic treatment. His shoes were removed and his feet thrust into a bucket of snow. Mrs. Warnick took him in charge, and she was a competent nurse.

It was four weeks before his feet healed sufficiently to enable him to leave the Warnick house, and by the time he left, he had thoroughly established himself in the good graces of the Warnick family. Had Polly still been at home, heart and fancy free, those four weeks might have wrought wonders. But Polly was married, and Abraham's frozen feet did not find the road to her heart.

But those four weeks were not wasted. Sheriff Warnick had in his home a copy of the Statutes of Illinois, and Lincoln read them industriously. Robert Warnick said:

"At the time he froze his feet, he stayed in our house

four weeks, my mother nursing him, until he was able to be out. I have heard my father say that it was at this time Lincoln began to study law. My father being sheriff had a copy of the Illinois Statutes, and this was Lincoln's text-book in law."

It was not his first text-book, for he had already read the Statutes of Indiana, loaned him by David Turnham, but this period of four weeks with little to read except the Statutes, and Polly not there to divert his attention from that alleged jealous mistress, the law, was one in which his study made good progress. His legal inclination received a new impetus.

Before the "deep snow" melted away, Abraham met Denton Offutt, a brisk and venturesome business man, who traded up and down the Sangamon. He had learned that Abraham Lincoln and John Hanks had had experience in navigating the Mississippi. He offered them fifty cents a day as wages if they would go to New Orleans for him. They accepted the tempting offer.

Polly did not mourn for Abraham Lincoln. But in after years she remembered with a happy thrill of pride that the tall lawyer who came to Decatur when court was in session, and put up at the Macon House, and was spoken of by her father in terms of increasing honor, had some times in a former year crossed the Sagamon River to visit her.

She saw him disappear in a canoe headed down the Sangamon in the spring of 1831. A little later he was on a flatboat headed for New Orleans. That was the boat that stuck on the dam of Rutledge's Mill at New Salem; and that was where Abraham Lincoln met Anne Rutledge.

CHAPTER XII

ANN RUTLEDGE

A RED-HAIRED girl in a linsey-woolsey dress and a slatted sun-bonnet, serving meals which her mother cooked for boarders in a log tavern, carrying baskets of dinner down the clay bluff to the mill at the river side, and stopping twice a week at the post-office to inquire after a letter that never came, has caught the imagination of the people in America in a manner that belongs to no other young woman, and makes the story of Ann Rutledge a chapter of especial interest in the life of Abraham Lincoln. To winnow the few grains of truth about it from the stacks of chaff that have been written, and tell the story as it really occurred, is far from being an easy task. It involves a study of the career of the future president during the first four of his six years in New Salem, and weaves itself into the whole web of his fortunes, commercial, intellectual and political.

After just one year of residence in the new state to which his father had removed when his son was twenty-one, Abraham Lincoln left Macon County, Illinois, in March, 1831, for the purpose of joining Denton Offutt and making a voyage on a flatboat to New Orleans. He and his associate found Offutt in Springfield, having a gay time in the Buckhorn Tavern. The boat was not ready. Abraham Lincoln, John Hanks and John D. John-

167

ston, thereupon undertook to build the boat. From "Congress lands" five miles north of Springfield, they cut trees, which were made into lumber for them at the Kirkpatrick Mill—a mill of the same name as that on Nolin Creek to which Abraham's family had conveyed grist on horseback in his childhood. In about four weeks the boat was built, loaded and started down the Sangamon.

In April, 1831, the boat stuck for a night and the better part of a day on the Rutledge dam at New Salem, a sporadic and short-lived town situated on a high and picturesque bluff about thirty miles from Springfield. The small population of the village gathered and watched the labor of getting the boat across. Abraham was conspicuous, with his trousers "rolled up about five feet" working industriously and successfully at getting the boat over the dam.

The voyage completed, Lincoln returned to New Salem. From there, he went in the spring of 1832, to the Black Hawk War; and after that brief and solitary military experience, he made his home in New Salem, until the little town "winked out" and Lincoln left it on March 15, 1837, having been a citizen of that ambitious and ill-starred little city during almost the whole of its corporate existence.

The six years from April 19, 1831, to March 15, 1837, were an important epoch in his development. In the middle months of that period lies his romance with Ann Rutledge.

The founder of New Salem was James Rutledge, who shared this honor with his nephew, Reverend John M. Cameron, a retired Cumberland Presbyterian minister. The town was surveyed on October 23, 1829, and the post-office was established on Christmas Day of that year.

Mr. Rutledge built a mill and a four-room cabin that served as a tavern.

During the summer of 1831, Denton Offutt, having returned from his flatboat excursion to New Orleans with Lincoln and his companions, contracted for a lot and erected a store building in New Salem. In that store Lincoln became a clerk.

Lincoln's return to New Salem after his trip to New Orleans was about August 1, 1831. Offutt's store was completed about the middle of September, Lincoln doubtless working with Offutt in the erection of the building. During this time, and for some time after the Black Hawk War, Lincoln boarded chiefly with Rowan Herndon.

Perhaps it is not quite accurate to speak of him as having a regular boarding place in the beginning. The stores of New Salem closed at sundown, and Lincoln spent the night where he was invited. Sometimes he was at Jack Armstrong's, over in Clary Grove. Sometimes he was at Uncle Jimmy Short's, across at Sand Ridge. Sometimes he was at Bowling Green's. Board was cheap, but hospitality was even cheaper, and Lincoln did much boarding around. When he worked for farmers, as he did now and then, he boarded with them. He was welcome everywhere, for he was an interesting guest, and the frontier had no lack of food for a visitor who brought an element of cheer into the loneliness that was inseparable from pioneer life. He did not pay for his board unless he had to do so.

Love was little in his thought when he went to New Salem. He was busy studying grammar under the instruction of Mentor Graham, and later was surveying under John Calhoun. He was writing papers for the debating society. He was acting as referee in wrestling matches. He was winning his own way with his palms and with his fists and with his wits. He had little thought of love. His world was a world of men.

Even before his departure for the Black Hawk War, Lincoln had announced himself as a candidate for Legislature, his published manifesto bearing the date March 9, 1832. The election was held August 6, 1832, and Lincoln was defeated. There were twelve candidates for four positions in the Legislature. The man who stood next above Abraham Lincoln was Reverend Peter Cartwright, with whom he was destined to cross swords again in later years. Cartwright's vote was eight hundred and fifteen and Lincoln's six hundred and fifty-seven. Lincoln stood remarkably well in his own county. His first speech at Pappsville was heard by a number of men who became his permanent and useful friends. Among these were Stephen T. Logan, who later was his law partner, Major John T. Stuart, whom he had known in the Black Hawk War, and who became Lincoln's first partner in the law, and William Butler, with whom Lincoln later boarded in Springfield, and who was capable of teaching even Lincoln a good deal about politics.

After his defeat, Lincoln returned to New Salem and considered how he was to earn a living. Offutt's store failed, and Lincoln was out of work. In the interval between his partnership with Offutt and that with William F. Berry, he considered the wisdom of becoming a blacksmith.

Lincoln had some thought, also, of going to Jacksonville, for a few months of schooling in Illinois College. Ann Rutledge's brother and William Greene pursued studies there, and Lincoln considered a brief course there as not beyond the bounds of possibility.

On May 7, 1833, Abraham Lincoln was appointed postmaster of New Salem, and held that honorable but not very lucrative office until it was discontinued in March, 1836. It was time for him to secure a regular boarding place, and he found one in the home of Reverend John Cameron. This Cumberland Presbyterian preacher and real-estate promoter was blessed with one son and eleven daughters. There was safety in numbers, and Lincoln ran that gauntlet without losing his heart. The girls joked about "old plain Abe" and were not in sympathy with his politics. The Rutledges were Whigs, but the Camerons were Democrats, and the Cameron girls would not have voted for Abe if they could. However, when he had chills and fever, and lay in bed burning up with heat and Mat Cameron supplied him with brimming gourds of water, he told her that when the Whigs came into power, and he became president of the United States, he would make her postmistress of the then to be great city of New Salem, if she would keep him supplied with cold water. He did not offer to marry her, however, and according to the Cameron tradition it would not have done him any good if he had done so.

Lincoln's office did not bring him much money, and he was in debt on the second of his commercial enterprises. Peter Van Bergen, to whom had been assigned a note of Lincoln's for $379.82, issued by Lincoln October 19, 1833, sued him and obtained judgment April 7, 1834. To satisfy this judgment, Lincoln's horse and surveying instruments were seized, and it would have fared ill with him if Uncle Jimmy Short, of Sand Ridge, had not bid in this

property, returned it to Lincoln, and given the young surveyor ample time in which to repay the money necessary
to recover his instruments and horse.

During all this time, which covered the first three of
his six years in New Salem, Lincoln had little time to look
at women. Hannah Armstrong repaired his clothing;
Mrs. Jack Kelso was good to him when he sat with her
rather idle husband reciting poetry; Mrs. Bowling Green
liked to have him come and visit her husband. His women
friends were married women, and they were his friends
because he was a friend of their husbands.

This brings the narrative down to the summer of 1834,
and Lincoln was a second time a candidate for the Legislature. This time he was elected. For the first time he had
promise of a small but regular income, three dollars a day,
while the Legislature was in session, which was less than
three months of the year. It was about this time that
Lincoln changed his boarding place, probably because the
Camerons were moving back to Sand Ridge, as we shall
later have reason to relate. Then it was that Lincoln
went to board at the Rutledge Tavern. He had known
Ann Rutledge for more than three years, but now for a
few months he saw her three times a day.

Moreover, at this time, his several commercial enterprises having failed, and having no store of his own in
which to house his post-office, he removed the few tan-
gible effects of that office to the store of Samuel Hill,
and was Hill's clerk, postmaster, surveyor, farm-hand,
and member elect of the Ninth General Assembly of the
sovereign State of Illinois.

Abraham Lincoln and Samuel Hill had occasion to talk
about a great many things, one of which was to remark

on the regularity with which, twice a week, Ann Rutledge came to inquire for a letter that never came. Both men grew very much interested in Ann's anxiety about that letter.

Lincoln and Hill were never partners, but Hill had had a partner when Lincoln first came to New Salem in 1831. The name under which he was known was John McNeil, and he had prospered in his business. He had no bad or expensive habits. He saved his money, and when some one had a farm that had to be sold quickly for cash, John McNeil always had a little money on hand to help him out of his difficulty in exchange for a warranty deed for one hundred and sixty acres of good prairie soil. It is necessary for us to form a more intimate acquaintance with this man, John McNeil, the man in whose house in 1831, Lincoln cast his first vote as a citizen of Illinois, and of the United States. The election was held in the house of John McNeil, but that gentleman, almost alone of the citizens of New Salem, did not vote. He had become a little reluctant to record his name in places where there might be subsequent investigation.

On November 4, 1831, "John McNeil" bought a farm for a very modest sum in cash, and the deed was drawn in that name. But a little more than a month later, McNeil came to Abraham Lincoln, and asked him to draw a deed for another farm which he was purchasing, and told him a secret. His name was not McNeil, but McNamar. He was beginning to feel uneasy lest his land-holdings under a false name might cause him trouble. Lincoln was not yet a lawyer, and that was probably the reason McNamar went to him. A lawyer would have charged him more. But Lincoln was a surveyor and accustomed to legal descriptions of land, and he drew the deed to John McNamar, Jr., grantee. Also he kept McNamar's secret.

The farm thus purchased, for cash and at a rock-bottom price, was that of Reverend John Cameron, and was situated on Sand Ridge, on the waters of Concord Creek. He was staking everything he had on the New Salem venture, and was already financially embarrassed. McNamar generously helped him out with money in exchange for an excellent farm.

McNamar explained to Lincoln that his home was in New York State, and that his parents still lived there. He had left them to make his fortune. His father had had financial reverses, and McNamar feared that if his father knew how to reach him he would send him pitiful appeals for assistance. He was determined not to answer any such appeals till he owned ten thousand dollars. That was a fabulous sum in New Salem in 1832, but John McNamar was within sight of possessing it. He was beginning to plan for a return to his old home, and he wanted to get his property in good legal shape for an absence.

On July 26, 1832, Abraham Lincoln drew the papers for another transfer. James Rutledge also was on the brink of a financial precipice, and he sold his Sand Ridge farm on Concord Creek to the benevolent John McNamar, who had a sufficient sum on hand in ready cash to make himself the possessor of another excellent farm adjoining that of Cameron.

By this time all New Salem knew that John McNeil was really John McNamar, and they knew the poor excuse he gave as a reason. Even if he told the truth, he had been an unfilial son, deserting his father when the father had need, and piling up money and extending his acreage until

Rutledge Tavern, where Lincoln boarded, in New Salem, Menard
County, Illinois, as rebuilt in 1925

The view from John McNamara's house to the corner of the yard
where stood the house in which Ann Rutledge died

Photograph by Hon. William H. Townsend

The Original Grave of Ann Rutledge

With the compliments of W. H. Fay, custodian of Lincoln's Tomb, Springfield, Illinois

The Ann Rutledge Grave at Petersburg, Illinois

he was the richest man in New Salem, while his aged parents suffered dire poverty and he hid from them under a false name. But not many people in New Salem believed this was the real reason. That he had gotten a girl in trouble and deserted her was the first conjecture, and was readily dismissed. John McNamar was not a man who permitted unreckoning passion to lead him into imprudence and possible expense. It was more likely to have been some fraud or bit of sharp practise, the people thought. But no one knew, and no one knows now. He may have told the truth.

Having secured as many farms as were for sale at bargain prices, with their land values increasing every day, and with New Salem's fortunes dribbling out, John McNamar left New Salem in the fall of 1832. He promised a speedy return, and announced his intentions of bringing his aged parents to live and die in New Salem in a home he was generously to provide for them. He did not return for more than three years, and by that time there was little left of New Salem.

Every one in New Salem knew that John McNamar had paid some attention to Ann Rutledge, but the general impression was that her parents distrusted him after learning that he was masquerading under a false name, and that if Ann ever loved him, her love was killed by his heartlessness and deception. Yet Lincoln and Hill knew that though McNamar had been gone two years, Ann was still looking for a letter that never came.

We can have no reasonable doubt as to why John McNamar jilted Ann Rutledge. She whom he had first known as the prospective heiress of the great fortunes of one of the founders of New Salem, was now a poor girl.

Her father had lost his mill, lost his farm, lost his courage. New Salem was a forlorn hope. Both Rutledge and Cameron were bankrupt. Both men had families likely to become dependent. John McNamar, who had left home when his own father was in financial straits, and had changed his name to escape financial obligations on his father's account (to accept as the least dishonorable his own account of the affair) was not the man to marry, if he could help it, into a family like that of the Rutledges or Camerons. He had their farms already, both of them, and that was the thing of chief concern. He could see in his mind's eye his own fine house erected in the Rutledge dooryard, and presiding at his table some thrifty woman who would bring with her land or cash. We go not far afield in ascribing to him the motives that were native to him. His second wife said he was an honest man, but utterly devoid of sentiment; and she knew.

Just what understanding existed between John McNamar and Ann Rutledge at the time he left we do not know. Her sisters, who were interviewed by the author many years afterward, were sure that if she ever loved him, her love was dead. But he left her heart dangling, and she was not free to choose another lover, or if she were, she lacked McNamar's formal release from whatever engagement had existed. And John McNamar treated her as he had treated his parents.

It is just possible that some feeling of loyalty to her parents made Ann Rutledge desirous of not needlessly offending John McNamar. The Rutledge tavern was a financial failure. The money which the Camerons and Rutledges had received in exchange for their farms had not availed to save their New Salem investment. The

Rutledges had to give up the tavern in the fall of 1834. Where could they go? John McNamar was not occupying or cultivating any of his farms. He was letting them lie peacefully out-of-doors and gaining their daily unearned increment while he tarried in New York State at some unknown but doubtless profitable undertaking. Whoever represented him locally in the payment of taxes and the little of business that was necessary, permitted the Camerons to move back into their old double log house on Sand Ridge, and occupy it as tenants by courtesy. And there the Rutledges joined them, both families living in the Cameron home.

This was the situation in the fall of 1834, and up to the time of the family's removal from New Salem, Ann was still looking for her letter. Sam Hill and Abraham Lincoln grew very interested in Ann's desire for a letter, and suddenly they discovered that they both were caring for Ann.

Whether they proposed to her individually, we do not know, but in some unmistakable manner she made her preference apparent. She no longer loved McNamar, and as between prosperous Sam Hill and his tall, awkward, raw-boned clerk, she preferred Abraham Lincoln. Women make strange choices.

Ann Rutledge was born in Kentucky, January 7, 1813, and was thus four years younger than Abraham Lincoln. The Rutledge family had been prominent in South Carolina, one of her relations being a signer of the Declaration of Independence. Ann was of medium height, well rounded in figure, and had the hair and complexion that Titian loved. She had a good mind, and at the time of her friendship for Abraham Lincoln was considering going to a Female Seminary in Jacksonville. Her brother David was then a student in Illinois College in that town.

With both Hill and McNamar eliminated from the contest, Lincoln was without rivals in the field. But Ann was penniless, and her family were in financial straits, and he was staggering under his debts. He had been elected to the Legislature, but what degree of success he could have in that assembly, no one could predict.

That they were ever formally engaged, we do not know. But that they cared for each other, and that each of them understood it, we are sure.

Toward the end of November, 1834, Lincoln left New Salem, in a new suit of clothes, bought with borrowed money, and he took the tedious stage-coach journey to Vandalia. The Legislature convened December first of that year and was in session until February 13, 1835. If Lincoln ever wrote to Ann while he was away, the Rutledge family did not preserve his letters nor any tradition of such letters, and they were accustomed to save their correspondence. When he returned to New Salem at the end of February, and resumed his duties as postmaster and his work as surveyor, the Rutledges had moved from New Salem, six miles north and a mile west, to the Cameron farm. There they put in a little crop on the otherwise untenanted land of John McNamar.

Of Lincoln's acquaintance with women and his romance with Ann Rutledge, Nicolay and Hay say:

"Besides his stepmother, who was a plain, God-fearing woman, he had not known many others until he came to live in New Salem. There he had made the acquaintance of the best people the settlement contained, and among them had become much attached to a young girl named

Ann Rutledge, the daughter of one of the proprietors of the place. She died in her girlhood, and though there does not seem to have been any engagement between them, he was profoundly affected by her death."

These two sentences, or three, omitting the one that introduces the subject, are all that Nicolay and Hay say of Ann Rutledge in all of their ten thick volumes.

This reticence is in striking contrast with the freedom which other biographers have taken with the incident; and we may as well learn the whole truth about it, if this is now possible.

Ann Rutledge was an attractive girl. Everything that we know about her leads us to think highly of her. Interest in her as the girl whom Lincoln loved has tended to exaggerate her accomplishments. Her cousin, James McGrady Rutledge, declared that she was of remarkable beauty. In his old age he said of one of the most attractive girls in Petersburg, that she was "the very picture of Ann Rutledge" and that girl's photograph has since become familiar. Parthenia Hill, widow of Samuel Hill, who knew Ann Rutledge well, said:

"Ann was a good girl, but not beautiful. She had red hair to begin with."

The older Cameron girls had to "work out" to earn a little money. Ann also appears to have worked for wages in the spring of 1835, in the home of James Short, a near neighbor. It is said that Lincoln once rode over and visited her while she was in the Short home. If this story had come from Short himself, it would be entitled to great weight; for Uncle Jimmy Short was reliable, and was in position to know. But Short wrote to Herndon in 1866, in reply to Herndon's inquiry, and said that the whole story of Lincoln's love affair with Ann Rutledge was new to him. The only possible reason why it could have been new to him was that there was not very much of it.

The summer of 1835 was one of unusual sickness. Typhoid malaria is what it might be called now. Ann was sick, and so was her father. And both died. She died August 25, 1835, in the Cameron house, then owned by John McNamar. She was buried, doubtless on the following day in the old Concord Cemetery, about a mile away from the Cameron house, and quite a different place from the present Concord Churchyard.

Probably there was no funeral at the time. It was not the custom, and her father was then fatally sick. Probably there was a public service later in memory of the two. Whether John Cameron preached, or the service was conducted by Mr. Berry, minister of the Concord Church, and father of Lincoln's dissolute partner, we do not know. The family tradition is too vague and confused at this point to be of any value in this matter.

About one matter we have a clear tradition, which comes through McGrady Rutledge, Ann's cousin: that he went to New Salem, informed Lincoln of Ann's serious sickness, and that Lincoln rode over about a fortnight before her death, and visited her. What they said to each other, no one knows.

Ann Rutledge died, and we have no reason to doubt that Lincoln's sorrow was sincere, but he was speedily in love again, and again and still again. No one in New Salem suspected that he had loved Ann Rutledge with an incurable affection.

The popular story is that Lincoln raved and contemplated suicide, and that for months he was incapable of doing business. Barrels of mingled tears and ink have flowed over his ravings in this period. As a matter of fact, Lincoln was steadily attending to business all that summer and fall.

A letter is in the Barrett collection written by Matthew S. Marsh, of New Salem, and read by the present writer at New Salem on May 8, 1926, before a joint meeting of the Mississippi Valley Historical Association and the Illinois State Historical Society. This young man had voted, as Abraham Lincoln also voted, at the New Salem election, August 3, 1835. Mr. Marsh, a native of Portsmouth, New Hampshire, wrote to his brother George in that place, under date of September 17, 1835, only a few days after the death of Ann Rutledge. He tells of receiving his brother's letter, and about the carelessness of the postmaster, Mr. Lincoln, who, however, is a "clever fellow" and a friend of Marsh. He counted on Lincoln's personal friendship to save his payment of postage, and he was not in error on that point. The letter bears Abraham Lincoln's handwriting on the outer side of the sheet. Lincoln addressed the letter, and wrote this frank:

"Free, A. Lincoln, P. M.
New Salem, Ill., Sep. 22."

Neither Marsh nor any one else in New Salem anticipated that Lincoln would be incapacitated for business, and he was not incapacitated. A few days after he had franked the Marsh letter, Lincoln surveyed a piece of land which Marsh had purchased from Bowling Green. The survey is in the Barrett collection. Lincoln made the survey carefully, drew the plat accurately and computed the area of the tract with a clear mind and wrote it all down in a firm hand.

On November tenth of the same year, he wrote a remarkably discriminating letter to Governor Duncan, asking a recommendation which was his right as a member of the Legislature, and from December 7, 1835, till January 8, 1836, he was back in Vandalia attending to his duties as a member of the Legislature. And not a single soul in New Salem or Vandalia made any record then or for decades afterward that Abraham Lincoln had gone crazy over the death of Ann Rutledge.

If Lincoln needed any other cure than work and politics for such despondency as he had over Ann Rutledge in the fall of 1835, he probably had it. The best cure known to medical science for hypochondria is malaria.* To burn with fever one day and sit on the next with chattering teeth is to take one's mind off all his other troubles. And when he recovers from malaria he is likely to be thankful enough for that recovery to forget that he ever worried about anything else. In the fall of 1835 Lincoln had chills and fever. We are not certain that he needed this cure, but he had it.

We are greatly indebted to Lincoln's third and last law partner, William H. Herndon, for invaluable knowledge of Abraham Lincoln. We also have somewhat against him on the score of prejudice and bad taste. After the death of Lincoln he was accustomed to go to Petersburg when court was in session there, and pick up a few cases. He boarded with his brother-in-law, whose name was Miles. He had to pay only for what he drank. The fall term of

* For interesting information relating to malaria as a cure for mental troubles, I am indebted to my friend Doctor William A. Evans.

court adjourned on Saturday, October 14, 1866, and on Sunday morning Miles drove Herndon to the Concord Creek and Sand Ridge district, and on Monday he visited the site of old New Salem—then long depopulated, with but a single log cabin standing. Herndon took notes on those two days, recording even the hour and minute of some of his interviews.

The first man on whom Herndon called on that Sunday morning was John McNamar. He was at home. He ran no risk of being offered an opportunity, such as might have come to him had he gone to church, of dropping a dime into the contribution box. He sat in his house, erected in the dooryard of the log home where Ann Rutledge died, and looked out over his broad acres and his fat stock.

Herndon asked him if it was true that Ann Rutledge had been engaged to him, and he said that it was true. When he undertook to explain why he had left her and for three years had not written, he said that for three weeks of that time he was sick. He modestly admitted that Ann Rutledge loved him so much that she never wholly loved Abraham Lincoln, and that she died of a broken heart on McNamar's account.

He intimated to Herndon that it was for love of her he bought the farm where she had died, and with trembling hand and choking voice he pointed out a currant bush that marked the spot in his dooryard where the corner of the old house had stood.

He was unable to identify the grave, however, or that of her own mother, who was buried near her and whose grave lay only a mile from his home. He had never visited either of them.

Fortunately, there were residents of the Concord neighborhood who were able to identify the graves. Herndon went to Concord Church, when services were in progress, interviewed some of the Berrys, and the Shorts, who were able to show him the grave of Ann Rutledge. Her body has not been permitted to remain there, however.

It was late in 1835 when John McNamar returned from New York with his widowed mother, who was not an expense to him very long. He did not need the Rutledge or Cameron farms just then. since no crops would be grown there during the winter, and he had other houses. With rare generosity for him he permitted the widowed mother of Ann Rutledge and the widow's fatherless children to occupy the cabin until spring, and then he turned them out. They had to make their weary way across the prairies to a new home in Iowa, leaving him to choke with emotion beside the currant bush.

It was on Sunday and Monday, October fourteenth and fifteenth, that William H. Herndon obtained this information. He let no grass grow under his feet. On Friday evening, November 16, 1866, a bare month after his investigation, he delivered his lecture in the Springfield Court House.

William H. Herndon hated the widow of Abraham Lincoln and he knew that she held him in contempt. In that lecture, which was heard with indignation by about a dozen people, but printed and given to the world, Herndon pilloried that heart-broken and already almost insane woman, stripped from her the garments of her widowhood, and proclaimed to the world that she was the unloved wife of her husband; that he had never loved but one woman, Ann Rutledge, that he married Mary Todd, because she nagged him into matrimony, and that he never gave his heart to the mother of his children.

The author of this volume has followed to its very limit every avenue of known information on this subject. He has crossed the continent to interview the last remaining sister of Ann Rutledge. He has made what he supposes to be the most careful examination ever made of all the evidence in the case, and he presents here what in his judgment is the truth, the whole truth and nothing but the truth about Abraham Lincoln and Ann Rutledge. The thoughtful will believe it, but the vast majority will prefer the mushy lies that have grown so popular.

If Ann Rutledge had lived, it is possible that Abraham Lincoln would have gone to college. In the only extant letter to Ann Rutledge, one written to her by her brother David, while a student in Illinois College in the summer of 1835, it appears that she was considering going to Jacksonville the next autumn to study in the Female Seminary there, and the Rutledge family has a consistent tradition that Lincoln had some thought of matriculating in Illinois College in the same city. At this time he procured a book of Greek exercises, and he apparently gave some thought to the possibility of a college course.

It has been assumed by most if not all writers on the romance of Abraham Lincoln and Ann Rutledge that if she had lived she and Abraham Lincoln would have married and lived happily ever after. Herndon himself thought that, and believed that such a match would have been unfortunate for Abraham Lincoln. He was by nature an indolent man, loving ease and unmolested comfort. If he had had a tenderly affectionate wife, free from outbursts of passion, making home alluringly comfortable,

Abraham Lincoln might have yielded to her seductive charm, have become a well domesticated and uxorious husband, and never have gone far in political life.

Herndon thought it well that Ann did not live to make Lincoln as affectionate a wife as she would probably have made him.

We do not know this. And we do know Abraham Lincoln.

Knowing his habit of mind, we are sure that had Ann Rutledge lived, he would have had periods of heart-searching and indecision. We can not with certainty declare what would have been the result.

We know the sorrows that come to us. We mourn over them as though the blessings they displace would have come unmixed with discomforts or pains. It is not so in life. There are no griefs harder to bear than those that we gain for ourselves in the answers to our own prayers. There is no more incurable remorse than that of men and women who, in the agony of impending sorrow, pray for its aversion, and get just what they pray for. We do not know what would have happened if Ann Rutledge had lived. But as Herndon has set the example by telling us that her love would have ruined Abraham Lincoln by making him a too affectionate and attentive wife, we, knowing almost nothing about her, may now safely rest our conjectures on our knowledge of Abraham Lincoln.

CHAPTER XIII

Mary Owens

All good women are match-makers. The women of New Salem were good women. They were mostly young married women, and it is highly complimentary to their satisfaction in their condition that they were interested in getting everybody else married. They all agreed that Abraham Lincoln needed a wife. Mrs. Bowling Green said so. Mrs. Jack Kelso said so. Mrs. Doctor Allen said so. Mrs. Jack Armstrong over toward Clary's Grove said so. Mrs. Bennett Able said so, and what was more to the point, she resolved to do something about it. And she did it.

It was the day of the August election in the village of New Salem on the Sangamon, and every man in the neighborhood was present. Exciting things were sure to happen on election day, and the arrival of a woman more or less might have passed with little notice if Mary Owens had not been the kind of a woman she was. Not a masculine eye belonging to New Salem or Clary's Grove but followed her from her first appearance on the street till she was out of sight around the bend in the road that led to the home of her brother-in-law and sister, Mr. and Mrs. Bennett Able.

"She wore the finest trimmings I ever saw," said one of the men who beheld her on that day.

When he was asked for a more particular description, he said:

"I am getting old. I have seen too much trouble to give a life-like picture of this woman. None of the poets or romance-writers has ever given us so beautiful a picture, or a heroine so beautiful as a good description of Miss Owens in 1836 would be."

The men ceased talking politics and discussed her beauty and the stunning character of her "trimmings." No such woman had ever been seen in New Salem. She herself had been there three years before, and had been beautiful even then. But now she had returned in her war-paint and feathers. She was fair as the moon, clear as the sun, and terrible as an army with banners. The heart of New Salem was at her feet that day.

She had returned to New Salem under promise to marry Abraham Lincoln, and he had promised to marry her.

It was a joke, or partly a joke, between the twain and Mrs. Able; but it was far from being wholly a joke.

The date of her arrival, as certified by the election returns, was August 1, 1836. Less than a year previous, on August 25, 1835, Ann Rutledge had died. No one in New Salem then, or for many years afterward, imagined that Lincoln's grief over Ann Rutledge, sincere as it was, precluded the possibility of his loving another woman. And it did not prevent Lincoln's prompt and vigorous courtship of Mary Owens.

A visitor to the site of New Salem, approaching it from Petersburg, may leave the highway, and walk through fields to the river where the old town stood. Just before he climbs the fence that bounds the new State Park, he stumbles over the meager vestiges of a human habitation. A few foundation stones, a few bricks from the hearth, a few bits of broken crockery, show that once a house stood there, just in the edge of New Salem. It is outside the official survey, just west of the village line as recorded in Menard and Sangamon Counties. The house stood on the level of the village, but appeared to be upon a hill, for a deep valley skirted the homesite and ran through the timber to the river above the town. There stood a frame building, eighteen by twenty feet, the home of Bennett Able. The visitor stands for a few moments lost in meditation. He has not yet set foot in New Salem, which lies just over the fence toward the river; but this first suggestion of the old town plunges him into the very midst of the Lincoln story. This was the house where Lincoln came, somewhat more than half a mile from his store and boarding place, to court Mary Owens.

All the women in whom Lincoln was ever interested, with the possible exception of the little girl in the prairie schooner, were of southern birth. Not only his mother and his stepmother, but Katie Roby and Polly Warnick and Ann Rutledge and Mary Owens and Sarah Rickard and Mary Todd, were born south of the Ohio River. Mary Owens was a sister of Mrs. Able, and her home was in Kentucky. But she had a stepmother at home. In October, 1833, Lincoln first met her, when she was on a visit of four weeks to her sister.

Even on this visit Lincoln found her an interesting companion, and he called occasionally at the Able house during the four weeks. Mary was related to a large fraction of the population of New Salem, including the Bales, the Greenes and the Grahams.

Mary Owens was a year older than Lincoln, and in

some respects the superior of any woman he had ever met. In a letter written August 6, 1866, she thus described to Herndon her appearance at the time of her acquaintance with Lincoln:

"Born in the year eight; fair skin, deep blue eyes, with dark curly hair; height, five feet five inches, weighing about one hundred and fifty pounds."

She weighed more later.

Her cousin, Mrs. Hardin Bale, described her:

"She was blue-eyed, dark-haired, handsome—not pretty—was rather large and tall; handsome, truly handsome, matronly looking, over ordinary size in height and weight. Miss Owens *was* handsome, that is to say noble-looking, matronly."

Johnson G. Greene, another cousin, agreed with Mrs. Bale in his general description, which is confirmed by quite sufficient testimony, so that with the single exception of Mary Todd, we know better the appearance of Miss Owens than any of the other women who at any time had a place in Lincoln's life. Mr. Greene added that she was "a nervous and intellectual woman, the most intellectual I ever saw, with a forehead massive and angular, square, prominent and broad."

"She had large, blue eyes, was jovial, social, loved wit and humor, had a liberal English education, and was considered wealthy," says one of her numerous cousins.

A few months after the death of Ann Rutledge, Mrs. Able received a letter from her sister. Lincoln delivered this letter at the house, not as part of his official duty, but still according to his custom of calling soon after the arrival of mail and making a little visit as he conveyed a newly received letter to any resident of New Salem who was not present when the mail arrived. Letters were not plentiful in those days, and the receipt of a letter was an event in the family and even in the village.

Mrs. Able talked with Lincoln about the letter, and told him she was planning a visit to Kentucky to see her sister. She proposed to him to bring her sister back with her, on condition that Lincoln should marry her. Lincoln, not more than half in jest, encouraged her to do this; affirming that if Mary Owens came back, and he did not marry her, it would not be his fault.

Concerning the courtship that followed, we have evidence in several letters of Lincoln, in the rather strikingly consistent recollections of Mrs. Owens's cousins, and in letters which Mary herself wrote to William H. Herndon in 1866, supplemented by her story as related in that year to her cousin Johnson G. Greene, who visited her about that time. Of Lincoln's love-story with Ann Rutledge we know very little. We have not a letter or other scrap of contemporary documentary evidence bearing directly on the case; and that which comes to us on the testimony of Herndon concerning Ann rests back ultimately upon the highly questionable narrative of McNamar. But in the matter of Mary Owens we walk on firm ground. We have her story in writing, and Lincoln's story in writing, and Lincoln's letters, and much corroborative material. We are not compelled to create the story out of our imagination, as large sections of the Ann Rutledge story have been created, nor even to fill in the gaps of our knowledge with many conjectures. We know all the essential facts in the story of Lincoln's wooing of Mary Owens.

Lincoln lost no time in the beginning of his courtship. He and Mary met, not as they had parted, acquaintances

and friends, but as two marriageable people, no longer to
be described as young, each of whom had confided to a
mutual friend a willingness to consider matrimony. Lincoln was unremitting in his attentions; "wherever she
went, he was at her side." It was quite the regular thing
for her to spend an afternoon with one of her many
cousins, and stay to supper, with the usual result that before or after supper Lincoln dropped in, visited for a little
while, and then walked with her to the Able house. It
was probably the most regular and industrious courting
that New Salem had ever seen, or that Lincoln had ever
done. A good part of the period of his interest in Ann
Rutledge was during her residence at the Sand Ridge
farm where he saw her only at intervals; Mary Owens he
saw almost daily, and that not by accident; and he walked
home with her almost nightly.

Nor was he long in fulfilling his promise of offering
himself as a husband. His love-making was straightfor-
ward, and soon brought him to a proposal of marriage.

But Mary Owens did not immediately accept him. She
had begun to doubt whether Lincoln was the man to make
her happy. She noticed that in many respects he was
sensitive to a fault. She was impressed with his getting
down from his horse to help a hog that was mired; but
when he and she were riding horseback in company with
a number of other couples, and she and Lincoln were behind all the rest, she noticed that when they came to a bad
ford all the other men were careful in assisting their respective ladies in finding their way across the stream; but
Lincoln rode ahead of her, never once looking around to
see whether she got safely through or not.

She chided him for this. She said:

"You are a nice fellow! I suppose you did not care whether my neck was broken or not!"

He laughed and replied that he knew she was "plenty smart to take care of herself." Apparently he thought she should accept this as a compliment, but she did not; she blamed him for his carelessness and lack of courteous attention, and she wondered how he would behave after they were married.

If they had been younger, many things would probably have been overlooked; but they were not young, and they both had to consider the full responsibilities of matrimony.

One day Mary and Abraham and Mrs. Bowling Green were climbing up the hill from the ravine that led from the Green house to the Able home. Mrs. Green had carried her baby the whole three-quarters of a mile, and the hill was yet to climb. The baby was large, fat and heavy, and inclined to be cross, and the hill was rather steep. Lincoln did not notice the opportunity which Mrs. Green tried to make apparent for him to offer to carry the baby up the hill. He strolled carelessly along, attentive to Mary, but indifferent to the fatigue of the tired woman with the cross baby.

Mary Owens thought of herself as the possible mother of a big heavy baby, and Abraham as wholly unconcerned while she struggled under the burden. She chided him, and told him he would not make a very good husband.

They had a quarrel over this affair,* and almost immediately afterward Lincoln went away on a surveying

* Miss Owens in 1866 denied the precise accuracy of the New Salem tradition of this quarrel, but of the quarrel itself, and the occasion for it there appears no reasonable doubt.

party. He was absent about three weeks in the vicinity of Havana, Illinois. When he returned, he met one of the Able children at the post-office, and asked whether Miss Owens was at home; and being told that she was, sent word that he would call upon her that evening. Miss Owens had planned to spend that evening with the family of Mentor Graham, and she determined to carry out her plan, and see if Lincoln would follow her there.

He called at the Able house in the evening, and finding that she had gone a mile and a half away, asked:

"Didn't she know I was coming?"

Mrs. Able, fearing that the match was in peril, stretched her conscience, and said "No," but one of the children said, "Yes, ma, she did; for I heard Sam tell her so."

Lincoln was displeased, and he did not follow her. He thought she had wearied of him. Miss Owens walked home alone, and was sorry later that she had put him to the test, for she was not ready to throw overboard so eligible a young man. But they were both obstinate and they parted unreconciled.

The Tenth General Assembly of the sovereign State of Illinois convened at Vandalia on December 5, 1836, and from then until a few days after its adjournment, March 6, 1837, Abraham Lincoln did not see Mary Owens. He did not forget her, but he had a new basis of comparison. A new state senator had been elected from Quincy. His name was Orville H. Browning. He was a native of Kentucky and a Whig. He had married, February twenty-fifth of that year, Eliza Hickman Caldwell; her middle name was the same as his, and she may have been a distant relative. She was a Kentuckian. She and her husband had passed their honeymoon in Quincy, but they had not been married long enough to be willing to live apart during a session of the Legislature, so he had brought her with him. They and Lincoln boarded at the same place. The business of that session of the Legislature, and of the session that followed rather quickly, beginning July tenth, and adjourning July twenty-second, and called on account of the financial panic, brought Lincoln and Browning in close relations. Like Lincoln, Browning had served in the Black Hawk War, but he had obtained a better education than Lincoln, and had married a handsome and attractive woman who became the nucleus of Vandalia's most brilliant out-of-town coterie.

Lincoln found himself in a gayer atmosphere than he had ever known. He began to wish that he was free from all entangling alliance with Mary Owens.

New Salem, at the time Abraham became a resident of that infant community, was the largest village in which he had ever lived. Vandalia, as compared with New Salem, was a city. But he was not long permitted to think of Vandalia as the largest or greatest town upon the map. Vandalia itself had a number of residents who were ready to speak disparagingly of it. For instance, there was the new Attorney General, the Honorable Ninian W. Edwards, who had recently come from Kentucky with his attractive wife, Elizabeth P. Todd. These were so promptly and incurably unhappy over the melancholy contrast between Vandalia, Illinois, and Lexington, Kentucky, that Mr. Edwards resigned his position and removed to Springfield, where he ran for the Legislature, and came back in 1836 determined to help remove the seat of government from Vandalia to Springfield. It was not difficult to win Lincoln over to the same cause, for Springfield was the seat of his own county of Sangamon.

Lincoln's idea of what ought to constitute an important town was in process of rapid evolution, and the same was true of the state, itself.   When Illinois was a territory, Kaskaskia was a satisfactory capital.   But when it became a state, a new site was selected with provision that the new town should continue to be the capital for at least twenty years.   Long before the twenty years were over, the agitation was in progress.   Alton, Peoria, Springfield and Jacksonville were eagerly contesting for the honor, while certain men held that the new capital should be situated in the geographical center of the state and named Illiopolis.   In this event, they argued, whatever profit there was on the sale of real-estate would accrue to the benefit of the state, and not of private speculators, and the whole state would be benefited in the matter of convenience of access.

But Vandalia was most unwilling to lose the capitol; and the building being objected to, the citizens tore it down without process of law, and erected a new capitol building, at a cost of sixteen thousand dollars, assured that the state would not look such a gift in the mouth. This was in the summer of 1836; but the Legislature, meeting in the new building, immediately set to work to consider the question of the future capital.   On Monday, February 28, 1837, on the fourth ballot, the two houses of the General Assembly in joint session, accepted Springfield as the future seat of government.   Stephen A. Douglas voted for Jacksonville, first, last and all the time, but with no assurance of success.   In that single encounter, the last till 1860, he was beaten by Abraham Lincoln.

Not because it is important in the matter of his love-making, but because it is important in the life-story of Abraham Lincoln, we must recall that it was while his love-affair with Mary Owens was hanging in the air, that he signed with Dan Stone his protest in which he affirmed his belief that slavery was "founded on both injustice and bad policy." That was March 3, 1837.

In the successful effort to remove the capital to Springfield, the Long Nine of Sangamon County had the full cooperation of the new Whig Senator from Quincy, and that cemented still more closely the friendship of Abraham Lincoln and Orville H. Browning. And Mrs. Browning was there with her husband, smiling her approval.

Mrs. Browning was not a pretty woman, but she smiled indulgently when her husband told her and told others of her charms. But she had the charm of personality, the grace and dignity of culture, which made her attractive. Lincoln admired her greatly, and had large faith in her judgment.

While he was in Vandalia, Lincoln wrote now and then to Mary Owens. His letter of December 13, 1836, is preserved, and it implies that there had been at least one previous letter and that she had written also to him. But he was thinking of other things than Mary Owens. The log-rolling with reference to the removal of the capital occupied his mind in the first session of the Legislature, and the collapse of the efforts to make the state rich by legislation filled his mind in the second and short session. But still, in his memory, Mary Owens was ever with him, and he sometimes thought he wished that she was not.

The first and long session of the Legislature adjourned in March, 1837, and Lincoln returned to his little village.

Not very much was left of New Salem. He had not returned to stay. He was going to live in Springfield.
Thither he went, after less than a week in his old home.
He saw Mary Owens, and they met as friends, almost but
not quite engaged to be married. They parted with their
relations still undefined.

He was soon back in Vandalia again, for the short session, and then returned to Springfield for the great banquet in which the Long Nine of Sangamon and the Senator
from Quincy were lauded for their virtuous action in moving the capital. To be sure, the capital was not yet moved,
and the exact time for removal was not yet set, and Vandalia was determined to try to get the Act repealed, but
Springfield was ready for the celebration, and did cele-
brate.

It was a brave celebration that was held in Rural Hotel,
when sixty or seventy gentlemen sat down and the resident and visiting law-makers received "a proper tribute
of respect for a faithful performance of their official
duties." Twenty-one formal toasts were proposed. The
toasts to which Abraham Lincoln and Stephen A. Douglas responded were in immediate juxtaposition. Douglas
had voted for Jacksonville, but with no ill will toward
Springfield, and Springfield had a warm welcome for him.
He toasted:

"The last winter's legislation—may its results prove no
less beneficial to the whole state than they have to our
own town." That was a safe wish and a futile one. The
legislation in the main had been unwise, and they all had
had a share in it.

Lincoln's toast was:

"All our friends. They are too numerous now to be

named individually, while there is no one of them who is not too dear to be forgotten or ignored."

But the hero of that occasion was the new Senator from Quincy, the Honorable Orville H. Browning, who was thus toasted:

"When the column and the dome of the Capitol shall be reared aloft, as we gaze upon its beauty and its grandeur, Sangamon in her gladness shall remember him, as introducing into the Senate the bill locating the seat of government. That pillar, that dome, shall be his monument."

The author of this volume, as it happens, is copying these words from the *Journal* in Springfield, on the opening day of the meeting of the General Assembly in 1927. He is tempted to stand in front of the capitol building this afternoon when the two houses of the Legislature adjourn, and to say to each Solon as he passes, "That is a beautiful dome, and a fitting monument to Orville H. Browning."

The author wonders how many of the members of the Legislature would remember ever to have heard of Browning. But the toast was not at the time so extravagant as it would now appear.

Senator Browning went back to Quincy and told Mrs. Browning about the honor that had come to him, and she had no doubt he deserved it. And Abraham Lincoln went back to his cheerless room above Speed's store, and began again a letter to Mary Owens, and tore it up.

In order to understand in any degree the manner of Abraham Lincoln's courtships, we must keep resolutely in mind, first that Abraham Lincoln was no philanderer, and secondly that he really liked women, but that his inordinate caution, which affected all things that he did, was morbidly apparent in all his relations with them.

When Herndon came to write of Lincoln's feeling toward women, he said:

"Mr. Lincoln had a strong, if not terrible passion for women. He could hardly keep his hands off a woman; and yet, much to his credit, he lived a pure and virtuous life. His idea was that a woman has as much right to violate the marriage vow as the man—no more, no less. His sense of right, his sense of justice, his honor, forbade his violating his marriage vow. Judge Davis said to me in 1865, 'Mr. Lincoln's honor saved many a woman,' and this is true to the spirit. This I know on my own knowledge. I have seen Lincoln tempted, and have seen him reject the approach of women."

Awkward as he felt among women, he liked to be with them. He was accustomed to attend concerts, and especially enjoyed those in which women participated. But in all the years of his traveling the circuit, and of his long absences from home, there are no traditions worthy of a moment's notice that link his name unworthily with that of any woman.

On the very contrary, when his personal relations with any woman approached a degree of intimacy, Lincoln appears to have suffered to a high and unusual degree an inherent inhibition that halted him a long way on the hither side of propriety.

It was not simply that he was a moral man; he was a morbid man. He was by nature a man given to irresolution, and that quality affected him painfully in matrimonial affairs. Other men have had the same morbid shrinking from matrimony that he had.

When we stop to think of the immeasurable responsibilities of matrimony, we might wonder that more men, not to say women, are not oppressed as Lincoln was. We perhaps should not wonder that now and then a prospective bride or groom commits suicide on the eve of the wedding. For marriage is more and other than the gay and flippant affair which is often assumed. Birth is a mere circumstance; death is not worth mentioning in comparison. There is only one thing more solemn than getting married, and that is not getting married.

Abraham Lincoln knew nothing of complexes and inhibitions, so far as those names were concerned. But he had them. We shall not understand his relations with any of the women whom he came to know with some degree of intimacy if we do not remember this. In part it was his too great consciousness of poverty and lack of culture. But that was not the whole of it. He and other men of the Lincoln family had a morbid shrinking from marriage, based on no physical limitation, and no bad habit, but on a congenital mental inhibition. Most of the Lincolns ultimately married, but the habit of indecision belonged to the family and ran in the blood.

This chronic trait in Lincoln, which he recognized and counted an almost fatal weakness in him, asserted itself in his dealings with Mary Owens.

He was a blundering love-maker at the best, and he certainly displayed small skill of women in his relations with this mature, thoughtful, affectionate but calmly calculating woman.

Lincoln had discovered flaws in her beauty. She was handsome, but not pretty. She was intelligent, but she had her own opinions. She seemed old and fat, and, as he thought, rather too willing to marry.

He postponed the evil day when he must repeat his
request that she marry him. He wrote her from Springfield on May 7, 1837, and again on August sixteenth of the
same year. These were very blue and downcast letters.
He reminded her that if she came to Springfield as his
wife she would see wealth and comfort, but could not
share it; that she would behold others "flourishing around
in carriages" but could not have one herself. Having
given her excellent reasons why she should not marry
him, he asked her to do so.

To his surprise, she flatly refused him; and then he
suddenly realized that he cared for her more than he
thought. He pressed his suit and she refused him again.
Thrice, and with growing ardor did he ask, and thrice
did she refuse.

He had been hesitant because he thought her a little
too eager to marry him; now he realized that he had been
"confoundedly well pleased" with Mrs. Able's proposal
to bring back her handsome sister on condition that he
should be her brother-in-law, and he was ashamed of himself and very much more disappointed than he had
thought possible. He had wished himself released from
his partial obligation to marry Mary Owens, and now that
he was released, he was very unhappy that she had so
completely released him.

Some months afterward, when Miss Owens had returned to Kentucky, and all was over between them, he
met Mrs. Able in Springfield, and learned that she was
about to visit Kentucky. He said:

"Tell your sister that I think she was a great fool because she did not stay here and marry me."

There were times when Lincoln was of the opinion that

it was he who had played the fool in the matter. The ending of it by her deliberate and repeated refusal left him thoroughly sick at heart. How much he really loved Mary Owens he did not know and we do not know. Had he loved her more, he could have won her love.

Miss Owens told her story in three letters to Herndon, dated May 1, May 22 and July 22, 1866. "Really, you catechise me in true lawyer style," she said in her second letter. Her letters are dignified and well written, and she and Lincoln do not contradict each other at any important point.

There is one item in her first letter which deserves mention. Herndon hoped to supplement his meager information about Ann Rutledge. He made inquiry of Mary Owens. *She could not remember that she had ever heard mention of Ann Rutledge's name.* Yet she lived in New Salem among the people who had known every fact about Lincoln's association with Ann Rutledge, her residence in the home of her sister, Mrs. Able, having continued from the summer of 1836, less than a year after the death of Ann, to the spring of 1838. During all that period of eighteen months, covering her own broken course of love with Lincoln, she never once heard, so far as she could remember, the name of Ann Rutledge! This certainly shows that these more recent years have heard too much of her in proportion to the truth.

Mary Owens wrote to Herndon in 1866 that she and Lincoln had much in common, and that in politics "we saw eye to eye, though since then we differed as widely as the South is from the North."

Mary Owens did not find Lincoln coarse or brutal or unkind. She said of him that her refusal was not based

on any moral objection. She was fearfully aware of his
defect: "Not that I believed that it proceeded from a
lack of goodness of heart; but his training was different
from mine."

For eighteen months, which were troubled months for
her as well as for Lincoln, she considered the matter. Her
age increased to thirty, and Lincoln was more than twen-
ty-nine. She was not disposed to discard or neglect a de-
sirable matrimonial opportunity. Lincoln was a rising
man, already prominent in the Illinois Legislature, and
had become a resident of the city to which he, more than
any other man, had procured the removal of the capital.
He was honest, he was upright, he was kind; but she refused him; and when the refusal brought him to a tardy
recognition of a greater interest in her than he had previously understood, she still, and definitely, refused.

She gave this reason:

"Mr. Lincoln was deficient in those little links which
make up the path of a woman's happiness."

A short time before her death Mary Owens wrote a
letter in which she thus characterized Abraham Lincoln:

"He was a man with a heart full of kindness and a
head full of good sense."

That was true, and we wish Abraham Lincoln had
shown a little more of his good sense in his courtship of
Mary Owens. But would it have been better for him
and the world if he had been sensible and married her?

Lamon, who first published Lincoln's letter to Mrs.
Browning, apologized for using it. He said:

"For many reasons the publication of this letter is an
extremely painful duty. If it could be withheld, and the

act decently reconciled to the conscience of a biographer professing to be honest and candid, it should never see the light in these pages. Its grotesque humor, its coarse exaggerations in describing the person of a lady whom the author was willing to marry, its imputation of tooth-less and weather-beaten old age to a woman really young and handsome, its utter lack of that delicacy of tone and sentiment which one naturally expects a gentleman to adopt when he thinks proper to discuss the merits of his late mistress—all these, and its defective orthography, it would certainly be more agreeable to suppress than to publish."

We can not be sure of the regret expressed in the fore-going paragraph; we could wish the regret had been suf-ficient to suppress the letter. But the letter has been public property for fifty years, and is a part of the inevit-able material for our knowledge of one of Lincoln's love affairs. Inasmuch as that unfortunate letter relates the full story, after the incident had closed, and also because the letter as printed by Lamon, and hence by all others, contains some errors, this chapter may properly close with the full text of the letter now first published in its cor-rect form:

"Springfield, April 1, 1838.
"Dear Madam:—
"Without apologizing for being egotistical, I shall make the history of so much of my life as has elapsed since I saw you the subject of this letter. And, by the way, I now discover that, in order to give a full and intelligent account of the things I have done and suffered since I saw you, I shall necessarily have to relate some that hap-pened before.
"It was, then, in the autumn of 1836 that a married

lady of my acquaintance and who was a great friend of
mine, being about to pay a visit to her father and other
relatives residing in Kentucky, proposed to me that on
her return she would bring a sister of hers with her on
condition that I would engage to become her brother-in-
law with all convenient despatch. I, of course, accepted
the proposal, for you know I could not have done otherwise, had I really been averse to it; but privately, between
you and me I was most confoundedly well pleased with
the project. I had seen the said sister some three years
before, thought her intelligent and agreeable, and I saw
no good objection to plodding life through hand in hand
with her. Time passed on, the lady took her journey, and
in due time returned, sister in company sure enough.
This stomached me a little; for it appeared to me that her
coming so readily showed that she was a trifle too willing;
but, on reflection, it occurred to me that she might have
been prevailed on by her married sister to come, without
anything concerning me ever having been mentioned to
her; and so I concluded that, if no other objection presented itself, I would consent to waive this. All this
occurred to me on hearing of her arrival in the neighborhood; for, be it remembered, I had not yet seen her,
except about three years previous, as above mentioned. In
a few days we had an interview; and, although I had
seen her before, she did not look as my imagination had
pictured her. I knew she was oversize, but she now appeared a fair match for Falstaff. I knew she was called
an 'old maid,' and I felt no doubt of the truth of at least
half of the appellation; but now, when I beheld her, I
could not for my life avoid thinking of my mother; and
this, not from withered features, for her skin was too full
of fat to permit of its contracting into wrinkles, but from
her want of teeth, weather-beaten appearance in general,
and from a kind of notion that ran in my head that nothing could have commenced at the size of infancy and
reached her present bulk in less than thirty-five or forty

years; and, in short, I was not at all pleased with her. But what could I do? I had told her sister I would take her for better or for worse; and I made a point of honor and conscience in all things to stick to my word, especially if others had been induced to act on it, which in this case I had no doubt they had; for I was now fairly convinced that no other man on earth would have her, and hence the conclusion that they were bent on holding me to my bargain. 'Well,' thought I, 'I have said it, and, be the consequences what they may, it shall not be my fault if I fail to do it.' At once I determined to consider her my wife; and, this done, all my powers of discovery were put to work in search of perfections in her which might be fairly set off against her defects. I tried to imagine her handsome, which, but for her unfortunate corpulency, was actually true. Exclusive of this, no woman that I have ever seen has a finer face. I also tried to convince myself that the mind was much more to be valued than the person; and in this she was not inferior, as I could discover, to any with whom I had been acquainted.

"Shortly after this, without coming to any positive understanding with her, I set out for Vandalia, when and where you first saw me. During my stay there I had letters from her which did not change my opinion of either her intellect or intention, but on the contrary confirmed it in both.

"All this while, although I was fixed, 'firm as the surge-repelling rock,' in my resolution, I found I was continually repenting the rashness which had led me to make it. Through life, I have been in no bondage, either real or imaginary, from the thralldom of which I so much desired to be free. After my return home, I saw nothing to change my opinion of her in any particular. She was the same, and so was I. I now spent my time in planning how I might get along through life after my contemplated change of circumstances should have taken place, and how I might procrastinate the evil day for a time, which

I really dreaded as much, perhaps more, than an Irishman does the halter.

"After all my suffering upon this deeply interesting subject, here I am, wholly, unexpectedly, completely, out of the 'scrape'; and now I want to know if you can guess how I got out of it—out, clear, in every sense of the term; no violation of word, honor or conscience. I don't believe you can guess, and so I might as well tell you at once. As the lawyer says, it was done in the manner following, to-wit: After I had delayed the matter as long as I thought I could in honor do (which, by the way, had brought me round into the last fall), I concluded I might as well bring it to a consummation without further delay; and so I mustered my resolution, and made the proposal to her direct; but, shocking to relate, she answered, No. At first I supposed she did it through an affectation of modesty, which I thought but ill became her under the peculiar circumstances of her case; but on my renewal of the charge, I found she repelled it with greater firmness than before. I tried it again and again, but with the same success, or rather with the same want of success.

"I finally was forced to give it up; at which I very unexpectedly found myself mortified almost beyond endurance. I was mortified, it seemed to me, in a hundred different ways. My vanity was deeply wounded by the reflection that I had been too stupid to discover her intentions, and at the same time never doubting that I understood them perfectly; and also that she, whom I had taught myself to believe nobody else would have, had actually rejected me with all my fancied greatness. And, to cap the whole, I then for the first time began to suspect that I was really a little in love with her. But let it all go. I'll try and outlive it. Others have been made fools of by the girls; but this can never with truth be said of me. I most emphatically, in this instance, made a fool of myself. I have now come to the conclusion never again to think of marrying, and for this reason: I can never be satisfied with any one who would be blockhead enough to have me.

"When you receive this, write me a long yarn about something to amuse me. Give my respects to Mr. Browning.

"Your sincere friend,
"A. Lincoln.

"Mrs. O. H. Browning."

CHAPTER XIV

MARY TODD

1. THE DAWN OF SPRINGFIELD'S GLORY

TO THE reader of this volume it may not greatly matter where or under what conditions any portions of it are written, but it matters to the author. It comes to him with a keen feeling of appropriateness, not unmixed with pathos, that, having made innumerable journeys to Springfield in quest of material for this book, he should now be where he is as he writes these words. The earlier portions of this book have been written, and the material is assembled for this last chapter which must be almost a book in itself, and the author is writing these lines above the hearthstone of the house where Mary Todd spent her unmarried months in that city, the house where she was married, the house where finally she died. For all the chapters in this book ample notes have been made in visits to the very scenes described, but somewhat more than that is true of this closing portion. The Centennial Building recently erected to commemorate the one hundredth anniversary of the admission of Illinois to the Federal Union flanks the State Capitol, and houses among other institutions the Library of the Illinois State Historical Society. In many previous visits much has been written in this library that must be incorporated into this narrative; and now the actual writing of the closing chapter of this book begins, as it happens, in this spot.

Here Abraham Lincoln wooed and won and married his wife, and here, after a varied career that conveyed her in succession to the White House, the insane asylum and into exile beyond the sea, she shut herself in her darkened room till the light of her life went out. If this story could be written easily in any place, this would be the place; but not even here can this task be lightly undertaken. It is one that is beset with the most serious difficulties. The narrative covers almost half of the lifetime of Abraham Lincoln, and involves in one way or another very nearly everything that he accomplished or undertook in his entire professional career. Furthermore, the task has been made the more difficult because concerning it much misinformation has been printed and on the debatable questions feeling runs high. Such approaches to this narrative as the author has already published have brought to him requests that if he knows any more of this story than he has already told, he forbear to tell it. But he intends to tell the whole cruel truth, and part of it is cruel, but to tell it with justice and sympathy. If he relates things which some readers will wish had been suppressed, he makes no apology. Too much has been written by others, and too much of error has been disseminated, to justify anything now but the whole truth.

And now before we introduce Mary Todd to a scene which on her arrival she will certainly dominate, let us take up the affairs of Abraham Lincoln, as they existed prior to her arrival in Springfield. He was rather new himself in that environment, and of his earliest experiences we have some account already. He had been admitted to the bar, and had one or two unimportant cases in Springfield before his partnership with Stuart actually began. His departure from New Salem was March 15, 1837, and the formal notice of his partnership with John T. Stuart was dated April twelfth, and duly published in the *Journal*. He was on the farther side of his Rubicon, and had burned his bridges behind him.

But while he had left New Salem forever, and knew that that town had no future, his heart was still there. Springfield was not as yet the home of his contented spirit. Often he wished himself back to share the fortunes, however forlorn, of the poor little vanishing town. Although he had left it, he experienced profound sorrow when he heard of others doing so. On May 7, 1837, not quite two months after he had taken his departure, he wrote to Mary Owens that the discussion of her sister, Mrs. Able, and her husband concerning selling out and moving from New Salem gave him "hypo." But Lincoln had already removed from that doomed town, and those of his old neighbors who had not already done so, followed soon.

Abraham Lincoln's six years in New Salem had done much toward his development, but they left him heavily in debt, and he did not recover from the onerous obligations which his New Salem residence assumed until he was in Congress in 1848. That debt had much more to do with his despondency than had his love for Ann Rutledge.

When Lincoln arrived in New Salem, he was able to read, to "make a few rabbit tracks" on paper, as he said when he assisted Mentor Graham on election day, and to cipher as far as the Rule of Three. He left New Salem with a knowledge of English Grammar, a working knowledge of surveying, and a sufficient knowledge of law to have admitted him to the bar. He was a young man of settled habits. He did not drink, nor use tobacco in any form. He did not use profane language. He was a member of the Legislature, which was thenceforth to meet in the city where he was about to reside, and he was recognized as a leader of the Long Nine who had log-rolled through the bill that took the capital away from Vandalia to Springfield. Had he been out of debt and settled in love and religion, he would have been a far happier man, but his religious development was a matter of growth, and at the time of Lincoln's removal to Springfield was in somewhat chaotic condition.*

As for his love affairs, they were in as bad case as his religious faith. He was still attached to Mary Owens, and wrote to her now and then from Springfield. He may have met her occasionally, either on some visit of his to New Salem or of hers to Springfield; but of only one such visit do we know. His letters, or some of them, we have.

Lincoln's first year in Springfield was one of the loneliest periods of his life. He did not attend church, not because he objected to it, but, as he said, because he felt he did not know how to act in such churches as were in Springfield.

Only one woman spoke to him, so he wrote, and she could not avoid it.

On Lincoln's arrival in Springfield he shared a bed with his friend, Joshua Fry Speed, above a store kept by the

---

* These matters are fully discussed in *The Soul of Abraham Lincoln,* by William E. Barton, published by George H. Doran Company, 1920.

latter. There he deposited his saddle-bags, containing all his worldly goods, and descending the stairs, said:

"Well, Speed, I've moved."

He had moved far.

In 1838 he was reelected as a member of the Legislature; and while his record was an honorable one, it can not be claimed that he showed that marked ability which later he displayed as a statesman. His most notable acts were as wise as those of his associates and no wiser.

Lincoln's first boarding place in Springfield was in the home of Honorable William Butler, whom Lincoln already knew. "Bill Butler" was an astute politician, and his advice was as valuable to Lincoln as were his bread and meat. Lincoln was very poor and in debt; nor did he use his long period of service in the Legislature in any way to alleviate that debt. Butler "took him in with little reference to board-bills and the settlement of accounts." Doctor Jayne may have put the matter too strongly when he declared that Butler fed and clothed Lincoln for years, but it was very nearly, and perhaps literally, true.

Lincoln came to Springfield already well known as a politician, but he had just been admitted to the bar and had no extended experience as a lawyer. His partnership with his friend and fellow soldier of the Black Hawk War, Major John Todd Stuart, was advantageous to him and continued for four years. It was dissolved because of political differences, Lincoln being a Whig and opposed to the further extension of slavery; Stuart being also a Whig but leaning toward pro-slavery views. But Lincoln and Stuart remained good friends.

The law is said to be a jealous mistress, but it was not so in those days. The foremost business in the offices which Lincoln inhabited was politics; and law came in second. Lincoln was a politician before he decided to be a lawyer. But he earned a precarious living at law, and his practise grew with his reputation not only for ability but for honor.

Before Lincoln became a resident of Springfield, but while the matter of his possible change was under consideration, he was invited to deliver an address in Springfield, and he rode over for that purpose. The Young Men's Lyceum issued the invitation, and Lincoln prepared his address and wrote it out with care. It was entitled "The Perpetuation of Our Free Institutions" and was received with favor and printed in full in the *Journal*. It was the first time an address of his had appeared in print, and he was proud of it. For that matter, it was five years before another oration of his appeared in full in the columns of Springfield's Whig newspaper. It may have disappointed him that Springfield should have sent for him to come over from New Salem and make a speech, and did not continue to make request of him when he had become a resident of the town. We are able to read this first published speech of Lincoln's and appreciate its merit while we take note of its defects. It was a florid piece of stump-oratory, showing Lincoln's feeling that he must be at his best in this cultured environment; it lacked the calm dignity of his mature style. But it showed that he was an orator of some ability.

In 1840 a joint debate was held in the First Presbyterian Church, in which Lincoln acquitted himself so well that there were people in Springfield who believed that some one else must have written a part of his argument.

These and other addresses, as well as his growing success in court, gradually won recognition for Lincoln in Springfield; while his nightly discussions with the group that habitually loafed in Diller's Drug Store widened his reputation as a story-teller, a debater and a man of growing power.

So far as Vandalia and the financial condition of the state were concerned, the last was a mournful session of the General Assembly. But there were compensations. If the removal of the capital to a point farther north and at the instance of Whig politicians was ominous, the Democrats were still in power. They "reformed" the Judiciary. They abolished the circuit courts, and sent the Supreme Court on an annual jaunt around the state. Three of the four Supreme Court judges were Whigs, which was a preposterous situation for a Democratic state. There was no legal way to displace them, but the Legislature added to the bench five good Democrats, one of whom was the brilliant young genius, Stephen A. Douglas. Although he did not remain long on the bench, being promoted by election to the United States Senate, Abraham Lincoln and many other of the friends of Douglas addressed him and spoke of him to the end of his life as "Judge Douglas."

But another matter of note occurred in that last funereal session at Vandalia. The gay Mrs. Browning was there again, and had with her two handsome unmarried sisters. Her court of love and beauty now shone more gaily than ever against the sorrowful background of Vandalia's desolation and the state's insolvency.

And so the days went by till June 30, 1839, when Governor Carlin proclaimed the official removal of the seat of government, to occur not later than July fourth of that year. And the Legislature shook the dust of Vandalia from its feet forever.

The city did improve, however. A number of people moved over from Vandalia, and built new homes in the south part of town. The new Governor's Mansion was located at Eighth Street and Capitol Avenue. This new and attractive part of Springfield was the Vandalia section. The home which a few years later Abraham Lincoln bought was in this section of the city, exactly one square from the Governor's Mansion.

On the tenth day of October, in the year of our Lord, 1839, the Honorable Abraham Lincoln and certain other of the younger members of the Legislature took a survey of Springfield, and decided that as compared with Vandalia it was deadly dull. It lacked the charm of polished society which belonged to the older and more settled community. These young members missed certain features of life which they had enjoyed in the earlier state capital. Especially they remarked the bevy of girls that swung in glittering orbit around that brilliant luminary, Mrs. Orville H. Browning, of Quincy.

The people of Vandalia had not been slack in warning the Legislature of the contrasts that would await them if they removed their capital to Springfield. In that frontier city they would have to eat venison, wild turkey, prairie chicken, mallard duck and quail; whereas in Vandalia they could have hog meat and with it other products of established civilization.

The first session of the Eleventh General Assembly of the State of Illinois convened at Vandalia December 3, 1838, and adjourned March 4, 1839. The second session of the same Assembly was to convene in Springfield, December 9, 1839. Here would be a contrast at the best. Would Mrs. Browning and her galaxy of girls attend in that primitive place? Abraham Lincoln was one of the members of the Lower House who felt some solicitude in that matter. He drew up a petition, which he and others signed.

"Springfield, Illinois,
October 10, 1839.

"Honorable Mrs. O. H. Browning:

"We, the undersigned, respectfully represent to your Honoress, that we are in great need of your society in the town of Springfield, and therefore humbly pray that your Honoress will appear forthwith to the seat of Government, bringing in your train all ladies in general who may be at your command, and all Mrs. Browning's sisters in particular; and as faithful and dutiful petitioners we promise that if you grant this our request, we will render unto your Honoress due attention, and faithful obedience to your orders in general, and to Miss Browning's in particular.

"In tender consideration whereof, we pray your Honoress to grant your humble petitioners their above request, and such further relief in the premises as to your Honoress may seem right and proper; and your petitioners as in duty bound will ever pray."

Her Honoress, Mrs. Orville H. Browning, was never deaf to a petition of this character, and her sisters and cousins and young lady friends were quite as much interested as she. There was scarcely a pretty girl in Illinois who did not scan her list of friends to see if there might not be among them a young matron who would invite her to spend a part of the winter in Springfield while the Legislature was in session.

Abraham Lincoln was hoping they would come. He had recovered from that settled gloom that rested on him when he first came to Springfield, and noticed that no woman spoke to him. He now was meeting women. He was still in debt, but his practise was growing. So far, Springfield had been between hay and grass. It was settled that the capital was to be removed, but the Legislature had not as yet assembled in the new capital. Law business was just beginning to pick up since the last meeting of the Legislature in Vandalia. It was time for him to be looking around.

Thus that becalmed mariner, Abraham Lincoln, having been somewhat buffeted by his affection for Ann Rutledge and Mary Owens, prayed for a breeze. So prayed Ulysses, and Æolus sent him a favoring wind, but gave him also a bag in which were confined the unfavorable gales. Homer says it was the seamen who grew curious; there was no Pandora present to blame for it; but we may wonder if it was not Ulysses himself. This only we know, that the god of the winds has many kinds in his cave, and when a voyager like Abraham Lincoln grows weary of watching his daily flapping sails, and prays to Æolus, he takes a chance. In his cave a gently perfumed breeze was beginning to stir, and by the time it reached Abraham Lincoln's little boat, the gentleman had no opportunity to reef his sails.

There was a grand cotillion ball in honor of the opening of the Legislature. There were printed invitations, as ostentatious as any that could have been produced in Vandalia. The caption "Cotillion Party" was set in a curve. That was a trick of high-grade job-printers calling for the use of plaster-of-Paris, and not every office had a

printer who could do it. Underneath was a spread-eagle,
with the motto "E Pluribus Unum." The invitation read:

The pleasure of your Company
is respectfully solicited at a
Cotillion Party, to be given at the
"AMERICAN HOUSE," on tomorrow
evening at 7 o'clock, P. M.
December 16, 1839.

M. H. Ridgely	J. F. Speed
J. A. McClernand	J. Shields
R. Allen	E. D. Taylor
W. H. Wash	E. H. Merriman
F. W. Todd	N. E. Whiteside
S. A. Douglas	M. Eastman
W. S. Prentice	J. R. Diller
N. W. Edwards	A. Lincoln

Managers.

2. THE GIRLHOOD OF MARY TODD

It has been recorded in a previous chapter that the then
Attorney General of the State of Illinois, the Honorable
Ninian Wirt Edwards, and his aristocratic wife, Elizabeth
Todd Edwards, had little liking for Vandalia, and that because of its undesirability as a place of residence in forlorn contrast with Lexington, Kentucky, Mr. Edwards
resigned his position and removed to Springfield. They
occupied the stately old home of Governor Edwards which
stood on the very spot where I am writing. In that large
and impressive home Elizabeth Todd Edwards reigned
with the prestige that belonged to the union of two families of the even then old Illinois aristocracy. She had
been reared a Presbyterian as had the Todds generally but
she had become an ardent Episcopalian, and her pound

cakes were the corner stones of the Episcopal church in Springfield. Her husband was speedily elected a member of the Legislature, and served with Abraham Lincoln in the adventures of the Long Nine that removed the seat of government.

But even before this was accomplished she was busy in seeking the matrimonial advantage of her sisters. To her home came her sister Frances, who married Doctor William Wallace, and then Ann, who after one matrimonial adventure became the wife of C. M. Smith, a Springfield merchant who in time became wealthy. In a town like Springfield it was no trouble at all to marry off the sisters of so talented and accomplished a woman as Elizabeth Todd Edwards. She had stepsisters, all of whom found husbands later without leaving Lexington. But she had also one remaining full sister, who was still single, in fact just out of boarding school.

Mary Todd, daughter of Honorable Robert Todd and his first wife Elizabeth Parker, was born in Lexington, December 13, 1818. She was not quite twenty-one when she first met Abraham Lincoln.

The becalmed mariner had prayed for a wind and he got a whirlwind.

Mary Todd was the daughter of a prosperous family and shared the ordinary life of a family in the capital city of the Blue-grass. Nowhere was soil more fertile than that which her father cultivated, and he owned a mill and was partner in a woolen factory. He was president of a bank, state senator, a citizen of dignity, probity and honor.

He owned slaves, but not in large numbers, and their condition was not one of rigor. The family was accounted rich, but that condition did not involve idleness or luxury. There were comfort and freedom from care. Blooded horses and fat cattle were in the meadow; sheep were abundant in the pastures. The life of the Todd family involved the use of a large and well appointed house in town, and the supervision of factory and field.

Political and military affairs bulked large in the life of Kentucky, and Mary Todd's father, as well as the fathers of her associates, had much to do with these concerns. Whisky was abundant and of excellent quality, but in the main it appears to have been used in moderation, though excess was by no means unknown. Religion was of deep concern to the people of Lexington, and it was a very real and earnest religion, but it did not depress the people who held its tenets. Its period of stagnation were offset by other periods of revival. What share she had in these we do not know, but she was reared and trained religiously by people to whom religion was a creed, but also a consistent life.

The death of her mother was followed by her father's second marriage. Mary was then about seven years old. A second large family followed. There were six children by her own mother and eight by her stepmother. The children of the first marriage left home one by one, not all of them happily. However there was no permanent break between the two sets of children; though the removal of three of the four daughters of the first marriage to Illinois added the element of distance to that of a different maternity.

Mary Todd had her education, not in the public schools of Lexington, nor yet in a convent, but in the then famous boarding school of Madame Mentelle, situated near the home of Henry Clay. In her later letters she sometimes said that her girlhood home was a boarding school. At Madame Mentelle's table no English conversation was permitted. The pupils spoke French. This language she learned to read, write and speak fluently. She had a quick, mind, an excellent vocabulary and a good literary style. In her letters she never used incorrect grammar or spelling or used the wrong word. She wrote a clear rapid hand and formed her letters and sentences with ease and precision.

She had unusual vivacity. Her answers came quickly and were to the point, sometimes too pointed, but always apt. She liked company, both of men and of women. Among women she was admired, rather than loved, but she was not without lovable qualities. She had a merry laugh, with just a bit of a sting in it. Her voice was pleasantly pitched and modulated, but sometimes she rasped a little. She had chestnut hair, and abundance of it. Her lips were cherry-red and alluring, but there was a hard line at the end of the mouth that showed a stubborn will. Her blue eyes flashed a challenging gaiety, with warning of a hot and uncertain temper. She was short of stature, plump, quivering with animation, an alluring armful for a courageous man.

Mary Todd had finished her work at Madame Mentelle's School, and on her return she did not long remain under the shelter of her father's roof. The new mother had her hands full with her own young children. There was more of freedom and a promise of interesting adventures in the home of Elizabeth Todd Edwards in Springfield. So thither went Mary Todd in the autumn of 1839.

3. WHEN THE BALL OPENED

The day so long and impatiently awaited came at last.
The time set for the convocation of the General Assembly
of the sovereign State of Illinois arrived. And just in
advance of it arrived the members of the two houses of
that body. They came on horseback and by stage-coach,
and they came to stay for the session. Now in these days
the senators and representatives arrive on the Tuesday
morning train and get away Thursday afternoon, and if
any additional legislative days are needed in that week
to push bills on to a second reading or advance them on
the calendar, the two chairmen of the steering committee
can dictate the proceedings of the day as they are desired
to be of record, and save the other members a great deal
of bother. But in the old days it was not so. Members
arrived for the session, and nothing but matters such as
death or an important political conference took them
away. The boarding houses of Springfield were filled.
Not a few members brought their wives with them, and
if there were marriagable daughters, they came, also. Besides these came visiting their married sisters or cousins
in Springfield half the pretty girls of Illinois. All roads
led to Springfield.

Springfield had no capitol building as yet, but the
Presbyterian Church had been rented for the use of the
House of Representatives, and the Methodist Church was
secured for the Senate. If Springfield lacked anything
that Vandalia had ever possessed, she intended to have
it in due time or something very much better. In time
she had it, the dignified old Capitol building in the very
heart of the town, now the Sangamon County Court-

House. At that time it was only two stories high instead of three, and what is now its Circuit Court room was then the hall of the House of Representatives. In that room Lincoln spoke often. But all that was later. His experience as a member of the Legislature was mainly in the Presbyterian Church. That church was swept and garnished early in December, 1839, awaiting the coming of the Legislature.

Springfield gave a grand cotillion ball at the American House in honor of the Legislature, an invitation to which the reader received a few pages back, and for whose occurrence we have been waiting more or less impatiently ever since. No one of distinction is known to have been missing. Even the Methodists and Presbyterians looked in, some of them buying a ticket as an official courtesy though not publicly dancing, while Episcopalians and others who had no conscientious scruples in such matters danced from seven o'clock until four the following morning.

A little late that evening came Mrs. Ninian W. Edwards, escorted by her husband, and with her, as with several of the young matrons, came a younger sister. Springfield quite generally knew that Elizabeth Edwards had brought on another sister, and people had a mild curiosity about her, but there were so many other things to talk about just then, she came in with relatively little gossip. But when she entered the ballroom, Springfield was aware that she had arrived.

Behold this plump, vivacious little woman, her blue eyes gleaming, her chestnut hair with a golden sheen, her changeable silk dress standing out over seven or eight starched or flounced white petticoats. She did not wear a great deal above her waist, for she knew she had attractive neck and shoulders, and she made the most of them. But nevertheless, she was dressed within an inch of her life. There was not a man there who did not turn and look after her, nor a woman who did not look after her without turning.

How she could dance! She knew the old-time dances, and had seen them and participated in them; but she knew the polka and the schottische and the complicated figures in the cotillion. She knew the meaning of the technical terms. She did not need to be told that "Do-si-do" which many people supposed was derived from the names of two of the seven musical notes was the old-fashioned "wring-the-dishcloth." She knew how it was to be done properly in the dance, and she knew that the proper form of the name was *"dos-a-dos"* which means "back-to-back." Other girls in Springfield were content with the pronounciation "sashay"; but she knew the meaning of *"chasez."* She knew how to do all the figures. She could even have waltzed, and a few months later she did so, for Madame Mentelle's school had taught her all that; but as yet there were too few people in Springfield who could waltz for that dance to have a place in the first formal ball of the General Assembly. However, it was sure to come in time. Had not that censor of good morals, Lord Byron, condemned the waltz as immodest? He told as much as he could that was bad about it, and said something like this:

> But here my Muse with due decorum halts,
> And lends her longest petticoat to waltz.

With such warning against the morals of it, Springfield

was certain before long to learn just how wicked the waltz was. Mary Todd knew about it already.

Mary Todd was a belle of that ball. It would be idle to pretend that she monopolized the glory of the occasion, but she had her full share of it, and a trifle more.

She met most of the young men of Springfield and the members of the General Assembly that night. Rather late in the evening she noticed a knot of men seated in one corner of the room, laughing and talking, and not doing their full duty in the way of dancing. She mentioned the matter to her cousin, Major John Todd Stuart. That gentleman told her that the center of the group was his partner, Abraham Lincoln, who did not do much dancing, but was a great story-teller, and that some of the young men cared more to hear his stories than they did to dance. Mary Todd commanded that this partner of her cousin be brought to her and properly introduced, and the same accordingly was done.

She held out her warm soft hand, and he took it in his big strong palm, and felt a thrill such as the handshake of a woman did not always impart to him.

Her Honoress, Mrs. Orville H. Browning, was there with both her pretty sisters. There were other girls from Quincy, and still others from Jacksonville and Edwardsville and Bloomington and Decatur and Paris and Peoria, but Abraham Lincoln wasted little time upon them that night. He held the hand of Mary Todd and looked down at her. "The long and the short of it," as he was later accustomed to say of situations involving himself and this same little woman, was that in an incredibly short time they were in love with each other.

4.   THE LONG AND SHORT OF IT

There would be no use trying to discover how many rivals Abraham Lincoln had after that night. If we are to believe all the gossip, we should need to compile a list of the young men of Springfield. If there were any of them, or any unmarried members of the General Assembly, who did not make advances toward Mary Todd that first winter, their names have somehow escaped the attention of those who help us by creating the myths which constitute one main tributary of recorded history. She was not lonely. She did not lack admirers. She had lovers enough among the men and admirers enough among the women, by whom she was admired rather than loved, for she had a keen wit and a sharp tongue.

Of her lovers, only two are of importance to this narrative. One of them was the gay brilliant Stephen A. Douglas, whom she rejected as a lover and retained as a friend, and whom she still found useful for an occasional flirtation; and the other was the tall gaunt Abraham Lincoln.

And she chose Abraham Lincoln.

There is no use pretending he did more than half the courting. She chose him out of the rather long list of eligible young men, and he chose her rather than either of the sisters of Her Honoress, Mrs. Orville H. Browning. Many reasons and conjectures are of record. The best reason I have been able to discover is that she preferred him to other suitors and that he wanted her.

She said repeatedly in after years that she had always believed and said he would be president, and she was accustomed to add, "That was why I married him; for you know he is not handsome." No, he was not handsome.

But he was a man of upright habits, a man who held and was likely to hold public office, a man who, though presently poor and in debt was likely to be able to give her a good home, a man whom she could respect and even love. It was a strange match, but most matches are strange, and this one as matches go was not so mysterious as some others. To the surprise of many people, Abraham Lincoln turned his back on several interesting matrimonial possibilities and made love to Mary Todd. To the surprise of an even larger number of people, the gay, brilliant, well educated daughter of an aristocratic Blue-grass family preferred Abraham Lincoln to lovers of more polished manner.

Just how or when Abraham Lincoln and Mary Todd became engaged to be married, we do not know. But we have the outside limits of the chronology of the first epoch in their relationships. Between December, 1839, when they were first introduced, and January 1, 1841, they had met, courted, plighted their troth, quarreled, made up, quarreled again and parted almost violently. We are able to discover the main order of events, but a connected narrative is impossible.

However, we shall be able to approach it more nearly than has ever been done hitherto.

Take another look at Springfield as Mary Todd beheld it. It was still far from being like Lexington, but Elizabeth told her it was much finer than Vandalia, and it was to Mary Todd more interesting than either of them. Springfield was becoming sophisticated. "Goods twenty-eight days from New York" spelled the doom of river transportation, and displayed the swifter possibilities of the lakes, but no one realized that. All they knew was that one might buy many articles of finery in C. M. Smith's store in Springfield such as were for sale on Broadway. There was less of bulk, and less of variety, but the Springfield stores were selling broadcloths, silks, satins, delaines and other rich goods, and there were women who were buying and wearing them. The men, too, while behind the women in matters of adornment, recognized certain standards of sartorial propriety as becoming to professional life. A dinner given by one of the Supreme Court judges in Springfield to the Governor and his Lady, and to a select group of distinguished members of the bar and their ladies, was an event of significance both as to the bill of fare and the dignity of those persons assembled. Springfield had its elements of undeniable crudity; but it had its standards, more inflexible than those of polite society in the large cities. It would be difficult to think of a place where a social error of sorts might more certainly doom a man to disgrace than Springfield, Illinois, about 1840. And of that social life, the Edwardses and Todds were on the crest. In that life Abraham Lincoln now had a share.

Moreover, Springfield was now sufficiently civilized to have all the then fashionable diseases. There were Indian and German root doctors, whose single prescription each was guaranteed to cure tic-doloreux, contraction, palsy, king's evil, salt-rheum, ring worm, eye-swelling, hemorrhoids, female weakness, snake bites, hydrophobia and milk sickness.

Let us see if we can visualize the life of Abraham Lincoln during the year between his first meeting of Mary Todd, in December, 1839, and January 1, 1841, on which latter date something happened.

It was, first of all, a time when the Legislature had to be busy. A considerable number of problems rose over the adjustment of the seat of government to its new situation. The disastrous after-effects of unwise financial legislation had to be reckoned with. There was much to be done.

All the year the political pot was boiling. For a week before the Legislature assembled, there were meetings in which the political issues of the day were discussed. Lincoln and Douglas there crossed swords, and the *Register* read Mr. Lincoln a lecture on his assumed clownishness and lack of dignity. It ventured to make out a list of "Committees of the Lobby," and it placed the name of Lincoln next after the chairman's on the committee on politeness and courtesy. That was sarcasm of evident intent.

On the day after Christmas, Lincoln and four political friends signed a confidential circular, and sent it out surreptitiously to Whigs over the state, announcing a campaign publication, under the ægis of the *Journal,* to be begun in January and run till the November election exposing Democratic fraud and setting forth the true principles of government. This publication, to be issued twice a month, made its special appeal to soldiers of the War of 1812, in the interests of General William Henry Harrison. It also had a column for young voters. It was called "The Old Soldier." It said very bitter things about President Van Buren, whom it called "King Martin," and it was far from being gracious and complimentary in its references to local Democratic politicians. In one article it said such biting things about Stephen A. Douglas that he assaulted the publisher, Simeon Francis, on the street.

There was a brief brawl, and no great harm was done.

The editors of this little newspaper, which was issued every two weeks from early in the year till the November election, were not named. A little later, however, the *Register* smoked them out, and the five men comprising the "association of gentlemen" who edited the paper issued a signed acknowledgment. One of the five was Abraham Lincoln. From the few copies that are preserved of this little paper one can pick out with reasonable certainty some editorials that by internal evidence appear to have been the work of Abraham Lincoln. He probably wrote more of the paper than the other four together.

In that summer he traveled rather far, making campaign speeches in favor of Harrison and against the Democrats. One of these journeys took him in June to southwestern Illinois, and brought him into conference with the Whigs of St. Louis. He decided to attend the Missouri State Whig Convention, which was held at Rocheport, Thursday, Friday and Saturday, June eighteenth to twentieth. He is believed with good reason to have gone up the river with the St. Louis delegation, which arrived by steamboat at eleven o'clock on Thursday, and the convention opened at noon. It is not known that he spoke there.

From Rocheport he rode by stage-coach twenty miles to Columbia. In that city Mary Todd was visiting her two uncles, Honorable North Todd and Judge David Todd. There he spent the week-end. He and Mary had not seen each other for about a month, and it was very pleasant for them both to meet where they were strangers to nearly all except each other. Even politics, for a day or two, lost something of its interest for Abraham Lincoln. But such seasons do not last. He went back to Illinois and plunged into politics, and in the early autumn he and Mary met again in Springfield. When she got back, he paid her as much attention as he well could pay when the political situation was calling for so much of his time. It was increasingly certain that the Whigs would win with their Log Cabin and their Hard Cider, and that the country would have, as it did have, "Tippecanoe and Tyler, too."

In the autumn of 1840 Abraham and Mary saw the elephant. For two days, October eighth and ninth, a menagerie and circus were in Springfield. The *Journal* had a two-column cut showing an animal of that name, and "a gigantic male elephant" was actually there, the first ever seen in Springfield. There was a giraffe and there was a bengal tiger. There were rope-walking and trapeze work, and a display of horsemanship, and an exhibit of the new dance known as the waltz. And Mr. Lincoln and Miss Todd were among those present.

They may even have gone together to the play *Therese* which was shown January 10, 1840. A lady who signed herself "A Play-Goer" and who announced that she had been "a regular attendant upon the theater for fifteen years" (where, one wonders?) wrote a letter addressed "Mr. Editor," commending the performance, especially declaring that the way Mrs. Ingersoll "came bounding across the stage showed that she had a proper conception of the character of Therese." What that character must have been, one blushes to conjecture, but it is alleged that "She had at her command all that elegance of manner and gracefulness of attitude so essential to make the character interesting." If this was not true, there were few people in Springfield who could have denied it.

Abraham Lincoln won Mary Todd against all competition. The Edwards family did not object. John Todd Stuart did not object. The Honorable Robert Todd, Esquire, of Lexington, Kentucky, did not object. Any who declare that Mary Todd's family looked down on Lincoln or thought Mary had made an unworthy match are misinformed. Robert Todd wrote a joint letter to his four Illinois daughters, declaring his satisfaction with their marriages, and admonishing them, in the precise and formal language of the time, to be good wives and prove worthy of the good men whom they had married. And that included Abraham Lincoln.

But when all competition was past, and every one understood that Abraham Lincoln and Mary Todd were engaged, then they began to quarrel. He did not come to see her as often as she thought he should. His excuses that he was occupied with political matters ceased to be valid after the November election. Sometimes he came and sat silent before the fire, and when Elizabeth Edwards came into the room, Mary was talking steadily and Abraham was watching her with a kind of vacant wonder and not saying a word.

They quarreled, and Lincoln began to fear that they would never do anything else. He wrote a letter to her, cancelling the engagement. He read that letter to Speed, who told him not to mail it, but go himself and tell Mary.

Lincoln did so. He was not prepared for what happened. Instead of accusing him, she accused herself. She cried dramatically, "The betrayer is betrayed!" She who had been a breaker of hearts had now to feel the breaking of her own. She wept. She denounced herself in passionate language.

Finally, Lincoln started to go, and she came forward to bid him a last farewell. He kissed her good-by, and in an instant he had her in his arms, warm, passionate, weeping, clinging.

Abraham Lincoln went back to his room above Speed's store, more undeniably engaged than ever.

5. MATILDA EDWARDS

When a stream is flowing swiftly, with full tide swelling to the tops of its banks, it will bear great logs upon its bosom and never think of them as impediments. But when it is trickling along an almost dry bed, a twig may slacken its current or deflect its flow. At any other time Matilda Edwards might scarcely have mattered, but just consider at what time she came.

So far as she was concerned, the time was opportune. Her father, Cyrus Edwards, of Alton, was a brother of old Governor Ninian Edwards, who had served as governor of the Territory of Illinois from 1808 until its admission as a state, its one territorial governor. Then from 1818 to 1824 Ninian Edwards was United States senator, and from 1826 until 1830 he was governor of the state which he had served in like capacity when it was a territory.

That was a remarkable record, and the Edwards dynasty was mighty on the earth. Cyrus Edwards, too, was a man of note, and came near being United States senator.

To the home of her cousins, Ninian W. and Elizabeth Todd Edwards, Matilda went. That was in 1840, and rather late in the year, about the time that Abraham Lincoln and Mary Todd were beginning to chafe a little within the bonds of their engagement.

Politics makes strange bedfellows, but the bedfellowship of Mary Todd and Matilda Edwards was not wrought by politics. In the critical period of her engagement to Abraham Lincoln, Mary Todd had, as her roommate in the Edwards house, a potential rival, Matilda Edwards. Accept any version of the story you like. This one will answer as well as any. Indeed, this is probably the nearest approach to the truth of the matter that at this time is possible.

Mary Todd had made her choice among the young men of Springfield and was engaged to marry Abraham Lincoln. He was tall, gaunt, awkward, but he had ability, character and promise of political distinction. And he wore a long coat, a silk vest, a satin stock and a tall hat, and was a man of note. She was in the habit of saying that she was about to marry a future president of the United States. She was a restless, nervous young woman, and she wanted activity and excitement. And she managed either to get it or create it.

Stephen A. Douglas was in town, and he was unmarried and unattached. He had always admired Mary Todd, and it was believed that he would have been glad to marry her. He still was attentive to her at parties and levees and balls. He was a graceful dancer, and she loved to dance.

It is said in Springfield that the matter did not stop there. It is alleged that she and Stephen A. Douglas were once seen in Springfield walking arm in arm in broad daylight. But let us hope that this is an exaggeration. It may not have been quite so bad as all that.

The worst of it was that her flirtation with Douglas did not make Abraham Lincoln jealous. Almost any other young man would have been wanting to shed the blood of Stephen A. Douglas, but Lincoln did not notice that anything was happening that called for his protest.

What is worse than a jealous lover?

The answer, as every woman knows, is, a lover who can not be made jealous.

That was the kind of lover Abraham Lincoln was.

And just then along came Matilda Edwards.

It is necessary for you to know what kind of girl Matilda Edwards was. As you know already, she was Matilda Edwards, niece of old Governor Ninian Edwards. She was tall and fair. She was blonde. Gentlemen are said to prefer blondes. The prevailing type of beauty in Springfield was brunette. The girls in Springfield were almost all Kentucky girls; Matilda was born in Kaskaskia, but her parents were from Kentucky. And she was tall and willowy and a blonde.

She and Mary Todd snuggled close together in Elizabeth's big goose-feather bed in which the sleepers could not lie apart if they tried, and they whispered to each other, and shared each other's secrets. But this whispering was with a measure of reserve. Each had some ideas of her own.

The next time Mary Todd went dancing with Stephen A. Douglas, practising the wicked waltz Springfield had seen at the circus, and Mary looked over her shoulder, Abraham Lincoln was not looking at her at all. He was talking to Matilda Edwards.

The matter grew serious. Elizabeth Edwards told her husband he ought to do something about it. She told him

that Matilda would make an excellent wife for Joshua
F. Speed. Speed was invited to the house. Mary and
Abraham were spirited away together, and Joshua and
Matilda sat out certain evenings. Joshua fell readily into
the trap, and that most willingly. He proposed to Ma-
tilda, and she refused him.

The next attempt was to divert Stephen A. Douglas
from Mary toward Matilda. That plan also succeeded.
Stephen A. Douglas also fell madly in love with Matilda
and is said to have proposed. She refused him, and never
slackened her pace.

And every time Mary Todd looked around at a party
or a ball, there in a corner, she could see Matilda Edwards
talking with Abraham Lincoln, and if Mary flirted with
other men, as she did, he simply let her flirt.

What could a girl do with a lover like that?

Mary now began to grow alarmed. Flirting with Stephen A. Douglas lost interest for her. She had real fear
of losing her lover, and she did not see how she could help
it. She and Matilda were still friends and bedfellows.
She could ask no favors of Matilda; her pride was too
strong for that. Moreover, she had a well-grounded suspicion that it would not do her any good. Matilda was going forward in her own sweet and smiling way, apparently
oblivious of the fact that she was breaking Mary Todd's
heart.

After some consideration Mary took the matter up with
Lincoln, and chided him for neglecting her and paying
attention to Matilda. To her bitter disappointment, he
did not defend himself nor pretend that he did not like
Matilda. On the contrary, she got the impression that he
really did care more for Matilda than he did for her. Mrs.

Edwards is authority for the statement that he confessed to Mary that he loved Matilda. Even with her statement, I am disposed to doubt his having said just that, but he did not give Mary Todd any comfort. She got the impression, or so her sister said, that he admitted that he loved Matilda and had never loved Mary. Elizabeth thought it "crazy talk." She thought it was always that way when people went insane or were on the verge of so doing; they denounced the people they most loved, and declared their love for strangers.

Matilda Edwards showed no mercy. She declared that if the young men liked her it was no fault of hers, and if Mary Todd could not keep her lover after she had him, she need not expect any help from other girls.

So Matilda Edwards ran full course and was glorified, if gossip is to be believed. She broke more hearts, male and female, than any other girl in the whole history of Springfield, and when she had had her little fling, she married none of the Springfield men who had gone tearing down the pike in pursuit of her. She picked an out-of-town lover to her liking, Mr. Newton D. Strong. She married him, and they moved to Reading, Pennsylvania, and lived happily ever afterward. So far as Abraham Lincoln and Mary Todd were concerned, she smilingly faded out of the picture.

One night, as Matilda and Mary were lying deep in the bosom of the big goose-feather bed, guarded by the four tall bedposts, each of them sworn to secrecy, Mary found courage to ask Matilda something she had long wanted to propound:

"Do you think Mr. Lincoln really ever loved you?"

She called him "Mr. Lincoln." Young ladies in Springfield did not call their beaux by their first names when they spoke of them to other girls.

"Mercy, no!" replied Matilda. "He only thought he did."

And again Mary screwed up her courage, and asked a question whose answer she feared:

"Did he ever propose to you?"

Matilda laughed a gay little laugh.

"Propose to me?" she giggled. "He never even paid me a compliment!"

6. THE FATAL FIRST OF JANUARY

Matilda Edwards had ceased from troubling, and Stephen A. Douglas was at rest or otherwise occupied. All should have gone well with Abraham Lincoln and Mary Todd. But just then occurred "the fatal first of January, 1841."

The phrase is Lincoln's own, and occurs in his letter to Joshua F. Speed, under date of March 27, 1842. No possible ingenuity can explain away the implications of this allusion. This, which set the date, and a letter of January 23, 1841, to his partner, John T. Stuart, showing plainly that Lincoln was alarmed at the prospect of his going insane, and the further fact as it appears in Speed's letters that this state of mind was involved somehow in Lincoln's relations with Mary Todd, set Herndon to investigating soon after Lincoln's death. He was able to secure most of Lincoln's letters to Speed, but was required to omit certain allusions, as will hereafter appear. He further obtained from Speed a letter addressed to himself, in which Speed affirmed that Lincoln's engagement with Mary Todd was broken on that date, and that Lincoln was so much depressed that his friends feared he would take his own life, and kept razors and knives away from him. He also said that Lincoln spent "several months" with him near Louisville that year. Speed sold out his Springfield store as of January 1, 1841, and soon afterward departed for Kentucky. Herndon's impression, and that of authors who depended upon him for their information, was that Lincoln went with Speed and under his care, toward the end of January, and that he was gone away from Springfield until autumn. It must be remembered that this inquiry of Herndon's was made twenty-six years after 1841, and that will account for some inaccuracies in Speed's recollection.

Herndon went to Mr. and Mrs. Ninian W. Edwards, and submitted this material to them. Mrs. Edwards went further than to admit that the engagement was broken. She said that the first of January was the date set for the wedding, but she explained matters by making Lincoln's insanity not the effect but the cause of the break:

"Lincoln and Mary were engaged. Everything was ready and prepared for the marriage, even to the supper. Mr. Lincoln failed to meet his engagement; cause, insanity.

"In his lunacy he declared he hated Mary and loved Miss Edwards. That is true, yet was not his real feeling. A crazy man hates what he loves when he is himself."

Her husband confirmed this story so far as the insanity of Lincoln was concerned:

"Lincoln went crazy as a loon," he said.

Herndon set all this down, and Lamon printed it in his *Life of Lincoln* in 1872. It made a furor in Springfield, and there were emphatic denials as well as confirmatory affirmations with added details.

In December, 1883, Jesse W. Weik was assisting Herndon to prepare Herndon's own book for the press, and Weik interviewed Ninian W. Edwards and his wife together:

"Mrs. Edwards said arrangements for the wedding were made; cakes baked; Lincoln failed to appear. At that point Mr. Edwards interrupted her and advised her to be cautious, as she was speaking to a newspaper man." But whatever was said by them was by way of confirmation of their statement to Herndon, made in 1866 and published in 1872.

With the Edwards testimony thus in effect repeated, seventeen years after its first declaration, Herndon elaborated the Lamon statement; his book appeared in 1889, and said, in part:

"The bride in grief disappeared to her room. The wedding supper was left untouched. The guests quietly withdrew; the lights of the Edwards mansion were blown out, and darkness settled over all for the night. By daybreak, after persistent search, Lincoln's friends found him. Restless, gloomy, miserable, desperate, he seemed an object of pity. His friends, Speed among them, fearing a tragic termination, watched him closely in his rooms, day and night."

Even in its elaborated form, of which this is only a part, it can not be charged that the story is an invention of Herndon.

But the relatives of Mrs. Lincoln came to resent this narrative, and to blame Herndon as its inventor. The accepted story among Mrs. Lincoln's relatives came to be that there really never was any "fatal first of January." They came to believe that the course of true love ran very smoothly with Abraham Lincoln and Mary Todd.

There is enough for which Herndon is to blame, and I am blaming him more than I once did, but I do not see how we can hold him seriously at fault in this matter. If he had had Lincoln's letter to Stuart of January 20, 1841, a letter which we presently shall quote, he would have been even more confirmed than he was in the opinion that Lincoln was on the verge of insanity, and that condition was certainly associated with his break with Mary Todd. There was no use in the Edwards family's denial of this clear implication, and it seemed to them to be better to let Lincoln's insanity go the full length. So, without intending to speak falsely, but still with intent to make all she could of the truth, Mrs. Edwards told Herndon that Lincoln did not appear on the first night set for his wedding, and that the reason was that he had gone insane. Her husband added the simile, "crazy as a loon."

But this was discovered to be an unsatisfactory alibi. Why should Lincoln have gone crazy at just that time? His insanity, if he was insane, would certainly, in that event, have been a result, no less than an occasion, of his trouble with Mary Todd.

Mrs. Lincoln's sisters and nieces were in a really hard situation, and they knew that the extent of Lincoln's aberration had been exaggerated. Still endeavoring to be truthful, as, having talked with them, I believe they wanted to be, but in straits to make a better story than Mrs. Edwards had done, they shifted their ground. The narrative on which they ultimately agreed, contradicting Mrs. Edwards and blaming Herndon, is that of Elizabeth

Edwards's next younger sister, Frances Todd Wallace. On September 2, 1895, she gave a newspaper interview which as yet has not found a place in any book on Lincoln, and which we need at this point: This gives the version of the story which now is generally accepted by Mrs. Lincoln's relatives:

"One of the most interesting interviews about Lincoln ever published was that obtained with Mrs. Frances Wallace of Springfield, Illinois, a sister of Mrs. Lincoln. This interview is regarded as having especial value because it is opposed to previous publications to the effect that Lincoln's home life was unhappy. Here is the way the newspaper man says Mrs. Wallace told her story:

" 'I came here in 1837 to visit my married sister, Mrs. Ninian Edwards. Her given name was Elizabeth. Both she and her husband are now dead. My father had quite a large family at home in Lexington, Kentucky, and Lizzie wanted me to stay with her. She said she needed me more than they did at home, and so I stayed here.

" 'I often heard Mr. Edwards speak of Mr. Lincoln, and one time I told him: "You are always talking of this Mr. Lincoln. I wish you would bring him down some time and let me see him." So Mr. Edwards had him come down, and that is the way I met him. Yes, he took me out once or twice, but he was not much for society. He would go where they took him, but he was never very much for company. I don't think he could be called bashful. He was never embarrassed, that I saw, and he seemed to enjoy ladies' company. But he did not go much, as some of the other young men did.

" 'He liked music, although in all my life I never heard him attempt to sing. No, I never heard him whistle, that I can remember. I don't know whether he could or not. But he liked to hear the piano, and he liked to hear us sing. My sister had a good piano. Mr. Edwards was quite prosperous and lived in very good style. My sister liked society, and gave a good many parties, considering that early day.

" 'I got acquainted with Mr. Wallace. He had come out from Pennsylvania, and he had some money, and he had been out in Iowa speculating. He stopped here on his way back and speculated some in property here. And then the Pennsylvania men wanted him to locate here, and so he did. And he and I kept company quite a while, and then we were married. My sister, Mrs. Edwards, gave us quite a big wedding. I was married in a white satin dress, I remember, and the invitations were printed, and it was quite an affair.

" 'At first we boarded for about a year, and then we went to keeping house. Mr. Wallace had opened a drug store. He didn't intend to practise medicine at first, but his friends wanted him to, and so he got to going out among their families, and so he got into the practise. And after we were married my sister Mary came out from Lexington to stay with Mrs. Edwards, just the same as I had done before I was married. And she stayed there only a little while till she and Mr. Lincoln got acquainted. And a year after I was married, they were married. They were married in 1842, November fourth.

" 'No, they didn't have a big wedding at all. As soon as Mrs. Edwards knew they were engaged, she wanted to give them a big wedding just the same as she had me, but they were both opposed to it. They both wanted a simple private wedding. So they wouldn't tell any one when they were to be married. They just went along together, and then one Sunday morning Mr. Lincoln came down to Mr. Edwards's house, and he and Mary were out on the front porch, and then they told Mrs. Edwards that they were going to be married that night.

" 'She was terribly disappointed, for she could not get up a dinner in that short time. It was Sunday, and Springfield was a very small town at the time, and she hardly knew what to do. But they would not have it any other way, so she wrote a note to me, and told me they were to

be married that night, and asked me if I could help her.
So I worked all day. I never worked harder all day in
my life. And in the evening they were married, and we
had a very nice little supper, but not what we would have
had if they had given Mrs. Edwards time.

" 'Only a few people were there, for there was no time
to prepare for a large company. I remember the minister,
Mr. Dresser, did not know of the ceremony in time to
announce to his morning congregation that there would be
no service in the evening, so he had to go down there to
the church in the evening and hold a short service, and
then come up to Mr. Edwards's house and marry them.
Mr. Herndon says in his history that the wedding was a
grand affair, and that there were several hundred invitations printed, and that some one stood up with Mr. Lincoln, and that Mrs. Lincoln wore a white silk dress, but I
know she never had a white silk dress in her life till she
went to Washington to live.

" 'After I was married I gave her my white satin dress
and told her to wear it till it got soiled, but then to give it
back to me, for I wanted to keep all things like that—my
wedding dress, you know. No, she was not married in the
white satin. It was too soiled. She may have been married in a white swiss muslin, but I think it was not a white
dress at all. I think it was delaine, or something of that
kind.

" 'After that they boarded a while, and then they went
to housekeeping. I don't see why people should say Mr.
Lincoln's home life was not happy, for I certainly never
saw a thing there that would make me think either of
them was unhappy. He was devoted to his home, and
Mrs. Lincoln thought everything of him. She almost
worshipped him. Why, she need not have married him if
she had not wanted to. She could have married Mr.
Douglas, I have no doubt. She had gone with Mr. Douglas to several places. They were very well acquainted,
and were very good friends.

" 'And Mr. Lincoln was not compelled to marry Mary.

The House where Abraham Lincoln and Mary Todd were married

The parlor of the house in which they were married

Photographs by Eugene J. Hall, Oak Park, Illinois

The Genuine Marriage License of Abraham Lincoln and Mary Todd
(The document shown in Nicolay and Hay and some other biographies is not the original)

He had become quite a promising young man, and we were all proud of him. He could have married any other girl, no doubt, if he had wanted to. But they did not lead an unhappy life at all. Why, she was devoted to him and to her children. And he was certainly all to her that any husband could have been.

" 'He was the most tender-hearted man I ever knew. I have seen him carry Tad half-way to the office, when Tad was a great big boy. And I said to him once: "Why, Mr. Lincoln, put down that great big boy. He's big enough to walk." And he said: "Oh, don't you think his little feet get too tired?" '

"Tears were standing in the kindly little old lady's eyes as she told of this incident. Her whole manner was so simple and unaffected; she seemed so really to be living those distant scenes; her white hair and her gentle manner so plainly marked her the lady that it was like a benison to sit by her, and hear the truthful tongue run on.

" 'They say that he had an affair with a young woman at Salem, and that he broke off one wedding with Mary because he was half distracted with love for his other girl. But he did not break off one wedding. The wedding I tell you about was the only wedding that was arranged. I would have known of it if there had been another. And there never was another. He may have offered himself to that other girl. I don't know anything about that. He and Mary may have had a lover's quarrel for all I know. But I certainly saw him the night he was married, and he was not distracted with grief, or anything else. He was cheerful as he ever had been, for all we could see. He acted just as he always had in company. No; no one stood up with him. Just he and Mary stood up alone, and Mr. Dresser married them.

" 'No one but members of the family were there, or almost none. As I remember it there were Mr. and Mrs. Ninian Edwards, Mr. and Mrs. Ben Edwards, Major Stuart and his wife, Mr. and Mrs. Dresser, Doctor Todd's family, and Mr. Wallace and myself. I don't think there was any one else there. There couldn't have been more than one or two more.

" 'And then they say that Mrs. Lincoln was an ambitious woman. But she was not an ambitious woman at all. She was devoted to her home. She was one of the best seamstresses I ever knew. She made all her clothes and her children's clothes; and they were better made than most any one else's. It was before the day of sewing machines, you know, and all her work had to be done by hand. And they always looked well.

" 'After Mr. Lincoln was elected president, he appointed Doctor Wallace a paymaster in the regular army, and stationed him first at Washington, but that was so far away from home that he asked to be removed to St. Louis, and so he was moved there. And he could come up and see us when he wanted to. He retained the office till his death.

" 'No, it was as I tell you. There never was but one wedding arranged between Mary and Mr. Lincoln, and that was the time they were married. And they certainly did live happily together—as much so as any man and woman I have ever known.' "

It must be remembered that Mrs. Edwards's first interview with Herndon occurred twenty-five years after the event she sought to explain and the second some seventeen years later, and that Mrs. Wallace's interview was fifty-four years and nine months after "the fatal first of January."

To this must be added that neither Speed nor Herndon helped greatly to simplify matters in their contributions made long afterward.

Let us discover, if we may, what Lincoln meant when he used that term "the fatal first of January, 1841."

In the first place, we are not at liberty to believe that Lincoln really ran away from his own wedding. The story

Mrs. Edwards told to Herndon, and which he elaborated, of the assembled company, the baked cakes and the waiting bride, is just about impossible. There was no license. There was no announcement in the Springfield papers. No single invitation has been produced, saved as a souvenir of what would have been counted by all Springfield as a notable event of tragic import. Springfield was a small town and was full of people, and Lincoln was prominent in politics and the Todds and Edwardses were among the most prominent people. Such an incident if it had occurred would of necessity have produced a sensation at the time, and we should not lack for evidence of it. Something happened, but it can not have been the event which Mrs. Edwards thought she remembered.

In the next place, the wedding did not occur at all as Mrs. Wallace thought she remembered it. The time was not Sunday, but Friday night; and most of the other details as she gave them are wrong. We have to go to other sources for whatever accurate information we are to possess.

In the next place, Lincoln did not go as stark mad as has been represented. He continued to attend the Legislature, and answered to the roll-call with reasonable regularity.*

On May 14, 1841, he dissolved partnership with John T. Stuart and became the partner of Judge Stephen Todd Logan, another relative of Mary Todd, and he attended to his legal business that summer until after the adjournment of all the courts.

---

* In my *Life of Abraham Lincoln* I have compiled a record of Lincoln's attendance on the daily sessions of the General Assembly from January 1, 1841, to adjournment.

This brings us to another point, which is that he did not leave Springfield under the care of Joshua F. Speed or any one else. Speed left Springfield soon after January first, and Lincoln remained in Springfield for months before he made Speed a visit. Speed many years afterward thought Lincoln was with him "several months." About ten years ago I began to discover in Springfield evidence that during most of the months of the year 1841 Lincoln was undeniably in Springfield or on the circuit. By the time I published my *Life of Abraham Lincoln* in 1925 I was able to say that his absence from Springfield occurred "late in the summer." Later research has confirmed this statement and I could make it more definite if it were necessary. I shall have occasion to mention this again, but this is all that need be said now.

But on the other hand, we have indubitable evidence that Lincoln was under great mental strain. Mrs. Edwards was quite right when she said, "Matilda Edwards was with us for about a year; it was a crazy year." Matilda appears to have been about the sanest of those who lived through it. It is not of record that she lost any sleep over the affair. If men chose to fall in love with her, that was their privilege and hers. There is something to be said for the system of Miss Edwards.

Something happened on January 1, 1841. I have searched the Springfield papers repeatedly to find account of any event which could with reasonable certainty be associated with a break between Abraham Lincoln and Mary Todd, and have not found it. There were the New Year's calls usual in that day. Mary may have thought that her lover stayed too long in some home where other girls were serving good cheer, and that she thus suffered neglect. They too may have gone to a New Year's party in the evening preceding, and when the lights went out at midnight he may have kissed some other girl. But we have no record of it. Probably the quarrel did not originate in any very great event. Abraham and Mary had quarreled before, and it may have been a mere trifle over which they quarreled on that day.

But we know in what state of mind Lincoln was. The heirs of Major John T. Stuart have the original of the following letter, which is not in any of the collected volumes of Lincoln's writings. It was written to Stuart, who was then in Washington, attending to his duties as a Member of Congress:

"Springfield, Jany. 20th, 1841

"Dear Stuart:

"I have had no letter from you since you left—No matter for that—What I wish now is to speak of our Postoffice—You know I desired Dr. Henry to have the place when you left; I now desire it more than ever—I have, within the last few days, been making a most discreditable exhibition of myself in the way of hypochondriasm and thereby got an impression that Dr. Henry is necessary to my existence—Unless he gets that place he leaves Springfield. You therefore see how much I am interested in the matter.

"We shall shortly forward you a petition in his favor signed by all or nearly all the Whig members of the Legislature, as well as other Whigs.

"This, together with what you know of the Dr's position and merits I sincerely hope will secure him the appointment—My heart is very much set upon it—

"Pardon me for not writing more; I have not sufficient composure to write a long letter—

"As ever yours

"A. Lincoln."

Now we know that Lincoln had medical attendance during that period, and that his physician was his long-time Whig associate, his fellow editor of *The Old Soldier*, Doctor A. G. Henry. We wish we had Doctor Henry's diagnosis. Lincoln called it "hypochondriasm." It was popularly called "hypo" and pronounced "hippo."

Three days later Lincoln wrote again to Stuart, and said:

"I am now the most miserable man living. If what I feel were equally distributed to the whole human family, there would not be one cheerful face on earth. Whether I shall ever be any better, I can not tell; I awfully forebode that I shall not. To remain as I am is impossible. I must die or be better, it seems to me."

The context of the letter shows that he thought it quite possible he would not long be competent to transact business. This can mean nothing else than that Abraham Lincoln was so mentally distraught by something that had occurred between him and Mary Todd on January 1, 1841, that he had grave fears for his own sanity.

But what started the trouble, no one knows, and it is not likely that any one will ever learn much more than is here recorded.

With an excitable temper like that of Mary Todd, and a morbid temperament like that of Abraham Lincoln, and an experience of quarrels already that might have wrecked most engagements, no very great event was necessary. Aristotle taught us that "The causes of war are profound, and the occasions of war are slight." Whatever the occasion of the quarrel, we know the cause. The occasion does not appear to have involved Stephen A. Douglas or

Matilda Edwards.   The fundamental reasons were inherent in Abraham Lincoln and Mary Todd.

7.   THE LANDLADY'S LITTLE SISTER

When Abraham Lincoln broke with Mary Todd on "the
fatal first of January, 1841" he had left on his hands two
tickets to a Thrilling Dramatic Entertainment.   They
were too valuable to be lost.   Broken-hearted he was, but
a show was a show, and there were not many of them in
Springfield.   Indeed, the girl who went with Lincoln that
night believed that it was the first dramatic exhibition
ever performed in that town.   But we remember *Therese*.
The girl who used the tickets with Lincoln was the first
one he met after he realized that he had the tickets and
that Mary was not to accompany him.   She was the little
sister of his landlady.   He took her to see the *Babes in the
Wood*.   The babes died and were covered over with leaves
by birds.   One would like to know how they managed that
in Springfield in 1841.

When Lincoln came to Springfield to live in the home
of William Butler, he met there this dark-haired girl of
twelve, a younger sister of Mrs. Butler.   Her name was
Sarah Rickard.   To Lincoln she was only a little girl, and
he petted and teased and liked her.   She liked Lincoln,
but thought of him as a big brother, a friend of her sister
and her husband, and a member of the family.

On January 1, 1841, or shortly after, Lincoln opened
his eyes, and there was little Sarah, now seventeen years
of age, and pleasant to look upon.   Lincoln felt that he
had made a mess of his courtships, and that he would
never be safe from folly in matters pertaining to matri-

mony.   He asked himself why he should not marry Sarah. Her sister, Mrs. Butler, was a woman whom he admired; Sarah was growing to be more like her; why not marry Sarah?

Sarah Rickard was the eighth child of Peter and Elizabeth Rickard, and was born in Virginia, March 2, 1824. She married Richard F. Barret, son of a well-known Springfield family, and a man whom she found "much more graceful and attractive" than Abraham Lincoln. After their marriage they lived in St. Louis.   The eldest surviving member of the Barret family when these investigations began was Mrs. Charles Ridgley, of Springfield, daughter of James Winston Barret.   She was born at Island Grove, Illinois, and the family was intimately associated with the Butlers.   She attended school in Springfield, boarding in the Butler home, and had a young girl's recollection of events narrated in this chapter, that recollection confirmed by her conversations in later years with others older than herself.

Certain details also were supplied by Honorable William J. Butler, grandson of the original William Butler. Although he did not remember Lincoln, or his great Aunt Sarah, he had heard very much from his father, Henry Wirt Butler, who was a boy in the home when Lincoln boarded there, and from his Aunt Salome, who spent her last days in his home.   Salome Butler knew Lincoln well and knew all his friends in Springfield.

Mrs. Ridgely said that in the family it was understood that both Mary Todd and Sarah Rickard received proposals of marriage from both Lincoln and Douglas.   She said that Mrs. Barret told her that she was not tempted to accept Douglas, but might have accepted Lincoln, not-

withstanding his age, if he had been as graceful and attractive as Richard Barret, whom she later married.

Both Mrs. Ridgely and Captain Butler agreed that
there was an offer of marriage made by Lincoln to Sarah
Rickard, Salome Butler being Mr. Butler's authority; but
neither of these relatives attached any considerable importance to the incident. "It was probably nothing more
than a flirtation," said Mrs. Ridgely; and Captain Butler,
who professed no personal knowledge, but relied on the
knowledge of his aunt, did not think of it in serious terms.
All the friends and relatives of Sarah Rickard thought
well of her good sense in declining a marriage so unsuit-
able on account of the disparity of age between herself
and Abraham Lincoln. Some of them even wonder if the
proposal was much more than a bit of persiflage. But in
general the proposal was accepted as genuine, though
hasty and ill-considered.

Lest some evil-minded person should raise the question
whether Lincoln's conduct toward Sarah had been honorable, and should wonder whether his fifteen months of
concern on her account had in it any element of contrition
for misbehavior, let that question be faced for a moment,
for it is a question which the author has propounded
bluntly to the nearest living relatives of Sarah. Their answer is emphatic. Lincoln had done nothing that changed
in any degree his relations with the Butler family, or with
the Rickards. He continued to board with the Butlers,
and he rode out every now and then six miles to visit
Sarah. She and her family liked him, and fortunately did
nothing to terminate matters abruptly.

Sarah was fascinated for a time; her little head was
turned, and no wonder. And Lincoln knew that he had

committed himself, and he was not disposed to leave her disconsolate. Fortunately that was not necessary.

Anyway, while Lincoln was thinking himself in love with Sarah, he was not in danger of doing anything else more foolish in the matter of his matrimonial future. And Mary Todd was still unmarried, and making no progress.

But while there was not much of the Sarah Rickard affair, there was more than has sometimes been assumed. In Lincoln's letters to his friend Joshua Fry Speed, during the stormy period of his courtship of Mary Todd, there are several anxious and troubled references to a person whose name is suppressed. The fact that Speed did not permit that name to be printed would of itself show that he regarded it as significant. And Speed knew just what that suppressed name implied. In three letters are references to visits of Lincoln to Sarah, who had left Butlers' and gone out to her own home, and these visits were a matter of anxiety to Lincoln. It was not so casual an affair as might have appeared. It lasted more than a full year, and it is evident that Lincoln, having really proposed to Sarah, did not easily rid himself of the feeling that he was obligated in some degree. Nor, since during that period he was keeping away from Mary Todd, is it certain that he did not sometimes think he really wanted Sarah. Fortunately, she or her sister, or both, had more sense in the matter than he.

Lincoln's letter to Speed, dated March 27, 1842, says:

"One thing I can tell you which I know you will be glad to hear, and that is that I have seen Sarah, and have scrutinized her feelings as well as I could, and am fully convinced she is far happier now than she has been for the past fifteen months."

In a letter of February third, preceding, he tells of seeing her, and finding her cheerful, and so not saying to her what he had planned to say, and had told Speed he intended to say.

If I were to indulge in a conjecture concerning the incident that caused the break between Lincoln and the woman to whom he was betrothed, I could give one which I regard as far more reasonable than any that others have proposed. It would be that Mary Todd, discovering before Lincoln did that Sarah had grown into an attractive young woman, thought of her as a possible rival, and by her jealous inquiries suggested the idea to Lincoln. That would account for the fact that for fifteen months prior to March, 1842, Sarah had been unhappy about Lincoln; for in the event of some such suggestion it would not be surprising that Lincoln's feeling of responsibility for Sarah went back almost if not quite to the time of his trouble with Mary. I do not give this as an opinion, for the reader knows how much and how little there is on which such an opinion might be based, but I advance it as a conjecture which has more merit than any that I have found in other books. I suggest it for whatever it may be worth and no more.

As for Lincoln, if he thought he had become indifferent to the happiness of Mary Todd, he was much mistaken. In the same letter of March 27, 1842, he says he is almost completely happy, and would be so, but for the fact that he had caused Mary to be sad:

"It seems to me I should have been entirely happy, but for the never absent idea that there is one still unhappy woman I have contributed to make so. That still kills my soul. I can not but reproach myself for even wishing to be happy while she is otherwise. She accompanied a large party on the railroad cars to Jacksonville last Monday, and on her return spoke, so that I heard of it, of having enjoyed the trip exceedingly. God be praised for that."

It should be recorded that long before Lincoln's reconciliation with Mary Todd he had recovered his health. He rode the circuit in the spring of 1841, and was in Illinois till midsummer. He had what we might now call a late summer vacation which he spent with the Speeds. While there he read such books as he found at hand, and though he was depressed at times he was already on the way to recovery. The courts of the Eighth Judicial District opened in Tazewell September sixteenth and moved to McLean September twenty-seventh. He returned to Springfield in time for the opening of court, and wrote his "bread-and-butter letter" to the Speeds from Bloomington on the twenty-seventh. He had not been absent from Springfield many weeks. He was "quite a man" by the time he got back.

He still was troubled about Sarah, and continued to feel responsible for her for the better part of a year. But he was not troubled forever. Sometimes when a man is wondering how he is to be rid of a girl, she renders him unexpected assistance. Sarah herself, aided and abetted no doubt by her mother and older sister, came to her youthful senses, and Lincoln knew that he had no further occasion to worry about her. No bones were broken or friendships sundered over this vexatious but superficial incident.

We have, therefore, from the nearest living relatives of the persons involved, and from Sarah Rickard's own letter, as accurate a narrative of the courtship of Sarah

Rickard by Abraham Lincoln as the world is likely ever to possess. It is a short story, but an interesting one, and it has its value for our knowledge of the man and of the evolution of his personality.

So this is the story of a slip of a girl who caught Abraham Lincoln's heart on the rebound, and held it more or less loosely in her little palm for a period of fifteen months, and then was sensible enough to toss it back to him, none the worse for anything she had done to it, and she none the worse for having had the big-brother love of a lonely man almost twice her age.

8. RECONCILIATION

Abraham Lincoln returned from his summer vacation, and had very pleasant memories of his days at Farmington, the home of the Speed family. He had enjoyed his companionship with Joshua Speed, and had formed a friendship for his brother James, who late in the Lincoln administration became a member of his Cabinet. The Speed daughters, also, were pleasant companions, especially the daughter Lucy. He held in especially grateful recollection the motherly ministrations of Mrs. Speed. He remembered them long years afterward, and sent her his autographed photograph after he had been elected President. Mrs. Speed gave him an Oxford Bible, telling him the Bible was the best cure for the blues.

While he was at this delightful home, he had an aching tooth extracted, and wished that he could have disposed of his other troubles as readily. He and Mary Todd had broken, but she was not married or engaged to marry any one else. Some time in September he was back in Springfield and riding the circuit, with plans for a visit to his father at Charleston. And he was busy with law and politics. On October twentieth he drew a call for a Whig Convention to nominate governor and lieutenant-governor. The convention was held on the third Monday in December and the political pot boiled. He had something else to think about besides Mary Todd.

There was no meeting of the Legislature in the winter of 1841-2, and he was giving more attention to law than he formerly had done. Judge Logan was requiring him to work, and that was good for Lincoln, though he did not like to do it. His legal papers drawn at this time are done with his habitual care and precision. They display no evidence of impaired mentality. This partnership was to Lincoln's advantage, except for one thing. Judge Logan wanted to be the next Member of Congress from his district, and Lincoln had no notion of standing out of his way, for he wanted the office himself. If any one has ever supposed Lincoln to have been a man of great modesty, one answer, among many, is his readiness to defeat his senior partner, if possible, in a race for a position which that partner felt he had earned by long and distinguished services. The partners did not quarrel immediately, but each watched the other with concern.

Early in 1842 Lincoln joined the Washingtonian movement, and was an active member of this temperance organization. He was a welcome addition to its membership, which truth to tell, was not wholly composed of the best citizens of Springfield. It was primarily a league of reformed men, and some of them were none too permanently reformed. They had "minds still passion-ridden; soul-powers frail." Lincoln was chosen to be their orator on Washington's birthday in 1842, and spoke in the Presbyterian Church at that time. This was the best prepared and most notable address he had thus far delivered. Unfortunately, Lincoln went out of his way to censure the church-members who did not care to join an organization of men so recently risen from the gutter. He appeared to reflect on their sincerity and also on their consistency. He did not need to do this, and it lost him friends. Otherwise it was a good speech, and set forth not only Lincoln's admiration for the character of Washington, but his hatred of rum and slavery. If Mary Todd heard him that night she had far more reason for pride than shame on his account; though he still had need to curb his tendency to invective and sarcasm.

In June of 1842, Martin Van Buren made a tour of Illinois, and planned to visit Springfield, but muddy roads halted him at Rochester, six miles away, and there he spent the night. A group of Democratic politicians went out to meet him, taking with them a hamper of what they deemed needful for the proper celebration of the event, and they invited Lincoln also to go with them. He and a few other leading Whigs went out and sat up until after midnight with the ex-president. Lincoln did not partake of the contents of the hamper, but he was in great glee. He had mercilessly opposed "King Martin" as a candidate for reelection, but that was two years before, and political bygones were bygones. The word that went back to Springfield was, that Van Buren had laughed himself sore over Lincoln's stories. Mary Todd must have heard this.

From the fatal first of January, 1841, till late in the autumn of 1842, Abraham Lincoln and Mary Todd kept

away from each other. He had found no more rest than
Noah's weary dove. He was rather more than ready to
pluck an olive branch and fly back to the ark. Mary, too,
had had her share of gaiety, and Abraham heard of it
and thought he was glad, but down deep in his heart he
was not happy about it, and she, if anything, was even
less happy than he. These two people, who were divinely
created to irritate each other, were also constituted in
such fashion as to be necessary to each other's comfort
and peace.

Two matters occurred to help in bringing them together. One was Lincoln's correspondence with his friend
Joshua F. Speed. Speed had been in love and hesitated
much as Lincoln did; but Lincoln had encouraged him to
go on and be married. Speed married, and Lincoln wrote
to him, asking questions such as one man seldom asks
another. Speed answered these questions frankly, and in
a manner wholly to his credit. He assured Lincoln that
his misgivings had been largely imaginary, and that his
married life was happy beyond his expectations. Lincoln
believed that Speed would not lie to him in so grave a
matter, and Speed's letters had weight with him, and
exerted no small influence in reuniting Lincoln and Mary
Todd.

The other affair concerned a prank of Mary Todd and
a friend, Julia M. Jayne, afterward her bridesmaid, and
still later Mrs. Lyman Trumbull. Lincoln had written
for the *Sangamon Journal* an article entitled "Letter from
Lost Townships" and signed "Aunt Rebecca." This article
held up to public ridicule James Shields, an Irishman,
prominent in Springfield politics and a rival of Lincoln.
The article excited much mirth, for Shields, though a

man of ability, was one whose characteristics easily lent
themselves to ridicule. Simeon Francis might have hesitated to publish an article so certain to provoke wrath,
had he not been a warm personal and political friend of
Lincoln. Herndon says of Francis, "He ran the Whig or-
gan, and entertained great admiration for Lincoln's brains
and noble qualities. The esteem was mutual, and it is no
stretch of the truth to say that for years Lincoln exercised
undisputed control of the columns of the *Journal*, himself.
Whatever he wrote or had written, went into the editorial
page without question."

Mary Todd, the future wife of a president, and Julia
Jayne, the future wife of a senator, wrote a second article,
in which the satire was carried further, and they signed
it with the same name, "Aunt Rebecca." This also was
published in the *Journal*. Shields, angered by the first,
was infuriated by the second article. He sent a friend to
Francis demanding the name of the author of the two
articles. Lincoln was out of town and could not be con-
sulted. Francis, compelled to reply, and feeling sure that
Lincoln would wish to shield the girls, gave Lincoln's
name. Shields, accompanied by a friend, followed Lincoln
to Tremont, where Lincoln was attending court, and chal-
lenged him to a duel. Lincoln, after some attempt to
avert such a proceeding, accepted the challenge. Happily,
the duel was called off by the good offices of mutual
friends, but not before the affair had become public, to
Lincoln's subsequent great mortification. He had the good
sense to be heartily ashamed of his part in the whole
matter. Mrs. Francis was an intimate friend of Mary
Todd. This matter, which had coupled the names of Mary
and Lincoln in much public talk, proved Mrs. Francis's

opportunity to bring the two together. They had a number of secret meetings at the Francis house; and at length reached a swift agreement to be married at once, with no more nonsense about it.

The next day was Friday. It was not a day which either Lincoln or his bride would have chosen for a wedding, for both were superstitious, but they feared nothing now so much as a delay, in which each would have opportunity to permit their resolution to be sicklied o'er with thought. The Springfield records contain the license, issued November 4, 1842, with the return of the minister, Reverend Charles Dresser, certifying that on the same day he married Abraham Lincoln and Mary Todd. The only contemporary newspaper reference is in the *Journal* of the following week, November 11, 1842, and may have been written by Lincoln himself. It is very brief and precise, as follows:

MARRIED: in this city, on the 4th, instant, at the home of N. W. Edwards, Esq. by the Rev. Charles Dresser, ABRAHAM LINCOLN to MISS MARY TODD, daughter of Robert S. Todd, Esq. of Lexington, Ky.

Reverend Charles Dresser, whose home the Lincolns were later to buy and occupy, was rector of the Episcopal Church in Springfield. This was the church which the Edwards family supported, and to whose social life Elizabeth Edwards was so constant a contributor. Mary had been attending church regularly with her sister, and had become a communicant there; but whether she was actually confirmed, her sister, Mrs. Helm, doubts.

This was Mr. Dresser's ninth marriage in Sangamon

County, and the Episcopal service was still a novelty in Springfield. The clause "with all my worldly goods I thee endow" excited its usual joke among the friends of the groom.

Informal as the wedding was, and hurried as were the preparations, Mary wanted bridesmaids, and had them. One of them was Julia Jayne, afterward Mrs. Lyman Trumbull, and the other was Annie Rodney, sister-in-law of Honorable William L. Day. Lincoln secured as his attendants James H. Matheney and Beverley Powell. The former was an associate at the bar, and a long-time friend; the latter was a dry-goods clerk, a popular young man, and admittedly the best dressed man in town. Although the preparations had to be made on that Friday, the securing of these attendants was not a matter involving any serious difficulty. Everybody knew everybody else in Springfield. Mary had only to send for her two friends and tell them to put on their best frocks and come over that evening and stand up with her. Lincoln had only to mention the matter to Jim Matheney as he crossed the state-house square, and then step in at the store and ask Beverley to come over to the Edwards home that evening and give him such assistance as was customary in the circumstances.

About forty people were present at the wedding, and Elizabeth Todd Edwards was there with one of her justly famous cakes; but the icing was still warm when it left the Edwards kitchen, and the cake was too new to cut well.

And Springfield people were happy over it, in the main, though now and then some one expressed wonder how such a strangely mated couple would get along together.

9. FAMILY CARES AND POLITICS

Lincoln and his wife were not in condition to make it possible for him to purchase a home. They took up their abode in the Globe Tavern, and lived there for nearly a year. They paid for board and room two dollars a week each, which was an increase over what Lincoln had paid for food at the Butler's, and as for room over Speed's store, that had cost him nothing. Even four dollars a week is four dollars every seven days. The Lincolns lived at the Globe Tavern until after their first child was born, their son Robert, who arrived August 1, 1843, and lived until July 26, 1926.

If Lincoln wrote any letter to Speed telling him of his reconciliation to Mary, and of his sudden marriage, as it would seem he could hardly have failed to do, that letter was among those that Speed withheld when he permitted Herndon to copy some of them, nor is it included in the complete list now extant.*

So far as we know, Lincoln's only written allusion to his wedding (for I do not accept the John Hanks letter cited by Weik in his *The Real Lincoln*) is that of his letter to Sam Marshall just a week after his wedding:

"Nothing new here except my marriage, which to me is matter of profound wonder."

This is the only known emotion which he confessed about it to any one, profound wonder that the thing could

---

* Mr. Oliver R. Barrett owns the Speed letters, and by his courtesy I have examined them all and have copies of them. The unfamiliar passages quoted in this book are mine by his kind permission.

have occurred. Yet, undeniably, at his elbow by day and by his side at night, there was Mary Todd Lincoln.

The prospect of maternity was immediate, and with regard to that we find our first suggestion of a growing separation between Lincoln and his intimate friend Speed. On March 24, 1843, in one of the unpublished letters, he wrote to Speed that he could not say "as yet" concerning the certain prospect that Speed would "have a namesake in Springfield."

As Mrs. Lincoln was at that time pregnant, and nearly four months in that condition, there would seem to have been no considerable degree of uncertainty about that fact. There had been an understanding that Lincoln's first son should be named for Speed. There was more than a measure of uncertainty about that. Mary Todd intended that her first son should be named after her father. Not quite two months later, on May eighteenth, Lincoln wrote to Speed rather fully about the "coming events" which were casting their shadows before in both families.

On July twenty-sixth Lincoln wrote to Speed:

"We shall look with impatience for your visit this fall. Your Fanny can not be more anxious to see my Molly than the latter is to see her, nor so much so as I am. Don't fail to come. We are but two, as yet."

Only four days longer were they two. The physician, probably, was Doctor Henry, who may have taken his fee in political friendship; or, as he was even poorer than Lincoln, may have accepted cash. Lincoln, let us hope, had a client who paid him liberally about that time. Doctor Henry had not succeeded in getting the post-office.

How Lincoln accounted to Speed for the fact that the

baby was not named "Joshua Speed Lincoln" we do not know. But we do know that the correspondence between these two friends grew less intimate. They were still friends, but their letters grew less frequent, and Lincoln's oft expressed "love to Fanny" became a distantly friendly greeting "to Mrs. Speed." Mary Todd Lincoln was not a woman who wanted her husband sending his love to other women.

One fact is of marked significance, and Speed did not permit it to be divulged. Lincoln had asked him the most intimate questions about Speed's satisfaction in married life, and Speed's declaration that he was more happy married to Fanny than he could ever have believed possible had much to do with Lincoln's decision to marry Mary Todd. This letter Speed permitted to be made public. What he concealed was that after Lincoln had been married about two months, Speed asked him the same question, and that Lincoln evaded a direct answer. In Lincoln's unpublished letter of January 18, 1843, he said:

"How the marriage life goes with me, I will tell you when I see you, which I hope will be soon."

That was an ominous answer, and Speed understood it, and did not look for any extended information.

Lincoln could not have said to Speed what Speed said to him, that his fears had proved groundless and that he was far more happy than he had dared to think he ever could be. But on the other hand, he did not say that he was more miserable than he had ever supposed possible. If married life was not as good as he hoped, it was not quite so bad as he feared. With all her faults, Mary Todd was an affectionate woman, and she loved her home. She had a keen eye for her husband's success, and she wanted the social prestige which that success would involve.

Her baby Robert was a care, and in due time he was followed by a brother. Lincoln may have had the naming of him, and we should like greatly to know why he was not named for Speed. The second boy was given the name of one of Lincoln's close political friends, Edward Baker. Was Mary willing that this should be, but did she feel some measure of jealousy of a friend who had been as intimate with her husband as Speed had been? Surely, she had reason to be grateful to Speed for the help he gave Lincoln in deciding to marry her. Lincoln made no explanation in telling Speed about this baby. It can scarcely have been by accident that, writing October 22, 1846, when Eddie was seven months old, he did not tell his name:

"Being elected to Congress, though I am very grateful to our friends for having done it, has not pleased me as much as I expected. We have another boy, born the tenth of March. He is very much such a child as Bob was at his age, rather of a longer order. Bob is 'short and low' and I expect always will be. He talks very plainly, almost as plainly as any body. He is quite smart enough. I sometimes fear he is one of the rare-ripe sort that are smarter at about five than ever after. He has a great deal of that sort of mischief which is the offspring of such animal spirits. Since I began this letter, a messenger came to tell me Bob was lost, but by the time I reached the house his mother had found him and had him whipped, and by now, very likely, he is run away again. Mary has read your letter, and wishes to be remembered to Mrs. Speed and you, in which I most sincerely join her."

Yes, Mary read the letters that passed between her husband and his old friend. And there was no longer any sending of love to Fanny, but a participation in Mary's greeting to Mrs. Speed.

Abraham Lincoln had become a well domesticated husband, at least so far as the sending of messages either to men or women that could be expected to rouse a spirit of jealousy in his wife. For it grieves me to record that in addition to her temper Mrs. Lincoln had in her a streak of jealousy as fierce as it was without provocation. Of it we shall have unfortunate examples later. And whatever the faults of Abraham Lincoln, he had none that could have given any reasonable woman occasion for that passion.

The letter already quoted goes a little ahead of the story in telling of Lincoln's success in getting himself elected to Congress. The Honorable Stephen T. Logan had been very desirous of going there, and wanted Lincoln to attend to the law business while the senior partner made stump speeches, but Lincoln preferred to look out for politics on his own account. Lincoln drove Logan out of the running, but had himself to reckon with other rivals. He wrote to a friend in March, 1843, "If you should hear any one say that Lincoln don't want to go to Congress, I wish you, as a personal friend of mine, to tell him you have reason to believe he is mistaken. The truth is, I would like to go very much."

A few days later there was a sort of Whig primary in Springfield, and he and Edward Baker were the leading candidates, but as the voting went on, Baker came to Lincoln, and proposed that the balloting cease, and Lincoln was glad to accept the suggestion. Baker had beaten him badly and was generous enough to be willing not to advertise the extent of Lincoln's defeat. For him as

already stated Lincoln named his second son, Edward
Baker Lincoln, who was born March 1, 1846, and died
February 1, 1850. But when the District Convention was
held, though Lincoln went as a delegate, instructed to
vote for Baker, and did so, the winning candidate was
John J. Hardin; thus many well laid plans went wrong
that year.

And now Lincoln made a sad discovery; his marriage
had not thus far helped him politically. There was a certain prejudice against the aristocratic families of Springfield, and Lincoln had to explain that he did not belong
to the silk-stockinged class. "I, a strange, friendless, un-
educated, penniless boy, working on a flatboat at ten dollars a month, have been put down here as the candidate of
pride, wealth and family distinction." The year 1844
brought the next presidential election, and Lincoln was
on the Whig ticket as a presidential elector, and stumped
a portion of Illinois, and also went to his old home in Indiana and made stump speeches for Henry Clay. But
Clay was not elected, to the sorrow of Abraham Lincoln.

About this time Lincoln's disagreement with his senior
partner, Judge Logan, reached a crisis. It was practically
certain that the Whig nominee from that district would be
elected to Congress, and Lincoln wanted to be the nominee and would not step out of the way for Judge Logan
or any one else. The partnership was broken off, and
Lincoln chose a new partner, William H. Herndon. Herndon was the son of an influential pro-slavery man, but had
been a student of Illinois College, where he became an
Abolitionist. He was several years younger than Lincoln,
and his personal habits were not wholly correct. He was
a member of the Washingtonian Society, and at one time

its president, but he did not stay reformed. When he was sober he was a capable man and in many respects supplemented Lincoln. He was impetuous, and rather a good judge of human nature. He had more initiative than Lincoln, and was much more given to diversified reading. He was a prolific correspondent, and his letters from Theodore Parker and other eminent men in New England and New York kept him in touch with some of the leading minds of his generation.

Lincoln was criticized for choosing Herndon as his partner, but said, "I know Billy Herndon better than any one else." All in all Lincoln had much reason to be thankful for such an assistant and associate. Mrs. Lincoln was not happy over her husband's choice; she did not like Herndon. Her feeling of repugnance dated from their first meeting. At a ball in Springfield, she danced with Herndon in that new and fascinating movement called "the waltz." Herndon greatly admired the lightness of her step and the precision of her rhythm; he attempted to pay her a compliment. He should have said, "You glide through the waltz like a bird," but unfortunately he said, "You glide through the waltz with the agility of a serpent." She resented the simile and ever afterward disliked Herndon. Although Herndon was a good lawyer and his qualities were such as to supplement those of Lincoln, his personality was offensive to her. When she entered her husband's office, she walked straight by Herndon, and was careful to hold her skirts a little aside. She never made a worse mistake. If Mrs. Lincoln had treated Herndon with a little more consideration, the world would never have heard of Ann Rutledge.

In previous books on Abraham Lincoln, I have paid

willing tribute to the fidelity of William H. Herndon as a
recorder of facts about Lincoln. This I have done the
more gladly because I believe that biographers of Lincoln
have, in general, been unjust to him, some of them mark-
edly so. I have acknowledged also Herndon's limitations,
and I regret to say that I have discovered more of them,
and some are not easy to reconcile with entire good faith.
I do not here and now make any charge, nor is this the
place for any general discussion, but one matter calls for
correction in this place, and that is the dates of Lincoln's
three partnerships.

As given by Herndon, Lincoln's partnership with John
T. Stuart began April 27, 1837, and ended April 14, 1841;
that with Stephen T. Logan began almost immediately
after the termination of the Stuart partnership and continued until September 20, 1843; and that with William
H. Herndon began on the dissolution of the Logan partnership and was never formally dissolved.

Herndon should have been accurate, at least as to his
own partnership, but for some reason he was not. I am
able to amend his dates, and it is important to do so.*

The Stuart and Lincoln partnership was formed April
12, 1837, and according to notice in the *Journal* was su-
perseded by that of Logan and Lincoln May 14, 1841.
Herndon is wrong when he states that he and Lincoln became partners in 1843; Herndon was not admitted to the
bar until December 9, 1844. However, he and Lincoln
must have had some form of partnership before that time,
although the Logan and Lincoln advertisements continue
to appear until March 27, 1845. The later uses of the

---

* For valuable information here I am indebted to Mr. Paul M. Angle
of the Lincoln Centennial Association.

old firm name were in connection with cases previously begun and continued.

The most reliable word we have on Lincoln's partnerships was discovered by Honorable William H. Townsend, and appears in his *Abraham Lincoln, Defendant*. Lincoln himself, writing of his alleged relation with a firm in which Mrs. Lincoln's father had been a partner, the firm of Oldham, Todd and Hemingway, said in his letter of September 13, 1852:

"I can prove by John T. Stuart, of Springfield, Illinois, that he and I were partners in the law from the Spring of 1837 to the Spring of 1841, and that, so far as he knows, we never had any business for O. T. & Co. By Stephen T. Logan of Springfield, Ills., that he and I were partners from the Spring of 1841 to the autumn of 1844, and that so far as he knows, he and I never had any business for O. T. & Co. By William H. Herndon of Springfield, Ills., that he and I have been partners from the autumn of 1844 up to the present time; and that so far as he knows, he and I never had any business for O. T. & Co."

Herndon certainly dated his partnership with Lincoln a full year earlier than it actually began, and his first year in Lincoln's office was before Herndon was admitted to the bar. As to the termination of the partnership, it is true that it was never formally dissolved. It is also true that when Lincoln left Springfield for Washington, in 1861, he advertised that his accounts and personal business would be attended to by Robert Irwin.

In all this we go somewhat ahead of the story, but this correction of all books about Lincoln, including in this instance my own, should be made at this point.

10. THE WIFE OF A MEMBER OF CONGRESS

In 1846, the promotion for which Lincoln had so long waited, came to him. He refused to be a candidate for further reelection to the Legislature and boldly set out to become a member of Congress. It was the presidential off-year and a bad year for the Democrats throughout the country, but no year was a good year for the Democrats in Lincoln's own district; it was the most solidly Whig section of Illinois. Hardin had had one term in Congress and Baker had had one, and now Lincoln and Logan were in line for promotion. Lincoln proved the more popular candidate of the two. A Whig Convention was held at Petersburg in May, 1846, and Logan reluctantly decided that he could not possibly be nominated, and himself presented Lincoln's name. There was a merry campaign that fall, for Lincoln had as his opponent the doughty Methodist preacher, Peter Cartwright. That valiant pioneer had forded streams and ridden through bottomless mud all through central and southern Illinois, holding revival meetings, thrashing bullies and consistently looking out for political possibilities. The first time Lincoln ran for the Legislature in 1832, Cartwright was his opponent and defeated him. Now fourteen years later Lincoln rode up and down the Congressional District and had the early satisfaction of knowing that he was quite certain to defeat Cartwright.

Mary Todd Lincoln was a happy woman when the November election showed her husband to be the new member of Congress from his district. She was going to Washington, where she was certain she would be a society belle; she had no doubt that her husband would go on from one

position to another, and she set no limit in her estimation
as to the honors which she might ultimately share with
him. Lincoln was the only Whig from Illinois. Among
his associates were John A. McClernand, of Shawnee-
town; O. B. Ficklin, of Charleston; Long John Went-
worth, of Chicago, and last, but by no means least, Stephen A. Douglas, who had been Lincoln's associate and
opponent ever since Lincoln's second term in the Legislature.

It was a happy day for Mrs. Lincoln when she and her
husband set out for Washington. They went by what was
then a fairly direct route, going to Indianapolis, Louisville, where they visited Joshua and Fanny Speed, and
Lexington, where she remained for a little time with her
stepmother and half-sisters. One letter of Mrs. Lincoln's
in that period is preserved; it is a pleasant, cheerful, gos-
sipy letter, such as an affectionate wife might be expected
to send her husband. Before very long he wrote her to
come to Washington, and she was with him through the
greater part of the long session of the thirtieth Congress.
They boarded at Mrs. Skaggs's boarding house near where
the Congressional Library now stands. It was a pleasant
and reputable but rather modest abiding place. They
were practising economy, for the last remnants of Lincoln's New Salem debt still hung like a mill-stone about
his neck. If he had put up at a good hotel, that debt
would have remained unpaid. Mrs. Skaggs's bill was
modest enough to enable them to get out of debt.

Mrs. Lincoln visited the Capitol with her husband, and
he pointed out to her the great men who were there: John
Quincy Adams, who had been president of the United
States, Daniel Webster, John C. Calhoun, Alexander H.

Stephens and many others. A great change had come over the complexion of the Lower House of Congress since the last election; the twenty-ninth Congress had seventy-five Whigs and one hundred forty-two Democrats, the thirtieth Congress had one hundred sixteen Whigs and only one hundred eight Democrats; it looked as though the good time coming was in sight for the Whig party and for Mr. and Mrs. Lincoln—nevertheless, her Washington experience was a deep disappointment. The wife of a new Member of Congress filled no very large angle in Washington society. Mrs. Lincoln did not have the social standing or the dry-goods necessary for distinction; she was an interested onlooker, but she subsided into inconspicuous obscurity. Yet if she saw that one term in Congress with her husband was not enough to give her standing in Washington, she also saw that the star of the Whig party was in the ascendant, and she had hope of a longer sojourn in that city at some later time.

Her husband was not long in letting himself be heard on the floor of Congress. That body convened on December 6, 1847; within a month Lincoln had made his first speech. The Mexican War was in active progress by the time Congress convened; Lincoln was opposed to it on principle, and lost no opportunity to register his opposition to the policy of the Administration. In this respect he gradually moved ahead of the sentiment of his own Congressional District without realizing the extent to which he had done this. Congress adjourned August 4, 1848, Mr. Lincoln went to New England to make speeches on behalf of General Zachary Taylor, whom in February he had helped nominate at Philadelphia as Whig candidate for president. He made most earnest arguments on behalf of Taylor and returned to Illinois by way of the Great Lakes. At some point on the return route Mrs. Lincoln joined him; apparently she had remained in Washington during the New England trip and met him in New York. She told the story of the return trip in a letter to one of her sisters, a rather cheerful and attractive letter, especially when it is considered that the experiences she related had brought her face to face with the realization of her poverty.

"The summer has strangely and rapidly passed away. Some portion of it was spent most pleasantly in traveling East. We visited Niagara, Canada, New York and other points of interest. When I saw the large steamers at the New York landing, ready for their European voyage, I felt in my heart inclined to sigh that poverty was my portion. I often laugh and tell Mr. Lincoln that I am determined my next husband shall be rich."

She and her husband must have enjoyed the westward journey by way of the Great Lakes, but part of the time her husband was abstracted; their boat stuck on a shoal and Lincoln set himself to work to invent a method of lifting vessels over shoals by atmospheric pressure. After his return to Springfield he spent some little time working on a model, and ultimately he got a patent for his invention. His model is in the Patent Office in Washington, but the invention was never found practical. Let us hope that Mr. and Mrs. Lincoln found time on this voyage for a little quiet love-making. It had become certain that Lincoln would not be asked to succeed himself in Congress, but he was not feeling very badly about that. The Whigs were pretty certainly coming into power and Lincoln had rendered conspicuous service for the party and its ticket.

On October 5, 1848, the boat which conveyed Mr. and Mrs. Lincoln steamed slowly up the mud-clogged channel of the Chicago River, and they walked down the gang-plank, and put up at the Sherman House. To her great delight their arrival was not without recognition. A com-mittee of Whig politicians waited on her husband and asked him to deliver a political speech the next night in the Court-House in Chicago. Lincoln was happy to accept the invitation. Hand-bills were printed and cir-culated, and with only thirty hours' notice the town of Chicago was made aware that the Honorable Abraham Lincoln, who was returning from a successful campaign in New England, would address the citizens of Chicago on the political issues of the day. The Court-House was packed, and Mary Todd Lincoln sat in the audience and heard her husband, who was almost a stranger in Chicago, applauded to the echo.

They went back to the Sherman House after the even-ing's entertainment, and sat and talked a while before they went to bed. The future had never seemed more rosy. The days of their Springfield residence were num-bered, Taylor would surely be elected and Abraham Lin-coln already knew just what office he wanted and what he thought he would get. He wanted to be Land Commis-sioner of the United States. If he secured that position he and his family would have a permanent residence in the Capital of the nation.

Zachary Taylor was elected, but the influence of Daniel Webster secured the land office for Justin Butterfield. Lincoln was so distressed that he made a special trip to

Washington in a desperate effort to secure the land office; he did not succeed. Moreover he found that his objections to the Mexican War had brought upon him and his party so much criticism, that while Judge Logan secured the Whig nomination for Congress, and while the Whig ticket in general went into office with Zachary Taylor, Logan was defeated, and, as he believed, largely on Lincoln's account.

It was a cruel home-coming for Mary Todd Lincoln. All her political hopes and social ambitions seemed to be at an end. There was nothing now to do but to go and live in Springfield and make the best of it. With many tears, as we must surely believe, and yet on the whole, with a courageous heart, and an ambition that, if hurt, was not killed, she set herself to her unwelcome task.

The services rendered the new Whig administration by Abraham Lincoln did not go wholly unrecognized. "Old Rough and Ready" Taylor died too soon after his inauguration to look up a suitable office for him, but Millard Fillmore promptly tendered Lincoln the Secretaryship of Oregon, which was virtually a territorial governorship. Lincoln was so discouraged he was tempted to accept this consolation prize, reflecting that Oregon would soon be a state and he might hope to be one of its first senators. That was precisely what had occurred in the case of old Governor Ninian Edwards. He was territorial governor of Illinois, one of the original senators from the new state, and then returned to be governor. But Mrs. Lincoln vetoed the proposition to go to Oregon. She had faith in her husband's political future after he himself had lost it. In Springfield they remained.

11. HOME LIFE IN SPRINGFIELD

Whatever faults Mary Lincoln had, she was not indolent; she looked well to the ways of her household and ate not the bread of idleness. She made most of the clothing for her children, was an excellent seamstress, and a most affectionate mother, though too excitable to be always a good one. Her home was well kept. Lincoln had difficulty in living up to her standards of propriety. It was not easy for him to restrain himself from going to the front door in his shirt-sleeves, welcoming in the neighbors and excusing himself till he could "trot out the women folks." Only by degrees did he learn that he must let the "hired girl" open the door, and that he must not put his own knife into the butter. Mary Todd Lincoln wanted an aristocratic home; it is said in Springfield that while Lincoln several times visited his father and stepmother in their home, his parents were never invited to visit Mrs. Lincoln in her home. It is said that when Hannah Armstrong, who had given Lincoln many meals when he first came to New Salem, visited Springfield after the election of Lincoln, she was not cheered by the welcome she received from Mrs. Lincoln. It would appear that Mrs. Lincoln desired to forget, and desired Lincoln and all his friends to forget, that he was not the son of one of the aristocratic families of Kentucky.

On February 1, 1850, death entered the Lincoln home. Little Eddie died, being not quite four years of age. The sorrow of Mr. and Mrs. Lincoln was profound. Up to this time she had been a communicant of the Episcopal Church, of which the Edwardses were leading supporters. Lincoln did not love a liturgy, though he liked a well pre-

pared sermon. When the funeral of little Eddie was arranged, Mr. Dresser was out of town, and the family
called in the Reverend James Smith of the First Presbyterian Church of Springfield. He was a large and vigorous Scotchman, with a Websterian head, and his sermons
were strongly logical. The Lincolns were profoundly
grateful to him for the comfort which he brought them.
They made a journey to Lexington soon after the death of
Eddie and there Lincoln found a book entitled *The
Christian's Defense,* of which Doctor Smith was the author. Lincoln read it in part and was impressed by it.
On their return to Springfield Mrs. Lincoln decided to
withdraw from the Episcopal Church and join the First
Presbyterian Church. Lincoln rented a pew and became
a more or less regular attendant upon Doctor Smith's
services. Comfort came to the Lincolns promptly in the
person of another son, William Wallace Lincoln, born December 21, 1850, not quite eleven months after the death
of Little Eddie. Robert was now a lad of seven and attending the public schools of Springfield. Mrs. Lincoln
had him to care for, and also the baby in her arms.

The arrangement which Lincoln made with his junior
partner was that Herndon should do the office work and
Lincoln should ride the circuit. He now was a lawyer of
repute and was able to form local associations in several
of the county-seats, whereby his practise was largely extended. Herndon, though often riding with his senior to
the nearer courts, remained, for the most part, in Springfield, and took care of the local practise and the extremely
simple bookkeeping. Lincoln now gave up all thought of
politics. He practised law more assiduously than he ever
had done before; he became a more thoughtful student

than he ever had been. He bought a book of logic and a
copy of *Euclid* and sought to remedy, in some degree, the
limitations of his early education. For him political life
seemed forever to be at an end, and he became, for the
first time, a really notable lawyer. The lines of the Eighth
Judicial Circuit shifted more or less, and the number of
counties varied. Usually there were fourteen. Lincoln
rode the entire circuit, and became well known in all the
county-seats. He was, indeed, one of the best known law-
yers in Illinois. He had an increasing number of cases in
the Supreme Court of Illinois. After 1855, the United
States Court, which had been meeting in Springfield, began to hold sessions in Chicago. In the six years between
1855 and 1860 Lincoln had nearly one hundred cases in
the Federal Court. He began to save some money; the
house was paid for and a modest and growing sum was
in the bank to his credit. The immaturities and crudities
of his earlier speech were gradually falling away; his style
of writing and speaking improved; he was a man of growing power, but he did not think that power lay in politics.

Mrs. Lincoln did not always have adequate domestic assistance. At first the reason had been one of economy;
this was no longer mainly the case, but she did not get on
well with her servants, and whether she obtained her help
from among Lincoln's friends in Menard Country or near
Charleston or whether she depended upon what she called
the "Wild Irish," her "hired girls" did not usually remain
with her long, nor when they left, did they speak of her
with any considerable affection.

Now and then the Lincolns gave a party. Of one of
the more ambitious receptions, Mrs. Lincoln wrote to her
sister:

"Within the last three weeks there has been a party almost every night, and some two or three grand fetes are coming off this week. I may surprise you when I mention that I am recovering from the slight fatigue of a very large, and I really believe, a very handsome and agreeable entertainment, at least our friends flatter us by saying so. About five hundred were invited; yet, owing to an unlucky rain, three hundred only, favored us by their presence. And the same evening in Jacksonville, Colonel Warren gave a bridal party to his son, which occasion robbed us of some of our friends. You will think we have enlarged our borders since you were here."

It was not Lincoln's fault if his wife did not have a cook. While he was in Washington in 1848, he wrote her:

"By the way, you do not intend to do without a girl, because the one you had has left you? Get another as soon as you can to take charge of the dear codgers. Father expected to see you all sooner; but let this pass; stay as long as you please, and come when you please. Kiss and love the dear rascals.

"Affectionately,
"A. Lincoln."

He wished her to keep help. Moreover, the time came when he bought her a carriage. It was not a coupe, but the familiar "top-buggy" of the prairies, and a very much more stylish affair than his open buggy, in which he drove around the circuit. Mr. Lincoln did not use, much less did he lend, his wife's carriage. In it she rode about Springfield, perhaps one afternoon a week, leaving cards where calls were due. Leaving cards had come to be a recognized social obligation, and Mary Lincoln did not go on foot, neither did she hire a hack. She had her carriage, and that was a distinction in Springfield.

We are about to consider whether Mr. and Mrs. Lincoln ever quarreled, and if we find they did, we may as well remember in advance that Mary Todd quarreled with other people besides her husband. She quarreled with the cook, and she quarreled with her sisters; there is documentary proof of both. Lincoln, too, quarreled with other people besides his wife. He was not always and unalterably gentle. Some of his political quarrels were bitter, and his part in them involved a stinging use of sarcasm. This he did not habitually employ toward his wife, but Mary Todd Lincoln had provocation. Not that he was untrue to her or unkind to her; the very reverse is true; but Lincoln's sluggish good nature, and thick-skinned imperturbability, and patient obstinacy, were irritating to a woman of her excitable nature. The idea of love must have appealed very differently to an easy-going, hesitant man of almost thirty-four, and a high-strung, passionate woman, in her early twenties. If, therefore, we say that Lincoln and his wife loved each other, we are to remember that love as Mary Todd felt it, was a passion of which in that particular form, Abraham Lincoln was incapable. He was as passionate in his way as she was in hers, but hers was a quick and hot flame, while his was much slower in kindling, yet burned deeply in his soul. If we speak of him as a man of sluggish feeling, that does not imply that he had no feeling. His passions were under control, but she rarely attempted to control her feelings, her utterance or her conduct. But if we say they loved each other, and mean that they had complete confidence in each other's integrity, that they respected each other, and were drawn toward each other, that they desired each other, and that each of them was supplemented and complemented by the other, then we speak truly. In that very important sense they loved each other as neither ever loved any one else. They were not always happy together, but each would have been unhappy with any one else, and neither would have been happy alone.

Letters which they exchanged before his presidency were generally not preserved, but those that remain are cheerful, chatty and affectionate. She wrote him all the local gossip, and he told her what was happening in Washington, or wherever he happened to be, that he thought would interest her. Their form of address and their expressions of affection and of concern for the children, were all that might have been expected from married people living in mutual respect, confidence and settled affection. That Lincoln missed Mary very greatly when he was away on the circuit may be doubted; he did not seek every possible opportunity to get home. That she was quite as happy to have him away a portion of the time may also be readily granted, but that they were glad to be together, that they admired each other, that their children were born of a mutual attraction which from the very beginning of their married life gave them promise of offspring, and that they were proud of their sons and that both parents loved them, is true.

James Gourley, for nineteen years their next-door neighbor, said they sometimes quarreled, but on the whole "agreed moderately well." Josiah P. Kent, who lived in the same block, and who, after Robert went away to school served as Mrs. Lincoln's coachman, receiving twenty-five cents for each afternoon he drove her carriage, said that, so far as he observed, and he often slept in the Lincoln home, the domestic troubles of Mr. and

Mrs. Lincoln were not so frequent or serious as had been represented. There was a general understanding that Mrs. Lincoln was a hard woman to get on with, but those who lived nearest were the ones who professed the least knowledge of actual disagreement.

Whatever disagreements the Lincolns had, they kept, or intended to keep, to themselves. Lincoln was by nature reticent, and he would have been wholly disinclined to discuss his domestic affairs with another man. Mrs. Lincoln, too, kept her temper for home consumption. Not even to her sisters did she make complaint of her husband. Like the sputtering spouse of the Reverend Doctor Syntax:

> No tongue she suffered to dethrone
> His reverend greatness but her own.

When she was in a temper her husband sought to avoid her as much as possible till she felt better. He said good-naturedly that her scoldings did her good and did not hurt him. He evaded an issue when he found it possible. He could usually remember something that needed to be attended to in the office, and so left her till he thought it was safe to come back.

A maid who had found life in Mrs. Lincoln's kitchen intolerable would tell other maids and they would tell their mistresses of her outbursts, and the women would express sympathy for poor Mr. Lincoln. But Lincoln asked for no sympathy from others.

Now and then there was approach to a public acknowledgment that all was not right, but this came inadvertently. Such an incident was that of Lincoln's correspondence with the editor of a short-lived newspaper, the

Springfield *Republican.* This newspaper was started by John E. Rosette, a personal and political friend of Lincoln. Lincoln did not favor the publication of this newspaper. His own interests were bound up with the *Journal.* However, if Rosette was determined to undertake the hazard of a new Republican paper, Lincoln had no mind to oppose him, and he let it be understood that he would pay for a single subscription.

Mrs. Lincoln was enraged when the paper was brought to the door, and demanded of her husband whether he had subscribed for another worthless little paper. Lincoln tried to evade the matter, and told her he had not ordered the paper to be left at the house. That was true; but he had not forbidden it to be delivered.

Mrs. Lincoln, unknown to her husband, sent an abusive message to the carrier, telling him her opinion of the paper, and ordering it discontinued. Also she said that Mr. Lincoln had not subscribed for it, and did not believe in it.

The *Republican* thereupon published an uncomplimentary paragraph regarding the matter, and as Lincoln did not reply, Rosette addressed a letter to him, demanding an explanation. The affair made Lincoln physically ill. He saw no way to avoid public knowledge of his domestic affairs. With deep sorrow he wrote to Rosette a letter marked "Private" in which he made the best he could of an undeniably bad matter:

Springfield, Ill., Feb. 20, 1857

"John E. Rosette, Esq.

"Dear Sir:—

"Your note about the little paragraph in the *Republican* was received yesterday, since which time I have been too unwell to notice it. I had not supposed you wrote it or approved it. The whole originated in mistake. You know by the conversation with me that I thought the establishment of the paper unfortunate, but I always expected to throw no obstacle in its way, and to patronize it to the extent of taking and paying for one copy. When the paper was brought to my house, my wife said to me, 'Now are you going to take another worthless little paper?' I said to her *evasively,* 'I have not directed the paper to be left.' From this, in my absence, she sent the message to the carrier. This is the whole story.

"Yours truly,

"A. Lincoln."

It was a humiliating necessity which evoked such a letter, and the offended editor was compelled to respect that necessity.

Once, when Mrs. Lincoln abused a neighbor, and the neighbor went to Lincoln in anger, Lincoln sadly and calmly said to him in substance:

"You can afford to ignore this single incident; you do not have to endure it all the time."

But such occasions were rare. Lincoln did not often find himself under necessity of explanation. He bore his burden in silence; and his domestic life was not always a burden. Mrs. Lincoln's periods of passion alternated with others in which she was as passionately affectionate. Far from hating her husband, she loved him with a love that was exacting and furious.

Herndon acknowledges that Mrs. Lincoln made her husband a great man, for he declared that she nagged him so unmercifully that he found home intolerable, and thus got out among men, and spent long weeks on the circuit, laying the foundations of political power. I am inclined

to believe that this is partly true, but I do not think that
this was all that Mary Todd did to make her husband
president. I think she was enormously proud of him;
and had greater faith in his ability than he had and that
is saying much. Lincoln was a man of great ambition:
he wanted office, and when he had secured one office, he
gave immediate thought as to how he could obtain a higher
office. His wife's ambition was even greater than his,
and she knew of practical ways of furthering their united
ambition.

Herndon recorded that Lincoln did not usually explain
his periods of depression, many of which, Herndon, rightly or wrongly, attributed to his domestic unhappiness, but
on one occasion he did explain, and Herndon was so profoundly moved by what Lincoln told him, that he did not
print it. I am assuming responsibility for publishing this
most unhappy story.

On a Monday morning Herndon came to the office and
found Lincoln already there, seated at the back of the
room, his hat pulled down over his eyes, himself the picture of self-accusation and despair. He barely responded
to his partner's "Good morning," and sat almost motion-
less until well toward noon. Then he went out, bought
some crackers and cheese, which, as it later appeared,
constituted his first meal that day, and having eaten his
sorrowful morsel, he told Herndon this tale:

On the preceding morning, Mrs. Lincoln had risen in
bad temper, and each trivial occurrence before breakfast
and at the table increased her anger. Lincoln himself was
not in a very good mood that morning, and though at first
he bore her scolding uncomplainingly, it rubbed hard upon
a sore spot in his spirit, and at length his own temper gave

way. Breakfast was over and he had left the dining-room, but he had occasion to reenter it by the door leading from the parlor immediately in front. She greeted his appearance with such vituperation that he lost his self-control. In his exasperation he caught her by the arm, and pushing her through the door into the kitchen, he forced her across the corner of the kitchen almost to the outside door on the Jackson Street side, saying, "You make the house intolerable, damn you, get out of it!"

The side door of the house stood open, looking down Jackson Street, and the line of vision through the two doors was such as to reveal them as they stood there. A number of people on their way to church were coming up the street, in plain sight of his performance. Lincoln did not feel sure that the light outside was enough clearer than that within to conceal his violence from the neighbors. He said he had never once in his previous life laid a hand even in restraint upon his wife, much less had he ever caught and pushed her as he did that day. The words he had used were such as he was not accustomed to employ, and never had employed toward her. He still was hurt and sore over her injustice and unreasonableness, but that weighed little in comparison with his condemnation of himself for his own lack of self-control. The hurt of it, the shame of it, the scandal of its possible publicity, cast him into the very depths of bitterness. The remainder of the Sabbath had been a torment. The night had been sleepless. With the first dawn Lincoln had risen and stolen away to his office, hating himself, wishing himself dead, and condemning himself beyond all hope of forgiveness in this world or the world to come.

But to admit the full truth of this sorrowful and dis-

graceful incident, and further to admit that this was by
no means their only quarrel, nor even the only time that
Lincoln lost his own temper, is not to say that Lincoln
and his wife were invariably or even usually at outs. She
did not always nag him, she had her hours of passionate
devotion; she loved him so demonstratively, so effusively
as to please and almost embarrass him; and he loved her,
in his big, indolent and genuinely affectionate way. When
he put his great arms around his plump little wife and almost crushed her with his bear-hug, she knew he loved
her, and Lincoln, slowly as ran the current of his blood,
liked to hold in his arms a warm responsive woman.

Some years ago there died in Springfield, Illinois, a beautiful and cultured woman, a near relative of Mary Todd
Lincoln. I had known her somewhat, and from her had
obtained valuable information. Her death brought together a considerable number of her scattered relations.
A group of these, all women, sat down together, and I was
privileged to hear their conversation as they discussed the
question what "Aunt Mary" saw in "Mr. Lincoln" that
made her willing to marry him. Without exception they
honored Lincoln, but it was a distant and formal reverence they felt for "Mr. Lincoln" as compared with their
belligerent sensitiveness for the reputation of "Aunt
Mary." They canvassed all the possibilities, and related
the traditions of all her matrimonial opportunities, and
decided that she must have married him because she loved
him. In the judgment of the present writer, they were
correct.

Lamon tried to account for the marriage of Abraham
Lincoln and Mary Todd as "a policy match" in which he
won the alliance with an aristocratic family and she gained

the name of a man whose growing power with the people was likely, as she coldly judged, to gratify her vanity. Herndon believed that she married him out of revenge for her hurt pride, and that she deliberately persecuted the man whose continued offenses against social usage gave occasion for her cruelty. Others have believed that she married Lincoln believing herself his superior, and discovering that he was greater and nobler than she ever could be, sank into a reasonless nagging which gave expression to her inferiority complex. But Mary Todd never had any inferiority complex, or ever supposed her husband to dwell above her on inaccessible heights; and if she had wanted to make a "policy match" or to avenge herself on Lincoln there were other ways less costly to herself.

The silly sentimentalists have their ready explanation, namely, that Abraham Lincoln loved Ann Rutledge so much that he could never truly give his heart to any other woman. That explanation is not supported by any known facts and is violently opposed to what we know of Lincoln's conduct and correspondence.

There remains one other possible explanation, which is that, spite of their wide disparity of temperament, this mismated couple cared for each other and needed each other and were loyal to each other. That is the opinion of the present writer.

Mrs. Helm relates that on one occasion she gently chided Mary for criticizing her husband for his lack of small social graces, and that she said to Mrs. Lincoln, "If I had a husband with a mind such as yours, I wouldn't care what he did."

This pleased Mary very much, and she said, "It is very

foolish of me; the things of which I complain are really very small."

It is my honest conviction that no woman among those whom Abraham Lincoln might have married would probably have made him so uncomfortable as Mary Todd; and it is equally my conviction that no woman of whom he ever thought seriously as a possible wife would have been so valuable to him as the woman he married.

One other fact may be mentioned as belonging to the home life of the Lincolns. Their fourth child was born April 4, 1853. Abraham Lincoln's father, Thomas Lincoln, had died two years previous: the baby was given his grandfather's name, Thomas. They called him Tad. He was born with a cleft palate, and all of his life had a serious impediment in his speech. He was petted and undisciplined, and he had an ungovernable temper, but he was a very affectionate child, and was destined to be widely known.

There is no reason to believe that Mary Todd Lincoln's ambition for her husband ever was conquered or that it received any permanent or serious set-back. In 1854 the repeal of the Missouri Compromise brought Lincoln back into politics. Again his wife had a vision of life in Washington, for there was a time when it seemed that her husband was to become United States senator. So sure was Mary Todd that her husband was to be nominated, that she and Elizabeth Edwards prepared a great reception to be given to Senator-elect and Mrs. Abraham Lincoln on the night when the two houses of the Illinois General Assembly, in joint session, were to have elected him as United States senator. That honor did not come to him nor to her. Lyman Trumbull and his wife, the girl who as Miss Julia Jayne had been Mrs. Lincoln's bridesmaid, received the honor which Lincoln failed to get. The reception at the Edwards house was given in honor of Senator and Mrs. Trumbull, but Mr. and Mrs. Abraham Lincoln stood beside them in the receiving line.

Disappointment had come again to Mary Todd Lincoln, but her spirit was unconquered; she still believed that honor might befall her and her husband, and that good fortune would ultimately return them to Washington. If this occurred, it meant that Abraham Lincoln was to be the next opponent of Stephen A. Douglas, as a candidate for the United States Senate.

For this contest Abraham Lincoln prepared himself, and his wife stood by him, not shoulder to shoulder, for his shoulder was eighteen inches higher than hers, but rather heart to heart.

12. LINCOLN AND DOUGLAS

Stephen A. Douglas, who was a member of the House of Representatives when Lincoln went to Washington in 1847, did not long remain in the Lower House. His meteoric rise had been without precedent in Illinois politics, and it continued without prospect of abatement. Almost immediately after Lincoln's election to the Lower House, Douglas was elected United States senator. On the expiration of the first term in 1852 he was elected for six years more, and it was certain that he would be a candidate to succeed himself in 1858. The Whig party had gone to pieces. Zachary Taylor did not live long after his inauguration as president; Millard Fillmore, though a good president, was not a brilliant one, and his party was not strengthened by his administration. In the meantime the slavery issue was becoming dominant. Lincoln hesitated long, but in 1856 joined the new Republican party, —at its organization in Bloomington he delivered his famous "Lost speech." That year he went far and wide, delivering campaign speeches in favor of John C. Frémont.

Mrs. Lincoln had some difficulty with her husband's politics, not indeed so much in his being a Whig, when he was a Whig, as in accepting Frémont, the Republican candidate for the presidency, instead of Millard Fillmore, who was an "American" or "Know-nothing." But how loyally she stood by her husband is shown in a letter to her sister, Mrs. Helm, in 1856:

"Your husband, like some of the rest of ours, has a great taste for politics and has taken much interest in the late contest, which has resulted very much as I expected, not hoped. Although Mr. Lincoln is, or was, a Frémont man, you must not include him with so many of those who belong to that party, an Abolitionist. In principle he is far from it; all he desires is that slavery shall not be extended, let it remain where it is. My weak woman's heart was too southern in feeling to sympathize with any but Fillmore. I have always been a great admirer of his —he made so good a president and is so good a man, and feels the necessity of keeping foreigners within bounds. If some of you Kentuckians had to deal with the 'Wild Irish,' as we housekeepers are sometimes called upon to do, the South would certainly elect Fillmore next time. The Democrats have been defeated in our state in their governor, so there is a crumb of comfort for each and all. What day is so dark that there is no ray of sunshine to penetrate the gloom? Now sit down, and write one of your agreeable missives, and do not wait for a return of each from a staid matron, and moreover the mother of three noisy boys."

Not even to her sister did Mrs. Lincoln speak of her husband as "Abraham," far less did she abbreviate his name. His name for her was "Molly" at first: then he changed and called her "Mother."

In the summer of 1858 Lincoln formally entered the lists as a candidate for senator against Stephen A. Douglas. The campaign which ensued was one of the most brilliant and picturesque in the history of the United States. There were processions and brass bands, cannon and fireworks. The most notable incident of the campaign was a series of joint debates between Lincoln and Douglas. In November it was found that the legislative choice gave Douglas a very small majority. For the second time Lincoln failed in his attempt to become a United States senator, yet he failed so narrowly as to give him promise of a successful political future. His popularity was growing, his name was becoming known outside of the limits of the state of Illinois. Mary Todd Lincoln every now and then repeated to her friends what she said when she married her tall husband, namely, that while he was not a handsome man, he would some day be president of the United States.

13. LINCOLN AND THE LADIES

Before we accompany Mr. and Mrs. Lincoln to the White House, and witness their absorption in the duties of that situation, it will be well to pause for a moment and consider the relations of Mr. Lincoln to women in general, and to little girls in particular. To each of these

groups of persons of the sex opposite to his own a short
sketch may profitably be devoted. This will of necessity
carry us somewhat ahead of the strict chronology of the
narrative, but may serve a useful purpose, and there will
be no opportunity for it later.

A good many men, first and last, believed that their
advice influenced Lincoln, but these were mainly men
who did not know him very well; those who were best
acquainted with him had sincerest doubts as to whether
any man's opinion weighed very much against the already
formed judgment of Mr. Lincoln. It was not so with
women; to their advice and suggestion he was particularly
susceptible. In all the years of his riding of the circuit,
being much of the time away from home for weeks at a
stretch, no single scandal grew out of his relations with
the women whom he met or was supposed to have met in
any of the fourteen counties where he practised. Harm-
less little tales are told of evenings spent in the rooms of
friends, and of his appreciation of the conversation and
companionship of women, but no one ever said that, like
a sailor, he had a wife in every port. Though a man of
austere morals, yet his fondness for women was great.
It was a period when women were coming to the fore as
they had not previously done in American life. There
were concerts with women prominent in the company,
recitations, entertainments and even occasional lectures,
in which women were the leaders. Lincoln was invariably
interested in these events. If his favorite form of amuse-
ment was a burnt-cork show, as it appears to have been,
his next was certainly a concert in which a considerable
portion of the singing was done by women.

He did not dance often or dance well, and he did not

greatly care for social events where he was expected to pass from one group of women to another and say pleasant nothings, but he did greatly enjoy the sparkle and the cheer of social life with women present. It is not true that Lincoln refused to take divorce cases; his was a general practise, and while now and then a case was refused for conscience's sake, in the main he took such business as came to him. Once at least, where his client was a woman suing for divorce from a brutal husband, his interest was very thoroughly aroused. Mr. Weik, in his investigations, learned of a case in which he had been the attorney for a woman keeping a disorderly house. Weik interviewed this woman and the net result of what she had to tell him was that in the doing of his duty as her legal adviser, Lincoln was always a gentleman, and nothing more or less.

Nothing aroused his indignation more than brutality of a man toward women. In Springfield there lived a shoemaker who was accustomed to get drunk, and whose sprees usually ended by his whipping his wife. One day Lincoln called this man aside, reprimanded him, and warned him that if he ever laid hands upon his wife again, he would himself suffer castigation. Lincoln informed two of his friends, James Matheney and Evan Butler, and they agreed to aid him when the time came. Before very long the shoemaker got drunk again, and the wails of the suffering wife were plainly audible in the Lincoln and Herndon office. Lincoln summoned his friends, and they took the shoemaker out to an open space, stripped him of his shirt, and tied him to a post. Then they sent for his wife, and when she came they placed a whip in her hands. She shrank from doing what they proposed, but they insisted and encouraged her to a vigorous performance of her duty. She thrashed her legal lord until his captors judged that he had had enough; then they replaced his shirt and warned him that if then or afterward he should take vengeance on his wife or ever again beat her, the whipping which she had given him would be a light thing compared with what they proposed to do to him. According to all accounts, this incident wrought a permanent reformation.

In 1855 Lincoln was attending court in the town of Clinton, Illinois, where fifteen women from a neighboring village in the county had been indicted, and were brought into court. Their offense was that they had invaded a saloon which was selling liquor to their husbands, and had smashed in the barrels and broken the glassware. Lincoln was not the attorney in this case, but the lawyer who had the defense in charge handled it badly, and the women were much disturbed. One of them, seeing Lincoln in the court-room, asked him if he would sit in as associate counsel. To this he consented. The conduct of the case changed immediately. When it came to his plea, he set forth the case of the women with such confidence and vigor that the judge took the case away from the jury, and discharged the women without fine or reprimand.

In the days when Lincoln was in the White House he was repeatedly imposed upon by women, some of whom borrowed widow's garb and possibly a baby, when intending to come to make a plea for some deserter or other evil doer. Lincoln could hear the voice of a baby crying in the corridor or a woman pleading with the door-keeper, when he was deaf to senators and high officials. Not infrequently they swerved him from sound judgment, so tender was his heart. Lincoln's letter to Mrs. Lydia Bixby, of Boston, is an illustration of the depth of his sympathy. He was informed by Governor John A. Andrew of Massachusetts, that Mrs. Bixby had lost five sons in the war. The report was not strictly accurate; she had not lost and did not lose so many as that, but Lincoln believed the information to be reliable and he had reason so to believe it. To this obscure woman he wrote the most beautiful letter ever sent by the head of a great nation to an individual as an expression of sympathy and comfort.

Lincoln had great sympathy for the Quakers. They were in a hard position. Their creed was opposed to war, but by the whole genius of their organization they believed in freedom. Mrs. Eliza P. Gurney, a notable Quaker woman, came to the White House in September, 1862, and made a brief address in approbation of the Emancipation Proclamation. Lincoln's carefully prepared reply to this address is a classic. Not only so, but some time afterward he wrote a letter to Mrs. Gurney concerning the war, as it might be interpreted by religious persons, and especially by those to whom war was hateful. He declared that if he had had his way there would have been no war, and that if he could honorably have ended it sooner, he would long since have done so, but he believed that an over-ruling God had His own purposes, dim to human observation, but to be discovered in faithful and sacrificial performance of duty. Viewed from any possible appreciation, the letter was a significant one. Mrs. Gurney, however, was far from being the only representative of religion who called on Lincoln. Scores and probably hundreds of ministers at one time and another, came to the White House to confer with the President. To no one of them nor to any other man did he write such a letter as he wrote to Mrs. Gurney.

It is a remarkable fact that in his first announcement of his candidacy for the Legislature in 1832, Lincoln proclaimed himself a believer in woman suffrage. How he came to believe in what at that time was a doctrine quite strange in ordinary political discussion, we do not know. Nor are we aware that he ever became a strong advocate of that principle. Perhaps he thought of it rather as a matter of abstract justice than as a method likely to present itself for adoption. But whatever the explanation of this early declaration, and of his silence about it afterward, the statement stands as he made it.

Thus hastily we survey the general relations of Lincoln to women whose lives lay outside the circle of intimate relationship, but who, in some fashion may be thought of as having influenced his decisions. The record throughout is one to increase our respect for the great heart, the magnanimity and the chivalrous spirit of Abraham Lincoln.

But while there were matters in which women were able to influence Lincoln, sometimes against his own better judgment, neither men nor women moved him in matters of vital conviction. Not even Mary Todd Lincoln could swerve him an inch in matters where he believed he discerned a clear moral issue. She might coo and coax, and she knew how to do both; she might pout and tease, and she could do either; she might upbraid him or fly into a passion, but it did her no good in great matters, and no one knew it so well as she. Very truthfully she said of him:

"Mr. Lincoln was mild in his manners, but a terribly firm man when he set his foot down. I could always tell when, in deciding anything, he had reached his ultimatum. At first he was very cheerful; then he lapsed into thoughtfulness, bringing his lips together in a firm compression. When these symptoms developed, I fashioned myself accordingly, and so did all others have to do sooner or later. When we first went to Washington, many thought Mr. Lincoln was weak, but he rose grandly with the circumstances. I told him once of the assertion I had heard coming from the friends of Seward, that the latter was the power behind the throne; that Seward could rule the President. He replied, 'I may not be a successful ruler, but certainly Seward shall not rule. The only ruler I have is my conscience—following it and God—and these men will have to learn that yet.'"

They did learn it, and women learned it, also. But it was easier for him to refuse men than women when matters were involved that appealed to the sympathy of Abraham Lincoln.

In a great many small matters, Mrs. Lincoln ruled her husband; but she was first to recognize the point at which her rule ceased and Abraham Lincoln was master.

14. LINCOLN AND THE LITTLE GIRLS

"I regret the necessity of saying I have no daughter. I have three sons, one seventeen, one nine, and one seven years of age. These, with their mother, constitute my whole family."

So wrote Abraham Lincoln to a little girl. His regret that he had no daughter, expressed in such a letter, has not been regarded as a matter of large significance; but

that regret was sincere, and Lincoln's feeling of depriva-
tion was far greater than the little girl imagined.

The letter was dated Springfield, Illinois, October 19,
1860, and was a prompt reply to her letter under date of
October fifteenth.

She wrote to him from a little town in western New
York, telling him she had seen his portrait on a campaign
broadside, and she thought he would look better if he wore
whiskers. She added that, if he would wear a beard, she
would endeavor to induce her two big brothers, who were
Democrats, to vote for him. She also suggested that if
he had not time to write to her in answer to her letter, he
might ask his little girl to do it instead.

Abraham Lincoln was just then receiving large numbers of letters, and he had had to employ a secretary and
an assistant secretary to take care of them, but he answered little Grace Bedell in his own handwriting. She
has the letter still that President Lincoln sent to her telling her he was sorry he had no daughter.

Perhaps some presidential candidates, responding to
such a letter, would have forgotten all about it; but Abraham Lincoln did not.

First of all, he began to let his beard grow. Almost
from the very day of her letter he decided that he would
wear a beard. He would have done so if he had had a
little daughter and she had asked him to do so; and he
did it at this little girl's request. Perhaps that is as
strange a story as can truthfully be related of any president or presidential candidate in the history of the United
States: that he consented to so radical a change in his personal appearance at the suggestion of a little girl.

Beards were not yet fashionable. The people of the

Private

Springfield, Ills. Oct 19. 1860
Miss. Grace Bedell
   My dear little Miss.
         Your very agreable letter
of the 15th is received—
   I regret the necessity of saying I
have no daughters— I have three
sons— one seventeen, one nine, and
one seven, years of age— They, with
their mother, constitute my whole family—
   As to the whiskers, having never worn
any, do you not think people would
call it a piece of silly affectation
if I were to begin it now?
         Your very sincere well-wisher
               A. Lincoln.

Why Lincoln Wore a Beard

Mary Todd Lincoln

As a bride   As a matron
In the White House   As a widow

United States were unfamiliar with the features of a bearded president. And the face of Abraham Lincoln had only just become familiar to them. All the portraits taken in Springfield and Chicago had been beardless; and the Brady photograph, made in New York when Lincoln had gone there to deliver his Cooper Union address, had come to be recognized throughout the country.

So far as is known, no senator or governor or prospective Cabinet member told Mr. Lincoln that he ought to wear a beard, but he gave the matter serious consideration when a little girl wrote and suggested it. Before he left Springfield he was twice photographed with a beard. In one of these pictures the black whiskers were just sprouting; the other, the McNulty photograph, is now one of the most highly prized and valuable, and is the one used for the engraving of Lincoln's face on the ten-dollar bill.

That might have been the end of the matter, but it was not. When the presidential train was on its way to Washington, it stopped at a small station in western New York, and the president-elect made a short address. Then he said, "I have a correspondent in this place, and if she is present, I would like to see her." No one came forward in response to this invitation. People began to call back to him, "Who is it? Give us her name." He replied, "Her name is Grace Bedell."

Then they took the little girl to the platform, half leading her and half carrying her, until she stood beside the tall man. As she was coming, Mr. Lincoln said, "She wrote me that she thought I would be better looking if I wore whiskers."

As she reached the platform he looked down and said, "You see, I let these whiskers grow for you, Grace."

Then, in the presence of that great crowd, and with all the newspaper reporters looking on and telling about it over the wires, he kissed her.

Mr. Lincoln was not unhappy with his boys; quite the reverse. He loved them and was proud of them, and he indulged them in their pranks when perhaps he should have punished them.

Lincoln was an absent-minded man, and he often passed boys without noticing them till they called, "Good morning, Mr. Lincoln." Then he always turned and spoke to them. He liked children; he noticed children. They liked him. But he sometimes walked to market, wearing his high hat and his gray shawl, having a market basket in the crook of his right arm, and holding Tad or Willie by the left hand, and walked along as though he had forgotten both the basket and the boy. He did not so often pass a little girl.

In those days they called little girls "Sis." Some little girls never outgrew it, and were called "Sis" as long as they lived. Mr. Lincoln called them "Little Sister."

Mrs. Lincoln's mother died and her father married again, and had a large family by the second wife. Her younger half sisters were almost like daughters to her when she went, a young matron, to visit her old home in Lexington. Then Mr. Lincoln would catch up the youngest of the sisters, Emily, and toss her almost to the ceiling, which was not very far above his own head, and laugh, a great loud laugh, and say, "Up you go, Little Sister!" It was terrifying, but enjoyable.

There were little girls in Springfield whose faces he knew, and whose parents he knew, but whose names he did not attempt to remember, but he always greeted them with "Good morning, Little Sister!" One of these was the little daughter of Mrs. Helmle, who made Mrs. Lincoln's bonnets. He sometimes called there on his way home from the office, to take home Mrs. Lincoln's millinery. Always he said, "Good morning, Little Sister." She met him one day shortly before he left Springfield for Washington, and he passed her without speaking. They passed each other on one of Springfield's precarious crossings, where no one could fail to see a person coming from the other way, but he had his head down, in deep and she thought sorrowful meditation, and he did not speak. She got to the other side, and stopped and looked back. She said to herself, "He is a great man now. He has forgotten me. He used to speak to me, but since he was elected president, he is too great a man to notice a little girl like me."

Mr. Lincoln also stopped, as though he had received a telepathic message. He turned around and saw the little girl on the other side. "Good-by, Little Sister," he called. And she never saw him again.

At the great reception at the Tremont House in Chicago, the one time Mr. and Mrs. Lincoln went there after the election, when Vice-President Hannibal Hamlin came on to meet them and receive with them, the whole procession had to halt while Lincoln wrote in eight autograph albums presented by eight little girls. Whatever other people asked and failed to get, little girls were rarely disappointed when they made requests of Lincoln.

When the family was at the Willard Hotel in Washington, and Mrs. Lincoln met a little girl named Julia Taft, she asked the little maiden to visit her often at the White House, because she was lonely, having no little girl of her own. Mr. Lincoln also welcomed her, called her "Joolie" and tossed her to the ceiling. When Congressman Dawes, of Massachusetts, who was later to succeed Charles Sumner as senator, called at the Willard and brought his little daughter Anna, the dignified statesman received somewhat less attention than the little girl of nine. Mr. Lincoln kissed her, and said he was very fond of little girls, and was very sorry that he had none of his own.

Yes, Lincoln loved boys; but how he would have loved the little daughter that never came!

15. MRS. PRESIDENT LINCOLN

Swiftly passed the months between the Lincoln and Douglas campaign and that of the election of 1860. Although Lincoln was in the habit of saying to men who spoke to him about the presidency that he thought there were other men more competent, that did not mean that ne was so modest as not to desire it. He did desire it very much, and his wife desired it if possible even more than he did.

In 1860 Mr. Lincoln went to New York City, as he first supposed to speak at a week night event in Plymouth Church, Brooklyn, of which Henry Ward Beecher was minister; but the place and character of the meeting were changed, and he spoke instead in Cooper Union. It was a notable address and was heard by an influential audience, and reported in the leading Republican papers, and afterward reprinted as a pamphlet.

From New York he went on to New England and gave a series of addresses in leading cities, including even Boston. He had been in New England in 1848, speaking on behalf of General Taylor's candidacy for the presidency; now he was speaking for the recognition of the principle of permitting slavery no further extension of area. These addresses greatly increased his reputation, not as a stump orator, or a successful jury lawyer, but as an orator, a statesman, a thinker and a man of coming power.

The second national Republican Convention was scheduled to occur in May of 1860, and by a clever stroke of those who wished to advertise the West, and also to promote its political interests, it was settled that this meeting should be held in Chicago, the foremost city of Lincoln's home state. He was far from being the most prominent candidate. William H. Seward held that place, and next to him stood Salmon P. Chase, but Lincoln, though a minority candidate, was in a strong position as a possible dark horse.

Nothing happened that spring in the political arena that passed Mrs. Lincoln's observant eye. She was the most interested of all those who had faith in the tall Illinoisan. In all the ups and downs of his career, that had in it no little of disappointment, she steadfastly believed in him.

On the concluding day of the Chicago Convention a telegram was received, stating that on the third ballot Abraham Lincoln had been nominated as president of the United States. A hundred evenings he had sat at the grocery store, swapping stories and apparently forgetting that he had a wife or a home, but in that high hour he hardly waited for the first congratulations of his friends. "Excuse me, gentlemen," he said. "There is a little woman down on Eighth Street who is interested in the result of this convention. I want to go and tell her." She knew before he got there, for the neighbor women had rushed in and brought her the information. No record exists of the manner of their greeting; it was decorous, without doubt, for Mr. and Mrs. Lincoln were not alone; but then, or later in the day we can not doubt that he took the plump little woman in his great arms and told her she was entitled to her full share of credit for the honor that had come to him.

The next evening the special train came from Chicago bearing the official delegates and a large company of distinguished people. Mr. Lincoln refused the offer of his neighbors to provide wine; the liquid served consisted entirely of water. He received his guests in the front parlor and they passed on to the next room, where Mrs. Lincoln was in waiting. It is much to her credit that the reporters and the critics who went away from that gathering carried a favorable impression of the wife of the president to be.

In 1860 it was not considered dignified for a presidential candidate to stump the country on behalf of his own ticket, or for a president-elect to boast ere he put on his armor, and Lincoln did not even deliver front-porch political addresses to visiting delegations. A simple word of thanks was all that he undertook. After the election which decided that Abraham Lincoln should be the next president and Hannibal Hamlin the vice-president, it was thought fitting that these two men, who had never met each other, should go to Chicago, attend a reception and be greeted by prominent people. Mrs. Lincoln accompanied her husband, and had her own place of honor at the reception.

The Lincolns were accompanied from Springfield by Senator and Mrs. Lyman Trumbull and Honorable and Mrs. Don Piatt. They were careful not to make any public announcement of their going, but there was a sizable crowd at the Springfield station to see them off. They rode in a well filled common coach, and had none too good accommodations. The Sheriff of Sangamon County was taking four ironed convicts to Joliet. He was a Douglas Democrat, and had no inclination to show marked courtesy to the president-elect. He managed to get his four convicts so seated as to separate the Lincolns from the Trumbulls.

The first town of importance through which the train passed was Lincoln, county-seat of Logan County. Several hundred people appeared, and their calls for Lincoln were loud and strong. They wanted to see "the President of the United States." He was not yet that, but he appeared, and in response to the greetings of the crowd he said:

"Fellow Citizens—I thank you for this mark of kindness toward me. I have been shut up in Springfield for the last few months, and therefore have been unable to greet you, as I was formerly in the habit of doing. I am passing on my way to Chicago, and am happy in doing so to be able to meet so many of my friends in Logan County, and if to do no more to exchange with you the compliments of the season and to thank you for the many kindnesses you have manifested toward me. I am not in the habit of making speeches now, and I would therefore ask to be excused from entering upon any discussion of the political topics of the day. I am glad to see so many happy faces, and to listen to so many pleasant expressions. Again thanking you for this honor, I will pass on my journey."

At Bloomington a crowd still larger assembled, and after many calls, Mr. Lincoln appeared and spoke.

These two little speeches are not great oratory, but

they are worth quoting. First, they are almost the only speeches we have of Lincoln after his election and before the day of his departure from Springfield. Secondly, no Life of Lincoln or book of Lincoln's speeches contains them, and they are veritable "lost speeches" which should be recovered, as has been done here. Thirdly, and for our present purpose most important, Mrs. Lincoln was part of the occasion that called them forth, and it is she of whom we are telling. Here is what he said at Bloomington:

"Fellow Citizens of Bloomington and McLean County —I am glad to meet you after a longer separation than has been common between you and me. I thank you for the good report you made of the election in Old McLean. The people of the country have again fixed up their affairs for a constitutional period of time. By the way, I think very much of the people, as an old friend said he thought of woman. He said when he lost his first wife, who had been a great help to him in his business, he thought he was ruined—that he could never find another to fill her place. At length, however, he married another, who he found did quite as well as the first, and that his opinion now was that any woman would do well who was well done by. So I think of the whole people of this nation—they will ever do well if well done by. We will try to do well by them in all parts of the country, North and South, with entire confidence that all will be well with all of us."

They fired a "federal salute" at Bloomington, shot probably not from a cannon but from blacksmiths' anvils.

Senator Trumbull also spoke briefly at Bloomington. And of Mrs. Lincoln it is recorded that "she received an ovation, as well as her husband. She bore herself admirably, bowing gracefully to the crowd, and shaking hands with those who approached her for that purpose."

Great and memorable was the reception tendered to Mr. and Mrs. Lincoln and Honorable Hannibal Hamlin in the Tremont House. It was by far the grandest affair Mary Todd Lincoln had ever had a share in, and worth a lifetime of struggle and disappointment. There was one feature of the visit which the newspapers did not know. Lincoln informed Joshua F. Speed of this visit in advance, and asked him to meet him in Chicago at the time, and to bring his Fanny to play with Lincoln's Molly while the men visited and Lincoln attended to political matters. It is good to know that this program was fully carried out. In the intervals between political and social duties, Abraham Lincoln and Joshua F. Speed had a good, friendly, old-time visit, and Molly Lincoln and Fanny Speed visited and shopped and had a happy time. That is an event worth recording, and one to be thankful for. The Lincolns and Speeds parted the best of friends.

The days between Mr. Lincoln's election to the presidency and his departure for Washington were crowded full. Delegates were arriving almost every day, and many of them visited the Lincoln home. In all this new, strange experience Mrs. Lincoln bore herself well.

Shortly before they moved out of their own home, they arranged two or three social events, in which their intimate friends came to spend an evening with them. Finally, on the night of February sixth, Mr. and Mrs. Lincoln gave a grand levee lasting from seven o'clock until midnight and thousands of guests are said to have attended. A report of this reception in the *Missouri Democrat* of St. Louis, says of her that she was dressed plainly, but richly, wearing a beautiful full trail, white moire antique, with a small French lace collar. Her neck was ornamented with a string of peals. Her head-dress was a simple one, a delicate vine arranged with good taste; she displayed but little jewelry, and this was declared to have been well and appropriately adjusted. The paper said:

"She is a lady of fine figure and attractive manner, and is well calculated to grace and do honor at the White House."

Within a day or two after the grand final reception, which occurred on Tuesday evening, the Lincoln family disposed of their furniture, which a few days previous had been advertised, at private sale, and gave up the home that had been theirs since Robert was a baby. They moved over to the Chenery House, Mr. and Mrs. Lincoln and Willie and Tad. Robert, too, had a room there. He had returned from Harvard to share in the final farewell, and accompany his parents to Washington.

Board in the Chenery House cost more than the four dollars a week which they had paid at the Globe Tavern, but still their expenses were not large, and their manner of living was modest. On the night before they started for Washington, their trunks were brought down into the office of the hotel, and Mr. Lincoln, with his own hands, roped them. He took some cards of the hotel, and wrote on the back, "Lincoln, White House, Washington, D. C." and tacked them on the trunks. Then he went up-stairs and he and Mary Todd Lincoln and the three boys spent their last night in Springfield together.

It had not been intended that Mrs. Lincoln should accompany her husband on the official train; she and her friends had thought that such a journey would be wearisome. It was planned that she should go to St. Louis and visit with friends until the presidential party neared Washington, and join her husband in New York or Philadelphia; but when General Scott sent a verbal mesage to Mr. Lincoln warning him of possible dangers on the way to the capital, Mrs. Lincoln declared her intention of going with her husband and sharing whatever danger should come to him. Whatever the faults of Mary Todd Lincoln, she did not lack courage or loyalty to the man she married.

Mrs. Lincoln did not, however, leave Springfield on the special train. The change of plan had been too sudden for her to make this convenient. He left in the morning and she followed on a later train on the same day, and she and the boys overtook him in Indianapolis and were with him for the rest of the journey.

On Monday morning, February 11, 1861, the day before his fifty-second birthday, Abraham Lincoln, President-elect of the United States of America, entered the rickety hotel bus and rode in a drizzling rain to the old Great Western Station, where the car in which he and those who were to go east with him stood on a spur track, with a group of neighbors and friends assembled about it. Just before the train pulled out, Mr. Lincoln appeared on the rear platform, and in a voice that he could with difficulty control, said:

"My friends: no one not in my situation can appreciate my feelings of sadness at this parting. To this place, and the kindness of these people, I owe everything. Here I have lived a quarter of a century and have passed from a youth to an old man. Here my children have been born and one is buried. I now leave, not knowing when or whether I may ever return, with a task before me greater than that which rested upon Washington. Without the assistance of that Divine Being who ever attended him, I can not succeed. With that assistance, I can not fail. Trusting in Him who can go with me and remain with you and be everywhere for good, let us confidently hope that all may yet be well. To His care commending you, as I hope in your prayers you will commend me, I bid you an affectionate farewell."

He reentered the car, choking with his tears. The train moved, and the old friends of Lincoln and his wife went home in the rain, and wondered how they would enjoy life in the White House. Frequently the train stopped and Lincoln made short speeches. Once, at least, before going out, he lifted "Mother" to the car seat, and she "fixed him up" a little before he showed himself. It was not exactly a triumphal procession. Lincoln's speeches at Albany, at Philadelphia and in other cities show that he did not then believe the South would really go out of the Union, or that there would be a war. But he grew more serious as he neared Washington, and he ended the journey under stress of a warning that sent him into Washington by night, attended only by a single companion, Ward Hill Lamon. It was an inglorious ending of a none too brilliant tour. But at length it ended. Mr. Lincoln took the oath of office, and the Lincolns found themselves at home in the White House. Then Washington stood agape, and at the first public reception there entered the room a very tall man, with a little plump woman on his arm, and Mr. Lincoln said, "Ladies and gentlemen, here is the long and short of the Presidency."

Mary Lincoln had arrived. She had refused the most brilliant man in Springfield under the conviction that he would never be anything more than a senator, and she wanted to be the wife of a president.

Two women constitute important sources of information concerning Mrs. Lincoln's life in the presidential mansion. One is her cousin, Mrs. Lizzie Todd Grimsley, who remained with her the first six months in the White House. She left in writing an interesting account of the visits of southern politicians, who, before their departure from the capital to take up arms against the Government, called to say "Good-by." One of them was John C. Breckenridge, a relative, who pleasantly said, "Cousin Lizzie, I should not like you to be disappointed in your expected stay in the White House. Remain here as a guest after the Confederates take possession." Mrs. Lincoln responded that Cousin Lizzie was quite welcome to stay that length of time, and in that event would be there a good while.

Mrs. Lincoln needed all of her practical wisdom, and more. Washington was full of Confederate spies. There were many high-born women of southern sympathy who were eager to hire out to her as chambermaids for the privilege of listening at keyholes. At least one woman got into the White House in some such fashion. One other was narrowly headed off from securing lodging there with intent to create a scandal. The newspapers had their representatives secretly employed. If Mrs. Lincoln made mistakes now and then, it was no wonder. No wife of any president ever met such a situation or was so little prepared for it.

Lincoln was very fond of Cousin Lizzie Grimsley, and professed to be much ruled and intimidated by her and her cousin Mary. The two women did force him to make one political appointment, or at least they said they did. Their old Springfield minister, Reverend James Smith, was a Scotchman by birth, but was by naturalization an American citizen. Doctor Smoth's son had been United States consul at Dundee under the Buchanan administration, and had died. Doctor Smith, retired from the active ministry, had been called back to Scotland by this event, and he desired to succeed his son as consul. He was a Democrat, and the Republicans were very greedy of political appointments. But Mary Todd Lincoln and Lizzie Todd Grimsley insisted that, regardless of his politics, the good old minister should have the place, and he got it.

But Cousin Lizzie wanted something else. Her son John Todd Grimsley was just sixteen, and she wanted him admitted as a student in the United States Naval Academy. The President had power of selecting a limited number of students. He promised Cousin Lizzie that Johnny should have the first appointment that the President made. The weeks went by, and Cousin Lizzie's six months in the White House were near their end, and still Johnny Grimsley was not appointed. One day the opportunity came. Lincoln had on his desk a curt note from Gideon Welles, Secretary of the Navy, notifying a student that, having been found guilty of neglect of duty, insubordination, and having in his possession a most obscene book, he was expelled from the service of the United States.

That order did not require any action on the part of the President; it was his notice that he might appoint a successor. But he paused to ask himself what would become of the boy so expelled and disgraced. He then

wrote on the back of Secretary Welles's letter an endorse-
ment that the President was under obligation to give his
first appointment to John T. Grimsley of Illinois, and no
recommendation by whomsoever made was to take prece-
dence over that promise. He then added that, nevertheless, he would be glad if this expelled boy might have
another chance.

I should not like to have been Abraham Lincoln when
he went to supper that night and was asked by Mary
Todd Lincoln and Lizzie Todd Grimsley whether he had
yet found the promised place for John Todd Grimsley, and
have had to reply that there had been a vacancy, but that
he had asked that the bad boy be given another chance.
Lizzie Grimsley had to go back to Springfield without having secured a place for her son. But a few weeks later
Lincoln learned, while on a visit to the War Department,
that there was another vacancy. He did not wait to get
back to his own office, but wrote a telegram on Stanton's
letter-head informing Cousin Lizzie that he had that day
appointed Johnny.

So much for Cousin Lizzie, of whom we shall hear later
in a letter from her cousin.

The other woman who has given us a close-up interior
view of the White House is Mrs. Elizabeth Keckley, a
negress. For thirty years she had been a slave. She
secured her freedom and became one of the best dressmakers in Washington. She had a son, and he was killed
during the war, to her deep sorrow.

As soon as Mrs. Lincoln got to Washington she let it be
known to all her friends that she would have need of a
dressmaker. Several Washington women whose husbands

were in official positions sent their dressmakers to the
White House to meet Mrs. Lincoln. They came at a
given hour, and when she catechised them she learned
that Mrs. Keckley had been dressmaker to the wife of
Senator Jefferson Davis, the new President of the Con-
federacy. That seemed to settle the matter in the mind
of Mrs. Lincoln. She told Mrs. Keckley, however, that
as she and Mr. Lincoln had just come from a small town
in the West, and were still poor, she could not afford to
pay high prices; she hoped Mrs. Keckley's rates would
be reasonable, and assured her that she would have abundant compensation in the fact that other women would be
glad to employ her when they knew that she worked for
the wife of the President. It was even so. Mrs. Keckley
soon had occasion to employ a large corps of assistants, and
her business prospered; she, however, became an increasingly intimate and influential person in the White House,
and was a confidential friend of Mrs. Lincoln for many
years afterward. She made Mrs. Lincoln's dress for the
first White House reception; it was a bright rose-colored
moire-antique, and she had to work hard to get it finished.
Indeed she was a little late on the evening of the reception, and Mrs. Lincoln had worried herself into a highly
nervous state for fear it would not arrive. When Mrs.
Keckley got there with the dress, Mrs. Lincoln was scolding over the delay and declaring she would not go down
at all. But after some persuasion she changed her mind.
When Mr. Lincoln came in and saw his wife so brilliantly
attired, he looked at her in unfeigned admiration.

Fifteen or sixteen dresses Mrs. Keckley made for Mrs.
Lincoln that spring and summer and the negress grew to
know quite intimately the White House family. She saw

Mrs. Lincoln in all of her moods, which were many, and the two women were drawn together by closer ties than those of business relationship. Mrs. Lincoln had an attractive neck and a rounded and well proportioned bust. Her arms were plump. These charms she liked to display, but what her dress lacked at the top it more than made up in the length of her train. The first time Lincoln saw her in a dress of this extreme character, he drew a low whistle, and said, "Whew, what a long tail our cat has!" When she questioned him as to whether he did not like her dress after all, he gave a qualified approval, but said that he thought it would look quite as well if the head and tail of it were a little closer together.

One White House custom Mrs. Lincoln found and for a time observed, but soon rebelled against. Traditionally the President offered his arm to some other lady, the wife of the Secretary of State or some one else whom he wished to honor, leaving Mrs. Lincoln to be escorted by some notable man. This caused her to go behind another woman, and she could not tolerate it. Once she compromised by having her husband lead Lizzie Grimsley down to a reception, but even this did not put the President's wife in the first rank. She declared that she herself, as "Mrs. President" should go on the President's arm, and no other woman should ever precede Mrs. Abraham Lincoln, the wife of the President of the United States. Not only this, but she kept a close eye on her husband at every public function, and any woman who succeeded in engaging him in five minutes' personal conversation suffered a black mark in Mrs. Lincoln's book. She did not fail to admonish her husband before each reception not to act like a beardless schoolboy and conduct flirtations with silly women.

He teased her a little by naming lists of women with whom he might possibly talk, choosing the names of those whom he knew to be least acceptable to his wife. She denounced them one by one as "hateful," "horrid," and all the rest. Then he would ask, "Well, Mother, who shall I talk to?" He should have said "whom," but he did say "who," and Mrs. Lincoln never succeeded in making out a list of the women she really wanted to see her husband talking with. Few women in the history of the world have had less occasion for jealousy than Mrs. Lincoln, and she knew that, but such matters with her were not wholly affairs of reason.

The White House was not always a cheerful place in those days. Scarcely had the Lincolns moved into it when they were constrained to drape it in mourning for Colonel Elmer Ellsworth, a member of their own household. Nor was it long until they draped it in mourning again, and this time for Stephen A. Douglas—a magnanimous act on Lincoln's part.

Douglas also had been magnanimous. At the counting of the presidential ballot, at the inauguration, where he held Lincoln's hat, and in a strenuous campaign in Illinois as the Civil War was breaking out, he showed loyalty and friendship. It is an interesting coincidence that the last meeting that was held in the Wigwam in which Lincoln had been nominated was one at which Stephen A. Douglas spoke ringing words in favor of the Union. He richly deserved the sorrow that was shown for him in the White House, and that sorrow was sincere.

Lincoln was a much photographed man, and his wife also posed often before the camera. She was not easy to please, and at one time she sent to Brady the photographer an imperative demand that he destroy every negative he had ever made of her. Fortunately, he did not do it. She and her husband were never photographed together; but when Brady's first picture of her husband after his election (for Brady's first photograph of Lincoln was made in New York at the time of the Cooper Union speech) and one of Brady's portraits of her were so combined as to bring her head up to the level of Mr. Lincoln's shoulder and to reduce her bust measure perceptibly, she liked that, and secured some of those pictures to give away. The picture of the Lincoln family group that became so familiar, was built up from a photograph of Tad and his father. Mrs. Lincoln and Robert were painted in, and a framed picture of Willie, then deceased, was shown hanging on the wall behind them.

One of the things which troubled Mrs. Lincoln in those days was the attitude, real or imaginary, of her old friends. It seemed to her that there was scarcely a person whom she had ever known who was not now either scornfully jealous of her or seeking to use her for some selfish advantage. From this tendency she did not think even her own sisters wholly exempt. After Lizzie Grimsley had returned from the White House to Springfield, Mrs. Lincoln wrote her a letter in which she commented with severity on the "intrigue" of Elizabeth Edwards, the ingratitude of Frances Wallace, and the falsity of Ann Smith.*

---

* Robert Todd Lincoln has been accused of buying up many books about his father and destroying them. I am able to state that the then owner of this unpublished letter, Mr. H. E. Barker, of Springfield, by whose courtesy I use it, before offering it for sale to others gave Robert T. Lincoln an opportunity to purchase it at a very modest price. Mr. Lincoln did not reply to the letter.

"Executive Mansion
"September 29th, '61

"My Dear Lizzie:

"I have been intending writing you for some days. I have been quite sick with chills for some days, this is my day of rest so I am sitting up. I am beginning to feel very weak. If they cannot be broken in a few days, Mr. Lincoln wants me to go North and remain until cold weather. Where so much is demanded of me I cannot afford to be delicate, if a different climate will restore my health. If at the close of this week I am still sick, I expect I will go up to Boston, take quarters at the Revere House for two or three weeks and return here in November. I trust however, I may not be under the necessity, yet I am feeling very far from well. September and early in October are always considered unhealthy months here, my racked frame certainly bears evidence to the fact. Have just received a note from Willis, with all his weaknesses he is kind hearted. Gov. Newell and Halstead are frequently here as *who is not?* I presume you are aware your brother is elected to Congress. I received a letter from Elizabeth E. the other day. Very kind and aff. yet very *characteristic*. Said if rents and means permitted, she would like to make us a visit, I believe for a season. I am weary of *intrigue*, when she is by herself she can be very agreeable, especially when her mind is not dwelling on the merits of fair daughters and a talented son-in-law. Such personages always *speak for themselves*. I often regret E. P. E. little weaknesses, after all, since the election she is the only one of my sisters who has appeared to be pleased with our advancement you know this to be so. Notwithstanding Dr. Wallace has received his portion in life from the Administration, yet Frances always remains quiet. E. in her letter said Frances often spoke of Mr. L's kindness in giving him his place. She little knows what a hard battle I had for it, and how near he came getting nothing.

"Poor unfortunate Ann, inasmuch as she possesses such

a miserable disposition and so false a tongue. How far dear Lizzie are we removed from such a person. Even if Smith succeeds in being a rich man, what advantage will it be to him, who has gained it in some cases most unjustly, and with such a woman, whom no one respects, whose tongue for so many years, has been considered 'no slander' and as a child and young girl could not be outdone in falsehood, 'Truly the Leopard cannot change his spots.' She is so seldom in my thoughts. I have so much more, that is attractive, both in bodily presence, and my mind's eye, to interest me. I grieve for those who have to come in contact with her malice, yet even that is so well understood, the object of her *wrath*, generally rises, with good people, in proportion to her *vindictiveness*. What will you name the hill on which I must be placed. Her, putting it on that ground with Mrs. Brown, was only to hide her envious feeling toward you. Tell Ann for me, to quote her own expression. She is becoming still further removed from 'Queen Victoria's Court.'

"How foolish between us to be discussing, such a person. Yet really it is amusing, in how many forms, human nature can appear before us. Nicolay told me, that Caleb Smith said to him, a few days since that he had just received a letter from Kellogg, of Cin. that he did not know why he had not received his appointment as Consul. Is not the idea preposterous? Did I tell you that 'Hollis' has been here, came to see me frequently, and always enquired with much interest, after you. The 'Cap' also dined here a few days since, still as refined and elegant as ever. I have so much to tell you, I do not know what first to write about. Wykoff, the 'Chevalier,' enlightened me about Baker's and Julia's proceedings in New York in Feb. Looked a little quizzical, about her not remaining in W. as she expected a long stay and much gayety. Did you say, she only numbered *5 months*. I thought she had gently insinuated, when she was here. Hill Lamon, I believe is now in Ill. mustering recruits. I know you will be sorry to hear, that our colored Mantuamaker, Elizabeth, lost her only son and child in the battle of Lex., Mo. She is heart broken. She is a very remarkable woman herself. The weather is so beautiful, why is it, that we cannot feel well. The air feels very much like the early days when I used to have chills in Ill., those days have passed, and I know I have no cause to grieve over my lot. If the country was only peaceful, all would be well. If I thought, sending your Father, a pass, would bring him here, I would do so with pleasure. Give my best love to them both. Mrs. Don Piatt, calls here in an hour's time. I must mount my white Cachemere and receive her. We now occupy the stately guest room. She spoke last winter of the miserably furnished rooms. I think she will be astonished at the change. I am not well enough to go down. Write very soon and very often to,

"Your attached Cousin,

"Mary Lincoln

"P. S. William has given me $3.00 to hand you. I will have it in bill shape, to send you in a few days, when I write next. Strange he called upon you."

Concerning some of the women mentioned in this letter, no explanation need be given, though all could be identified if it were necessary. But "Kellogg of Cin." was her brother-in-law, husband of her half-sister Margaret. He was the only relative of this group, children of her stepmother, who was on the side of the Union, and his letter to a Cabinet member professing surprise that he received an appointment, whose secret was no secret to Mary, gave opportunity for grouping Margaret and her family with those of her full sisters, Elizabeth, Frances and Ann. She sometimes thought she had hardly a sincere and unselfish or grateful friend in all the world.

The war lengthened beyond anybody's anticipation; and Lincoln came to see as soon as most men near him that it could not be short or easy. To a delegation that called on him when the war was midway, he wrote a brief note, which has never been published hitherto:

"Gentlemen:
"Nobly sustained; as the (our)government has been by all, you must send more soldiers to the field, more nurses to the hospitals, and more prayers to Heaven.
                                                    A. Lincoln."
"May 16, 1863."

He himself was sending many of those prayers to Heaven, and Mary Todd Lincoln was helping him.

Mrs. Lincoln was keenly interested in the hospitals, and in the sufferings of soldiers. She had a tender heart. In the fall of 1861, when a soldier, William Scott, was sentenced to be shot for going to sleep while on picket duty, she grew very nervous. General William H. Smith, commander of the Vermont brigade, had no intention of letting Scott be shot, but he gave his soldiers a nine-days' scare. Then he sent to General McClellan a recommendation of pardon, which McClellan promptly issued. Lincoln had no intention of overriding McClellan, and had no doubt the boy was to be pardoned; no Union soldier was shot during the Civil War for going to sleep on picket duty; but Lincoln went over to the Washington house McClellan had rented, and told him "the Lady President" greatly hoped the boy would be pardoned. McClellan was used to having the President make requests of him, and of doing as he pleased about granting them; but he wrote his wife that he considered it "another bouquet" of which he was getting many, that "the Lady President" was begging from him "the life of a man I had ordered shot."

The Lincoln boys were in and out of the hospitals, and they contracted measles. It was believed, and probably correctly, that this infection came from the hospital. Mrs. Lincoln had no natural aptitude for nursing; she was an over-solicitous mother, and one who lacked steadiness of nerve. She was a Christian woman, and her faith was a comfort; but her temperament had in it nothing that helped her to bear the strain of anxiety or the calamity of grief. These crushed her.

After the death of Willie, Mrs. Lincoln was almost frantic; she never again entered the room where he died and where his body lay awaiting the funeral. At one time she expressed her grief in such passionate terms that her husband led her to the window, and pointing out to the insane asylum, said, "Mother, do you see that large white building yonder? Unless you control your grief I am afraid we shall have to send you there." Lincoln himself was almost prostrated by grief over little Willie's death, but he was a man of self-control, and that was something Mrs. Lincoln never learned.

More than once, as just after the Battle of Bull Run, the family of the President was advised to leave Washington. Mrs. Lincoln was by nature a woman of great timidity, but she refused to go, and her presence was an encouragement to her husband. Lincoln did not know how to bear lightly his terrible load of responsibility. His wife contrived to invite old friends to meals at the White House, especially to breakfast. She laughed and joked with them as they talked of old days in Illinois; she even shared the fun at the expense of herself and her sisters, all but one of whom, like herself, married lean men, when an old friend made free to tell an old story, familiar in the family, that Major Wallace had been the only man who had been able to put on flesh while tyrannized over by a

Todd. The story was almost exasperating, but Mrs. Lincoln let it pass for the sake of the fun it gave her husband, who, like all tall men married to short women, complain of their helpless subjugation.

Mrs. Lincoln assumed a benevolent despotism over her husband, and compelled him to drive with her every afternoon, a blessed relief, and one he would not have taken had her sway over him been less absolute. Her attempts to lift the cloud of gloom that hung over the White House were not wholly successful. If she gave a reception, she was criticized for displaying joy at a time when the nation was suffering defeat upon the battle-field and sorrow in its homes. But if she did not permit some festivity in the White House, as for some time after the death of Willie she did not, this, too, was charged up against her as adding a needless element of gloom to a situation already depressing.

In March, 1865, President and Mrs. Lincoln went by the steamer *River Queen* from Washington to City Point, and anchored under the bluff on which stood the headquarters tent of General Grant. Mr. and Mrs. Lincoln slept on board the steamer, and took most of their meals there; but sometimes they dined ashore with General Grant and some of his officers. On March twenty-sixth a somewhat distinguished company, among them the French minister, Monsieur Geoffroi, came from Washington, and an excursion was made to the front of the Army of the Potomac about twelve miles from the landing. A portion of the journey was made upon a military railway. At its end, the men of the party were mounted on horseback, and the two ladies, Mrs. Lincoln and Mrs. Grant, were sent forward in what in military parlance was termed an ambulance, but which was a kind of half-open carriage. General Adam Badeau was detailed to escort the ladies, and he sat on the front seat with the driver, the two ladies sitting behind.

As they drove, General Badeau chanced to remark that they would meet one other lady, the wife of General Charles Griffin, who was a personal friend of Mrs. Grant. He said that on account of the approach of hostilities, all women had been ordered to the rear, but that Mrs. Griffin had a special permit from the President to remain for a day or two with her husband.

Mrs. Lincoln was instantly alert. How had that woman seen the President to obtain such a permit without Mrs. Lincoln's knowing of the interview? "What do you mean, sir?" she demanded. "Do you mean that she saw the President alone? Do you know, sir, that I never permit the President to see any woman alone?"

General Badeau attempted to return a soft answer, but she said, "That is a very equivocal smile, sir. Let me out of this carriage at once! I will ask the President if he saw that woman alone!"

Mrs. Grant here interposed. She knew Mrs. Griffin, who had been a Carroll, and was of an honored family and a most exemplary woman. But Mrs. Lincoln was not to be reasoned with. She thrust her arms past General Badeau and laid hold on the driver, ordering him to stop.

With difficulty Mrs. Grant prevailed on her to wait till the whole party alighted. There General Meade became her escort, and she at once turned upon him with a demand that he take her to the President and learn if "that woman" had seen him alone. General Meade took in the situation and excused himself. Presently he returned, and gave to Mrs. Lincoln very comforting information. She went back to the vehicle almost completely reassured. General Meade had made inquiry and learned that it was Secretary Stanton and not the President who had issued the pass to Mrs. Griffin. For which little white lie may the soul of General Meade receive no punishment hereafter.

The next day the same party went on the north side of the James to visit the army under command of General Ord. They sailed for a distance up the river in a steamer, and then Mrs. Lincoln and Mrs. Grant were driven ahead in an ambulance while the others rode horseback. Mrs. Ord, as wife of the commanding general, had remained with her husband, and for a little time she rode beside the President. Those who knew of her outbreak on the day before had no mind to mention this fact to Mrs. Lincoln, but Major Seward, nephew of the Secretary of State, chanced to speak of it in her presence. Mrs. Lincoln turned upon him so savagely that his horse became unmanageable, or so he affirmed, and he had to back away and disappear.

When the ambulance arrived, Mrs. Ord rode up to greet the ladies, but Mrs. Lincoln denounced her, calling her abusive names, and demanded what she meant by following up the President. Mrs. Ord went away in tears.

That night the President and Mrs. Lincoln entertained General and Mrs. Grant and the General's staff at dinner on the boat, and Mrs. Lincoln in the presence of them all, demanded of her husband the removal of General Ord. General Grant spoke up, declaring that General Ord was a brave and competent officer.

Lincoln turned patiently to Mrs. Lincoln, calling her "Mother" and trying to calm her down, but with only partial success. She continued to rant about Mrs. Griffin and Mrs. Ord during the time she and the President were at City Point.

A day or two afterward, Captain Barnes of the Navy, who had accompanied Mrs. Ord on the day of her ride, was accosted by Mrs. Lincoln as he came on board the boat, and when he declined to say that Mrs. Ord was to blame, she turned upon him with vituperation.

The President asked Captain Barnes to step to the President's stateroom, to look at a map. While there, he spoke no word as to what had happened. He did not rebuke his wife or speak of her behind her back; he simply showed that he was not offended with Captain Barnes.

While these cheerful events were in progress, General Sherman was coming by steamer for conference with President Lincoln and General Grant. He arrived on the twenty-eighth. Grant and Sherman went together on board the *River Queen* and had an hour's visit with the President, and returned to Grant's headquarters, where Mrs. Grant had tea waiting for them. She asked about their visit, and as they did not mention Mrs. Lincoln she inquired how they had found her. Grant replied that he had forgotten to mention her, and Sherman said he did not even know she was on board the boat, or anywhere in the vicinity. Mrs. Grant said, "You are a pretty pair!" and added that their neglect to show proper courtesy to Mrs. Lincoln was unpardonable. Mrs. Lincoln shared this opinion; for when, on the following day, these two generals, duly instructed by Mrs. Grant, went back on board the steamer, and, after a brief visit with the President stated that they would like to pay their respects to Mrs. Lincoln, Mr. Lincoln conveyed the mesage to her stateroom, and brought back word that Mrs. Lincoln was not well. Neither of the generals had the slightest difficulty in a diagnosis of her illness, and Mrs. Grant offered them little sympathy. It was just what she expected.

Mrs. Lincoln made an attempt to lionize General Grant on the day when he appeared at the White House to accept command of the armies. She had announced a reception in his honor that night. But General Grant hurried to Culpeper to be with the army. Mrs. Lincoln grew to dislike General Grant. He was finely loyal to Lincoln when there was a suggestion that Grant might be a candidate for the presidency in 1864; but even after Lincoln had been reelected, she did not get out of her mind that Grant was in some sort a presidential rival. She was not far wrong in her conjecture that he might be the Republican nominee in 1868. She referred to this matter, none too graciously, in conversation with Mrs. Grant. Mrs. Grant modestly said that she and her husband were quite content where they were, but Mrs. Lincoln did not feel any too sure of this.

There has been no little curiosity as to why General and Mrs. Grant, after having accepted invitations to attend Ford's Theater with the President and Mrs. Lincoln on the night of his assassination, sent a note of regret, and hurried to Burlington, New Jersey, where their boys were in school. The boys, it would seem, could have waited one more night. One reason, as General Badeau learned from the Grants, when he was assisting General Grant in the writing of his books, was that Mrs. Grant, warned and worn by past experience, and also by a conversation with Mrs. Stanton, would not sit in the box with Mrs. Lincoln. Perhaps she saved her husband's life in that way.

This is far from being cheerful reading, but it is the worst that can be said in truth, though far from being the worst that has been said.

Mrs. Lincoln has been accused of treason. While she was living and later, it was openly alleged and industriously whispered that she was in constant communication with southern leaders. In order to protect her from this charge as well as to save her from receipt of vile letters, her mail was opened by Mr. Stoddard, one of the President's secretaries; she was not even permitted the privacy of her correspondence.

When news of a Union victory brought joy to official Washington, her participation in the rejoicing could not afford any cloud of expressed personal sorrow because of loss of life among her own kindred. When Grant won at Shiloh the first notable victory of the Civil War, she could display no grief over the death there of a Confederate soldier, Samuel B. Todd, her brother. She participated in the rejoicing of the nation over the two victories at Gettysburg and Vicksburg, though she knew that in the capture of the latter city her brother, David Todd, was fatally shot through the lungs. The success of the Union forces at Baton Rouge had to be accepted as a thing to be thankful for, even though the news of it came with tidings that her brother Alexander was killed there.

Her three brothers died, one by one, in the Confederate Army, and she was not permitted to shed a tear for them where any one could observe it. When President Lincoln wired her of a Union victory, she being at the time in Philadelphia, and included in the message news of the death of her brother-in-law, Major-General Ben Hardin Helm, he could not permit himself the expression of a syllable of sympathy. When her sister Mrs. Helm came to the White House under a flag of truce, and was there as a guest in her widowhood, Mrs. Lincoln was permitted to display the very minimum of sisterly sorrow, checked by the consideration that even this might possibly be interpreted by some key-hole listener as sympathy for the Confederate cause for which her sister's husband had died.

It has been assumed even by some who were disposed to be friendly toward Mrs. Lincoln that her southern sympathies were to an extent responsible for Lincoln's hesitation and slow movement toward emancipation. This, I am satisfied, is the reverse of truth. Lincoln was conservative, cautious, disinclined to rashness, while she was impetuous and ready for immediate action. When her husband left the Whig party and became a Republican, she went with him and beyond him. "I always urged him to be an ultra-Republican," she said truthfully. She gave up her friends and kindred for her husband's cause. Whatever her personal prejudices on the negro question, and her intimacy with Lizzie Keckley shows how thoroughly she got over those in at least one particular, and however often her trials with domestic help prompted her to say that if she were free to choose her residence it would be in a slave state, she became if not an abolitionist in her personal sentiments, at least a believer in abolition as a military and political necessity, and in this she was more emphatic than her husband. It was not in her nature to do things by halves.

I venture even to soil a page at this point to refer to those loathsome and contemptible rumors which have cast their putrid odors about the White House in almost every administration, and very seldom with any truth or reason, and which whispered the vilest insinuations concerning the moral character of Mary Todd Lincoln. The soldiers around the camp-fire sang her name in ribald jest linked with the name of Jefferson Davis, and this was by no means the worst of the indecencies indulged in with respect to her. With how many men, some of whom she may never have seen, was she alleged to be ready to elope? And of it all there was not a syllable of truth.

Mrs. Lincoln was very fond of the attentions of men. She gloried in the stately and formal courtesy of the polished Charles Sumner, whom she liked better than her husband did, and she liked the subtle flattery of diplomats and men in uniform. But her life was lived in the blazing focus of a fierce white light, and no single approach to an impropriety was ever discovered in her.

Traps enough were set for her and for her husband, and she at least recognized the importance of guarding him. Moreover, this was quite to her liking. He came through that burning fiery furnace without the smell of fire upon his garments. She, though closely watched and constantly misrepresented, committed no act in any degree disloyal to her husband.

Mary Todd had not received a sufficient preparation for the task before her, nor had any other American woman. The mistress of the White House at that juncture would have needed to be super-woman to meet the distressing and complicated situation. Mrs. Lincoln had not the patience, the tact, the self-control, essential to her position. But she was loyal to Mr. Lincoln and to the Government of the United States. Peace came at last, and there was mercifully granted to Abraham and Mary Lin-

Mrs. Lincoln's Grand Reception

President and Mrs. Lincoln greeting General and Mrs. Grant

From a contemporary lithograph with many portraits of prominent people

The Lincoln Family

This famous group is based on a photograph of Lincoln and Tad by Brady. Mrs. Lincoln, Robert and the portrait of Willie were painted in by Frank B. Carpenter

coln a brief interval in which they were permitted to build castles in the air. Few and crowded were the days, but she treasured their memory, and counted like beads of a rosary the conversations which she had with him after peace was really assured. One of them was to her unspeakably precious. On the very last day of Abraham Lincoln's life she stole him away, as was her custom, and took him for a drive. They went beyond the city limits of Washington, out into the country, on that April afternoon, and in the days that followed she told the story, over and over, of the things they talked about.

Up to the time of Lincoln's second election, he and his wife had rather assumed that when they left the White House they would return to Springfield to live. Now there opened before them longer vistas. They would see the second term of office through and the wounds of the country healed; there would be a policy of forbearance and forgiveness and good will. Their period of office which had begun under the cloud of war would end in the sunlight of peace. Then they would travel; they would take the boys and go to Europe; they would visit the Holy Land; when they returned they would go to California, and see men digging out the gold that was to pay the national debt. They were no longer sure that they would return to Springfield; if their hearts pulled them back to their old home, well and good; but if otherwise, they would find a home where it might seem best. In the meantime there was peace, and the work of rebuilding the desolate places and healing the wounds which the strife had caused. And under the stars and stripes there was not a single slave. These were the things they talked about on their daily drive, even to the last afternoon before he died. These were the castles they built in the air. So far as we know the story of those last days, no cloud came between Abraham and Mary Lincoln. At evening time. there was light. Then came the assassin's bullet and the dark.

16. A SORROWFUL WIDOWHOOD

Even the shocking tragedy of her husband's murder did not protect Mary Todd Lincoln from situations in which she displayed herself at a disadvantage. When it was determined to convey the body of Lincoln back to Springfield, a meeting was held in that city, and a site was selected for his tomb. It was a most attractive spot, on the opposite side from the Edwards home of the present site of the State Capitol. The land was owned by a family named Mather, who agreed to sell it for the purpose. A vault was erected, men working day and night to have it ready for occupancy when the body should arrive. The brick work was actually completed, or so nearly so as to assure its readiness for use by the time the funeral train came to Springfield; it was later to be veneered with marble. But Mrs. Lincoln made emphatic protest, and declared that her husband's body should remain in Chicago, or be taken back to Washington unless the location was changed. So the interment was had in the receiving tomb at Oak Ridge, and there, later, a stately monument was erected.

Mrs. Lincoln had no inclination to make her home in Springfield. After the funeral she returned to Chicago with her two sons, Robert and Tad. Robert was grown and engaged to be married, but still for a time he was with his mother. He and she were not always happy together. In some respects they were too much alike to be congenial. They took rooms for a week at the Tremont House. She was sadly at home there. In that place she had stood, in November, 1860, with her tall husband on one side, and Vice-President-elect Hannibal Hamlin on the other, and received an ovation at the hands of all Chicago and the Northwest; and now she was a secluded stranger, heavily crêped and veiled, with few who dared approach her, and none too many so inclined.

Summer approached, and the three went to Hyde Park, near where the University now stands. It then called itself a summer resort.

Springfield was as nearly unanimous in its demand that Lincoln be buried in the tomb upon the Mather plat as it ever has been on any subject in all its history. Oak Ridge was a new burial ground, and few people went there willingly. Who would ever see a monument erected in that remote and lonely place? But the Mather place was of the extent of four city blocks, gently sloping toward the town and the Alton railroad. A monument erected there would be visible to passengers as they went through, and the new tomb, when coated with marble, would be beautifully appropriate. The Association had consented that Lincoln's body should be placed in the public receiving vault, but only as a temporary necessity. The city was determined to bring Mrs. Lincoln to her senses, and bury her husband's body in the fine new tomb on the Mather property.

How attractive their plan was, can be well estimated by those who view the location from the state-house, now located upon the Mather property. But Mrs. Lincoln was obdurate.

On May thirteenth, nine days after the interment of Lincoln, the *Journal* announced that the Association that had been formed to secure a monument "wisely resolved to retain the Mather block" as the place of permanent interment and the site of the monument.

Springfield went forward assured that Mrs. Lincoln would presently give her consent. On the contrary, she wrote from Hyde Park on June fifth, stating that unless within ten days she had the positive pledge of the Association that the tomb and monument should be at Oak Ridge and not on the Mather land, she would positively remove the body and take it back to Washington, and cause it to be buried under the dome of the Capitol in the empty tomb originally constructed for the body of Washington.

The Association determined not to yield to her. It voted to send its President, Richard J. Oglesby, and its Secretary, O. M. Hatch, to Chicago, and to set forth the manifold advantages of the Mather location.

Mrs. Lincoln learned through the papers of the Committee's approach, and refused to see them. Instead, she sent her son, Captain Robert T. Lincoln, to meet them at the train and send them back to Springfield with a letter from her, dated, "Near Chicago, June 10, 1865," saying that five of her ten days of grace were already gone, and unless she had the positive pledge of the Association that her demands were to be complied with, she would remove the body.

The two gentlemen returned to Springfield and, on the night of the fourteenth, they made their report. The Association voted by a majority of one vote to comply with

Mrs. Lincoln's wishes. But even this was not published till the twenty-second. They held the vote of record in case it should be needed to present to the officers who might be sent to replevin the body, but they did not publish until they were forced to do so the fact that Mrs. Lincoln had compelled them to give up their plan. She had her way, but she did not add to the list of her friends. Indeed, it would be difficult to conjecture just whom she counted her friends at that time.

Congress declined to pay her the full salary of her husband for the four years of the second term, and this was a bitter disappointment to her, for she had need of the money. However, she was voted a lump sum of twenty-five thousand dollars. Of this she invested sixteen thousand dollars in a new white-marble-front house on West Washington Street, facing south, between Elizabeth and Ann Streets. There she and the boys removed in the fall.

She was continuously unhappy. Often she wished herself dead, and Robert was not always a reason that reconciled her to life. So far as records permit an unbiased judgment, Robert had much to exasperate him in those days.

She had few friends in Chicago, and she did not seek to add to the number. Tad entered the Brown School, and became one of the editors of the little school paper. His speech improved; to his mother it seemed almost perfect. He made friends, and now and then brought one of them home with him, but those who made those visits and who still live have no cheerful memories of Tad's mother.

She kept away from her old friends in Springfield. In the fall of 1866, September ninth, she made a surreptitious visit to her husband's grave, and by appointment, met

William H. Herndon, not at his office, nor at the home of any of her sisters, but at the St. Nicholas Hotel. Considering their former relations, she was very courteous to him, and gave him valuable information for the biography of her husband which he was preparing to write. Scarcely was she back in the whited sepulcher of her marble-front Chicago home, when he delivered his Ann Rutledge lecture. Mary Todd had a dim recollection that her husband had had a young sweetheart who had died, but she did not remember that she had ever heard Ann Rutledge's name, when Herndon told the world that Abraham Lincoln loved this girl so well he had no heart left that he could have given to a wife. Her friends and relatives in Springfield were furious, and her old minister, Reverend James Smith, then retired and in Scotland, denounced Herndon through the press. Fortunately, Mrs. Lincoln herself bore this disgraceful attack in silence. But she suffered as only a proud and humiliated woman could suffer.

A distressing condition arose out of her financial situation. Mrs. Lincoln, during the latter months of her life in Washington, unknown to her husband, had bought from New York merchants, silks, furs, laces, diamonds, shawls and other finery to a total of seventy thousand dollars. How she expected to raise the money to pay for this no one knows. When she left Washington, she insisted on taking with her, not only all her new finery, but trunk after trunk of worn or half worn dresses, that were a burden to her.

After it had become evident that Congress was not to give her the one hundred thousand dollars she asked, the merchants pressed their claims. Mrs. Lincoln grew desperate. She packed some trunks with dress goods, and in September, 1867, went secretly to New York.

She registered at the St. Denis on Broadway as "Mrs. Clarke." She felt her helplessness and wrote her former dressmaker and confidential friend, Mrs. Elizabeth Keckley, asking her to come to New York and assist her. Elizabeth came, but was not admitted. The St. Denis would not permit a negro in its main dining-room. Mrs. Abraham Lincoln might have secured her entrance, but "Mrs. Clarke" could not accomplish this result.

"Mrs. Clarke" and her friend Mrs. Keckley, removed to "Union Place Hotel" where there was no prejudice against negroes. She looked over a New York paper and found the name of a firm of commission merchants. To them she wrote, dating her letters "Springfield," and Mrs. Keckley became her medium of communication.

The commission merchants evolved what they thought a clever scheme. Election was approaching in several states, New York among them. The results were likely to have a bearing in the following year when the Republicans would rally to repudiate Andrew Johnson and all his works. The Republican politicians could scarcely afford to see Mrs. Lincoln selling her wardrobe because her husband's party in Congress left her in poverty. It was determined therefore, to show Mrs. Lincoln's letter to prominent Republican politicians and endeavor to shame them into an appropriation, the commission merchants to profit by the deal.

The Republican politicians refused to stir. Mrs. Lincoln ran out of money and secured an advance of six hundred dollars from her merchants.

Meantime, "Mrs. Clarke" and Mrs. Keckley were attracting some attention. They went to the country for three days, and, returning to New York, put up at a poor and dirty place called the Brandreth House, where she registered as "Mrs. Morris."

Still no money came in, and she resolved to go over to the enemy. The leading Democratic newspaper in New York was the *World*. This newspaper was authorized to print her letters concerning her poverty. Very cheerfully the *World* assumed this duty, and held up to reproach the political party that professed to honor the name of Lincoln and was permitting his widow to starve.

The *New York World* had been bitter in its criticism of Mr. Lincoln. It had been suspended at one time by order of the Government, and its editor, Manton Marble, was arrested. It certainly was not a tactful performance on Mrs. Lincoln's part to give her tale of woe to the nation through its columns.

On the other hand, the attitude of the leaders of her husband's own party, who were appealed to at this time, merits stern disapproval. Foolish as she had been, in purchases she ought never to have made, and in the employment of methods for financial relief which she ought never to have undertaken, she deserved assistance which no one gave to her. In all this pitiful experience no man of influence and sound judgment became her adviser, or came near to save her in her frantic efforts to free herself from financial ruin, or from the public ridicule and abuse which followed.

This article appeared Thursday, October 3, 1867, a month before election. On the same day Mrs. Lincoln left New York for Chicago, arriving Saturday morning. The *World* went westward on the train with her.

On Saturday she wrote to Lizzie Keckley a rather full account of her journey from New York to Chicago. She had kept up her *incognito* and had overheard some things about herself. Also she met a man she knew, and found the meeting a mutual embarrassment. Her letter is dated October 6, but this is evidently a mistake. It was written on the day preceding:

"Chicago, October 6th, [1867]

"My dear Lizzie:

"My ink is like myself, and my spirits failing, so I write you today with a pencil. I had a solitary ride to this place, as you may imagine, varied by one or two amusing incidents. I found, after you left me, I could not continue in the car in which you left me, owing to every seat's berth being engaged, so, being simple *Mrs. Clarke,* I had to eat 'humble pie' in a car less commodious. My thoughts were too much with my 'dry goods and interests' at 609 Broadway to care much for my surroundings, as uncomfortable as they were. In front of me sat a middle-aged, gray-haired, respectable-looking gentleman, who, the whole morning had the page of the *World* before him, which contained my letters and business concerns. About four hours before arriving at Chicago, a consequential-looking man, of formidable size, seated himself by him, and it appears they were entirely unknown to each other. The well-fed looking individual opened the conversation with the man who had read the *World* so attentively, and the conversation soon grew warm and earnest. The war and its devastation engaged them. The bluffy individual, doubtless a Republican, who had pocketed his many thousands, spoke of the widows of the land, made so by the war. My reading man remarked to him: 'Are you aware that Mrs. Lincoln is in indigent circumstances, and has to sell her clothing and jewelry to gain means to make life more endurable?' The well-conditioned man replied: 'I do not blame her for selling her clothing, if she wishes it. I suppose when sold, she will convert the proceeds into five-twenties* to enable her to have means to be buried.' The *World* man turned toward him with a searching glance, and replied, with the haughtiest manner, 'That woman is not dead yet.' The discomfited individual looked down, never spoke another word, and in half an hour left his seat, and did not return. I give you word for word as the conversation occurred. May it be found through the execution of my friends, Messrs. Brady and Keys,† that 'that woman is not dead yet,' and being alive, she speaketh and gaineth valuable hearers. Such a life! Those who have been injured, how gladly the injurer would consign them to mother earth and forgetfulness! Hoping I should not be recognized at Fort Wayne, I thought I would get out at dinner for a cup of tea. I will show you what a creature of *fate* I am, as miserable as it sometimes is. I went into the dining room alone, and was ushered up to a table, where, at its head, sat a very elegant-looking gentleman—at his side a middle-aged lady. My black veil was doubled over my face. I had taken my seat next to him—he at the head of the table, I at his left hand. I immediately *felt* a pair of eyes was gazing at me. I looked him full in the face, and the glance was earnestly returned. I sipped my water, and said: 'Mr. S. is this indeed you?' His face was as pale as the table-cloth. We entered into conversation, when I asked him how long since he had left Chicago. He replied, 'Two weeks since.' He said, 'How strange you should be on the train and I not know it?'

"As soon as I could escape from the table, I did so, by saying, 'I must secure a cup of tea for a lady friend with me, who has a head-ache.' I had scarcely returned to the car, when he entered it with a cup of tea borne by his own

---

* United States five per cent. bonds, payable in twenty years.

† The commission merchants at 609 Broadway, who had charge of the sale of her goods.

aristocratic hands. I was a good deal annoyed by seeing him, and he was so agitated that he spilled half of the cup over my elegantly gloved hands. He looked very sad, and I fancied 609 Broadway occupied his thoughts. I apologized for the absent lady who wished the cup, by saying that 'in my absence she had slipped out for it.' His heart was in his eyes, notwithstanding my veiled face. Pity for me, I fear, has something to do with all this. I never saw his manner so gentle and sad. This was nearly evening, and I did not see him again, as he returned to the lady, who was his sister-in-law from the East. What evil spirit prompted me to go out and get that cup of tea? When he left me, woman-like, I tossed the cup of tea out of the window, and tucked my head down and shed bitter tears. At the depot my darling little Taddie was waiting for me, and his voice never sounded so sweet. My dear Lizzie, do visit Mr. Brady each morning at nine o'clock and urge them all you can. I see by the papers Stewart* has returned. Tomorrow I will send the invoice of goods, which please do not give up. How much I miss you, tongue cannot tell. Forget my fright and nervousness of the evening before. Of course you were as innocent as a child in all you did. I consider you my best living friend, and I am struggling to be enabled some day to repay you. Write me often as you promised.

"Always truly yours,
"M. L.

The elegant-looking Mr. S. whom she had seen in Chicago, and whom she met that day in Fort Wayne, was no other than Charles Sumner. And he had seen and read her letters in the *World!* No wonder his face was pale as the table-cloth, and that she rushed back to the car in confusion. No wonder she imagined his thoughts were of her publicly displayed clothing, and that in their mutual

---

*A. T. Stewart, prominent New York merchant, to whom she was heavily in debt.—W. E. B.

embarrassment her gloves were ruined by spilled tea! Of all men in America he was most certain to be horrified by what she had done, and there were few men in whose eyes she more earnestly desired to appear well. Sumner was on a lecture tour, and it was not strange that she should have met him, but it was horribly inopportune.

On Saturday evening Robert Lincoln, who had been out in the city, returned to the house, having read in the Chicago papers the articles copied from the *New York World*. His anger was almost that of insanity, or so at least it seemed to his mother. He felt humiliated and disgraced. He was furious, and he talked to her in no gentle terms. But, however she might have met his anger with her own, she was humbled before his grief. He was ashamed of his mother. After a night of weeping, she rushed again to her ink-bottle, and if her ink still was dry, she could have wet it with her tears. From this time on she wrote almost daily to Lizzie Keckley. This is her Sunday letter:

"Chicago, Sunday morning, Oct. 6, [1867]
"My dear Lizzie:
"I am writing this morning with a broken heart, after a sleepless night of great mental suffering. R. came up last evening like a maniac, and almost threatening his life, looking like death, because the letters of the *World* were published in yesterday's paper. I could not refrain from weeping when I saw him so miserable. But yet, my dear, good Lizzie, was it not to protect myself and help others, and was not my motive and action of the purest kind? Pray for me that this cup of affliction may pass from me, or be sanctified to me. I weep whilst I am writing. I pray for death this morning. Only my darling Taddie prevents my taking my life. I shall have to endure a

round of newspaper abuse from the Republicans, because
I dared venture to relieve a few of my wants. Tell Mr.
Brady and Keyes not to have a line of mine once more in
print. I am nearly losing my reason.

"Your friend, M. L."

She wrote again on Tuesday:

"Chicago, Oct. 8, [1867]

"My dear Lizzie:

"Bowed down with suffering and anguish, again I
write you. As we might have expected, the Republicans
are falsifying me, and doing just as they did when they
prevented the Congressional appropriation. Mrs. _____
knows something about these same people. As her husband is living they dare not utter all they would desire to
speak. You know yourself how innocently I have acted
and from the best and purest motives. They will howl
on to prevent my disposing of my things. What a vile,
vile set they are! The *Tribune* here, Mr. White's paper,
wrote a very beautiful editorial yesterday, in my behalf;
yet knowing that I have been deprived of my rights by the
party, I suppose I would be mobbed if I ventured out.
What a world of anguish this is—and how I have been
made to suffer! You would not recognize me now. The
glass shows me a pale, wretched, haggard face, and my
dresses are like bags on me. And all because I was doing
what I felt to be my duty. Our minister, Mr. Swazey,*
called on me yesterday, and said I had done perfectly
right. Mrs. F_____ says every one speaks in the same
way. The politicians, knowing they have deprived me of
my just rights, would prefer to see me starve, rather than
dispose of my things. They will prevent the sale of any-

---

* The Mr. Swazey to whom Mrs. Lincoln makes allusion in her letter
to Elizabeth Keckley of October 8, 1867, and the "Mr. S." in her letter of
the 9th, was Reverend Arthur Swazey, pastor of the Third Presbyterian
Church, residing on West Washington Street not far from where Mrs.
Lincoln lived.

thing, so I have telegraphed for them. I hope you have received from B. the letters I have consigned to his care. See to this. Show none of them. Write me every day.
                                                      "M. L."

Robert Lincoln could endure this no longer. He fled from Chicago, joining a group of young men who were going for a camping trip in the Rocky Mountains. There he would be safe for a time from the daily papers and from his mother's erratic conduct. His mother was frankly glad to see him go. In her letters she classed him with the men she counted her enemies. She did not trust him. "He is very deep," she said.

From that time on, something happened almost daily that drove her to her writing desk, and her letters to Lizzie Keckley are tragic. A perusal of the editorial comments in the newspapers of the time sufficiently indicates a part of the occasion of her perturbation. Mrs. Lincoln, always a traitor at heart, according to some of these periodicals, had made this shameful exhibition of her own extravagance, and at the same time had so trafficked in her own folly as to betray the personal and political interests with which her husband had been identified.

Again she wrote to Lizzie. But the close of her letter shows that she was capable of folly even greater than that which she had already shown. She authorized her agents to announce that she would accept donations.

                              "Chicago, Wednesday, Oct. 9th
"My dear Lizzie:
"It appears as if the fiends had let loose, for the Republican papers are tearing me to pieces in this border ruffian west. If I had committed murder in every city in this blessed Union, I could not be more traduced. And

you know how innocent I have been of the intention of doing wrong. A piece in the morning *Tribune*, signed 'B,' pretending to be a lady, says there is no doubt Mrs. L. is deranged, has been for years past, and will end her life in a lunatic asylum. They would doubtless like me to begin it now. Mr. S., a very kind, sympathizing minister, has been with me this morning, and has now gone to see Mr. Medill, of the *Tribune*, to know if he sanctioned his paper publishing such an article. Pray for me, dear Lizzie, for I am very miserable and broken hearted. Since writing this, I have just received a letter from Mr. Keyes, begging and pleading with me to allow them to use my name for donations. I think I will consent.

"Truly yours,
"M. L."

She was glad of Robert's absence for more than one reason. When she saw his utter humiliation, she had promised to call off the publicity, so far as it was in her power to do so, and she had so written Lizzie Keckley to furnish no more material to the press. But the *World*, glorying in the rebuke it was administering to the ungrateful Republicans, wrote to Mrs. Lincoln, and proposed, if she should consent, to open a subscription, and receive cash donations, to be acknowledged in its columns, the money to be given for the relief of Mrs. Lincoln. Mrs. Lincoln knew very well what Robert would say to that, but Robert was away. She wrote to the *World* and authorized that newspaper to solicit contributions for her, and the *World* printed her letter.

But the money did not flow in. At last Mrs. Lincoln's last shred of pride left her. Frederick Douglas, an eminent negro leader, and Reverend H. H. Garnet, pastor of a negro church in New York, proposed that the colored people of America should raise a fund to save Mrs.

Lincoln from poverty. Mrs. Lincoln consented to this proposal, and wrote Lizzie Keckley that if it succeeded, Lizzie should have five thousand dollars of it after Mrs. Lincoln died. Mrs. Lincoln was insistent that a circular be issued, one hundred and fifty thousand was the number of copies she desired, pleading for money.

But the comments of the press were drastic and in some cases cruel. Election passed, and the enthusiasm of the Democrats waned. The attempt to gain money from the negroes proved futile. The whole foolish scheme failed.

The old clothes situation now took on an aspect which would have been ludicrous if it had not been so tragic. Lizzie Keckley had some old dresses that Mrs. Lincoln had given her, and a glove that Lincoln had worn at one of his receptions, and that had been white when he drew it on, and it occurred to her that since people were showing so much interest in Mrs. Lincoln's garments, Lizzie might set up an exhibition of her own. So, while Mrs. Lincoln was writing her to encourage the colored people to contribute money to Mrs. Lincoln through the *New York World*, Mrs. Keckley was working out another plan. A negro bishop was soliciting from Lizzie a contribution for his school, and proposing that it take the form of a memorial to her dead son. She presented the clothes to him to be exhibited in different cities in America at twenty-five cents admission, and if the plan worked well, then in Europe; the money received to create this endowment. Mrs. Lincoln was horrified when she learned of this. She wrote:

"Dear Lizzie:
"I am positively dying with a broken heart, and the

probability is that I shall be living but a very short time.
May we all meet in a better world, where such grief is unknown. Write me all about yourself. I should like you
to have about four black widow's caps, just such as I had
made in the fall in New York, sent to me. Of course you
would not suppose, if I had you come out here and work
for me six weeks, I would not pay your expenses and pay
you as you made each dress. The probability is that I
shall need few more clothes; my rest, I am inclined to
believe, is near at hand. Go to B. & K. and have my
clothes sent me without further publicity. I am feeling
too weak to write more today. Why are you so silent?
For the sake of humanity, if not me and my children, do
not have those black clothes displayed in Europe. The
thought has almost whitened every hair of my head.
Write when you receive this.

"Your friend, M. L."

Mrs. Lincoln gave up her west side house, and lived in
the Clifton House on Washington Street and Wabash
Avenue. Tad attended Chicago Academy, only a block
away. He had grown to be a very tall, raw-boned boy, in
stature almost like his father, but still he was in some respects almost feminine. He was far behind in his studies,
and did not learn readily, though his mind was not defective. Robert came and went and sought to be patient
with his mother's moods, but at times he lost his temper.

Reports that Mrs. Lincoln was insane now grew widely
current. Just about this time Judge David Davis presented to the court of Sangamon County a statement of
Mrs. Lincoln's assets, showing that her husband had left
a fortune of about one hundred and ten thousand dollars.
The newspapers attacked her again, and Mrs. Lincoln
tasted the last bitter dregs in the cup of sorrow and humiliation.

17.   A CLOUDED MIND

The November election brought to an end the publicity concerning Mrs. Lincoln's wardrobe. The *New York World* lost its enthusiasm for holding up to public sympathy the widow of the first Republican President, shamefully deserted by the party of her husband. None of the schemes that had been tried had brought her money. The Republican politicians refused to make appropriations. The public declined to make donations. The negroes did not hasten to contribute money to the wife of the man who had made them free. Fortunately, the merchants from whom the goods had been purchased were disposed to be generous. The accounts were settled without further publicity, and Mrs. Lincoln was relieved from the high tension of her financial obligations.

But she never learned to stop buying what she could not afford and did not need. Economical and even penurious in matters of bread and cheese, she was extravagant beyond all reason in matters of apparel. While she wore mourning till her death, she bought dress goods. When Robert became conservator of her affairs in 1875, he returned to Chicago merchants considerable invoices of goods she had purchased and for which she had no use.

Robert married, and brought his accomplished and charming bride to Chicago. Fortunately for every one, he procured a home of his own. Mrs. Lincoln returned to her marble-front house on the north side of Washington Street. She was an almost constant attendant at the Third Presbyterian Church, but the First Congregational Church was almost across the street from her home; Tad joined its Sunday-school, and she often slipped in at a service. She shrank, however, from any approach to intimacy, and lived practically in solitude.

She and Tad went abroad and lived for more than a year. They were in London, in very modest lodgings, when General Adam Badeau, who was Consul General, learned of her being in that city. He called upon her, and she was pathetically grateful for his visit. She and Tad were on the Continent for some months, and she read French novels which she liked, but kept away from her countrymen.

Estranged from her own kindred, and almost estranged from Robert, she was indeed in solitude. Few of her letters of this period are known to exist. Learning that a woman whom she believed to be a friend was in Paris, and knowing that this woman was the sister of a senator, Mrs. Lincoln wrote to her a long letter, on eight pages of black-bordered paper, to tell her that Charles Sumner was still hoping to obtain a pension for her from Congress, and she wanted all the help she could get in securing its passage.

She was very confidential, and wished the letter to be burned. She was anything but gracious in her reference to Mrs. Grant, then in the White House. Her comments on Mrs. Elihu B. Washburn, wife of the American ambassador to France, were unkind. She was the *"little wife"* of the ambassador, her insignificance emphasized by the underscoring. The letter was well written, and touched on many subjects, but for us its significance is in its sense of isolation. She writes with the rain beating against her window, and out of a heart filled with dreariness. She remembers with constant sadness the death of her husband, "whose noble attributes make me each day worship his memory more and more." She is comforted in the presence with her of her little Taddie, and he is her only joy. One sentence is enough to reveal her heart:

"The loneliness of this winter words could not express, nor pen write its terrors."

Mrs. Lincoln had not long to wait after writing to her friend in Paris. Mrs. Oine wrote her two letters which cheered her greatly, and gave her some gossip and other matters to think about besides herself. In one of these letters Mrs. Oine inclosed one to herself from Charles Sumner. That gentleman had long remained a bachelor, and was still unmarried when he was accustomed to visit the White House while Mrs. Lincoln occupied it. In June, 1866, he buried his aged mother, and in October following he was married to Mrs. Alice (Mason) Hooper, daughter of Jonathan Mason of Boston, and widow of William S. Hooper. Her sister was the "middle-aged" lady whom Mrs. Lincoln encountered with Sumner on his lecture tour as she met him at Fort Wayne on her returning journey to Chicago after her adventure in the matter of her clothing. Senator Sumner and his wife did not get along very well together, and on May 10, 1873, were divorced. The affairs of the Senator and his bride were causing gossip by the time of Mrs. Lincoln's correspondence with Mrs. Oine.

No one who knew either Charles Sumner or Mrs. Lincoln could doubt that their relations were wholly platonic; but Mrs. Lincoln was the type of woman who saw in every man a potential lover of some woman, and all really elegant gentlemen were in her mind possible lovers of herself. There is no probability that Sumner ever wanted to marry her, or that she wanted to marry Sumner; but Mrs. Lincoln was not the woman to see a man like Sumner married to another woman, and suffering at her hands, and writing letters of dignified and cultured admiration to a third, without having a number of thoughts about it. This letter has in it no unkindness, and is worth reading.

FROM MRS. ABRAHAM LINCOLN TO MRS. OINE

Frankfort-on-the-Main
Dec. 2d, 1869

"My dear Mrs. Oine:

"Your two letters arrived at the same time a day or two since. I cannot tell you how glad I was *once* more to hear from you. I greatly feared you were sick. I hope you are now much better—you must take care of your cough. I was confined to my bed on yesterday, with a neuralgia headache, and am feeling very far from well today. Dear, charming Mr. Sumner, did I not tell you, *he was all right.* If Congress was entirely composed of *just* such men—there would be no more sleepless nights and trembling fearful days such as I am now experiencing. Regarding our business, I am grateful that Congress *so soon* meets, and I hope a decision may be made *before Christmas.* I trust not an *adverse* one, or I shall have to emigrate to *Australia* or some such region.

"Those bright sunny letters of yours! how cheery they are to my sorrow-stricken heart. If success comes—it will all be through you. God will bless you in this life for your noble efforts in behalf of a widow suppressed—what think you your reward in that hereafter will be for all your goodness!

"I have given you a day or two to read over the letters of your other beaux ere I return to you Mr. Sumner's. I have so many such treasures of his in America. The 'Yours faithfully' appears very familiar to me. In future I will be deserted by him for *you,* but I will forgive you both—in my great regard for both parties. In your future acquaintance with him you will find him the most agreeable and delightful of men. How could his wife have acted as she has done? It was a great mistake he made in marrying so late in life!!

"You will not forget, my dear friend, any LITTLE NO-TICES pleasant *or otherwise.* The latter will *surely* come. Please send me such as soon as read. My face begins to *burn*—but may perhaps grow *ghastly* pale when the DE-CISION reaches me.

"Tell me all about yourself when you write. Susie, I hope, is well, and Sallie is not dimming her very sweet eyes by *too* hard study—I am sure—if she is with you, you will often make her laugh and forget her book. Oh that I could see you! I believe I never fail in this expression in all my letters. From my heart it is written.

"Taddie is hurrying me greatly—to mail the letter. Do write just as soon as you receive it. Please present my best love to your dear daughters. Taddie sends his best love.

"Believe me, always most truly and gratefully,
                    "Lovingly yours,
                        "Mary Lincoln."

Mrs. Lincoln did not receive her pension before Christmas, as she hoped, nor very soon thereafter. But she was not mistaken in her expectation that Sumner's introduction of her bill would bring down severe criticism upon herself.

Mrs. Lincoln returned from Europe in the spring of 1871, and Tad became very seriously ill. There is a tradition, which I have not been able either to confirm or disprove, that his illness was due to his very strong temperance principles. Neither Lincoln nor his wife drank wine in their own home, and both were in a measure opposed to it. Tad, however, was as extreme as his mother in all his preferences and convictions, and he was an emphatic foe of intoxicating liquor in all its forms. Good drinking water was not abundant in France and Germany in 1870, and Tad returned with the germs of typhoid fever, alleged to have been the result of his refusal to drink wine when the water was bad. After a painful illness, he died, July 15, 1871, and Mary Lincoln made another sorrowful journey to Springfield to lay his body beside that of his father and his two brothers.

More than ten years afterward, on April 5, 1882, Robert T. Lincoln wrote this in a letter concerning his youngest brother:

"Poor Tad was a good boy, and extraordinarily affectionate and firm in his friendships. After you knew him he studied diligently and overcame the defect in his speech. He was only eighteen when he died, but he was so manly and self-reliant that I had great hopes of his future. He was cut off by his death after a torturing illness."

Once again the personal affairs of Mrs. Lincoln came in scandalous fashion before the country. While Mrs. Lincoln was abroad, she wrote a petition for a pension, addressing it, through the Vice-President, to the Senate. Charles Sumner presented the petition in February, 1869. Sumner moved that an annual life pension be paid to Mrs. Lincoln, and named five thousand dollars as the sum. That was the annual salary which the senators had voted to themselves, he explained, and it was interest on the seventy-five thousand dollars that the nation would have paid to Lincoln had he lived to the end of his term.

A very few senators favored the bill. Let us be thankful that the disgruntled Lyman Trumbull was one of them. But Richard Yates, the other senator from Illinois, was bitterly opposed, and the manner of his saying so was shameful. All that winter Sumner waited and pleaded in vain. Senator Edmunds of Vermont was chairman of the Pensions Committee, and his hostility was virulent. The bill was lost.

Sumner introduced the bill again the following year, and after much debate which at times partook not only of partisan rancor, and that on the part of Republicans against the widow of their own great leader, but even of scandalous innuendo, the bill, amended to a grant of three thousand dollars a year, passed the Senate, and Mrs. Lincoln received that sum from the government as an annual pension.

Viewed from this distance, the parsimony and petty spite of those Republican senators appear contemptible.

Mary Lincoln had been foolish and wilful and misguided. But reverence for her husband and chivalry toward her should have moved those men to far worthier contemplation of her condition. Their treatment of her is a national disgrace. Abraham Lincoln would never have treated any woman as his political friends treated his widow. If anything could have been meaner than the spite of the Republicans, it was the willingness of the Democrats to profit by it.

In his last passionate appeal on her behalf, an appeal that won the bill's passage in the Senate by a reluctant vote of twenty-eight against twenty, with four senators absent, Charles Sumner, with tears in his eyes, said:

"Surely the honorable members of the Senate must be weary of casting mud on the garments of the wife of Lincoln; those same garments on which one terrible night five years ago, gushed out the blood and brains of Abraham Lincoln. She sat beside him in the theater, and she received that pitiful, that holy deluge on her hands and skirts, because she was the chosen companion of his heart. She loved him. I speak of that which I know. He had all her love. And Lincoln loved, as only his mighty heart could love, MARY LINCOLN."

I believe that Charles Sumner nobly spoke the truth.

Mary Todd Lincoln had very little left to live for.

In the winter of 1874-5 she was in Florida. On March 12, 1875, she wired to the family physician, Doctor Isham, imploring him to save Robert's life, and telling him that she was taking a train for Chicago. Robert was not sick, and he and Doctor Isham met her at the train.

She was shocked and overjoyed in finding Robert alive and well, and soon grew cheerful and animated. She talked pleasantly concerning her winter in Florida, and about the journey, which had been a pleasant one, except for an attempt which she believed had been made to poison her at Jacksonville. She bought a cup of coffee there, and was confident that it contained poison. She refused to go home with Robert, but went instead to the Grand Pacific Hotel, and insisted that Robert should remain with her.

Robert remained in the hotel that night and subsequent nights, sleeping in the room next to that of his mother. Every night, and several times a night, she would rap at his door, and tell him she was in danger. Sometimes he had to finish the night sleeping on a lounge in her room; sometimes she came in with him, and he gave her his bed and got what sleep he could on a couch. She wore him out, and did much the same for the chambermaids and

other people in the hotel.   An Indian, she said, was pull-
ing wires out of her brain.   The doctors were taking steel
springs out of her head.   People were trying to murder
her.

By day she visited the stores, and in one of them she
bought three hundred dollars' worth of lace curtains, having no longer a home to hang them in.   The manager of the
hotel and all who had to do with her became apprehensive,
and wished for her removal to some more suitable place.
To Robert's home she would not go, and she was unfit to
be alone.

At length Robert felt compelled to apply to the County
Court of Chicago to have her declared insane.   No little
care was taken to hide the records, and when the present
writer instituted a search for them, the oldest clerks in
the office declared that such papers did not exist; subsequent investigation, however, revealed them, and the
author supposes himself to be the first person who had
seen these papers since they were carefully hidden away.

So far as the records show, the sad thing was done as
decently and with as much dignity as possible.   Robert's
lawyer was Leonard Swett, and Mary Lincoln's was Isaac
N. Arnold.   Judge Wallace was on the bench.   The complaining witness was, of necessity, the son Robert.   The
jury was composed of twelve as prominent men as Chicago
had at that time.   It would appear that everything was done
that legally could be done to carry out what was deemed
necessary, with as little publicity and with as much regard
for propriety as possible.   No docket number appears to
have been given to the case, and the papers were con-
veniently mislaid; but the court record is there, with the
names of judge and jurors; and they are of such character

as to forbid the suspicion that they acted hastily or
through prejudice. Mary Lincoln was found insane and
a fit subject for confinement in one of the State Hospitals
for the Insane in the State of Illinois. She was not taken
to a State Hospital, but to a private asylum at Batavia.

Robert T. Lincoln was appointed by the court conservator of his mother's affairs, and he set to work to restore
them to order. It was no small task, and his accounts
are on file. At first it seemed that a merciful solution had
been reached of a very difficult problem. If Mrs. Lincoln would be content to remain in her shelter in Batavia,
and finish her tempestuous life in that harbor, it would
be well. About two weeks after she had been sent there,
he wrote a long letter about her, and said, under date of
July 1, 1875:

"My mother is in appearance more in comfort and happiness than she has been since my father's death. I have
been exceedingly fortunate in being able to procure for
her proper care and treatment in a place where all the
surroundings are of a most pleasant character, with nothing to suggest restraint. In the absence of all excitement,
there are no very pronounced insane actions, but her mind
is weak."

Not long was she content to remain there. She prevailed upon her sister Elizabeth to petition for her release,
and Ninian W. Edwards after conference with Robert T.
Lincoln, instituted proceedings for her legal restoration
to reason. The services of Isaac N. Arnold, who had been
her attorney before, and who wrote a very gracious and
not very valuable biography of Lincoln, were again secured. Another trial was held, and Robert T. Lincoln
very cheerfully consented to his mother's release, Ninian

W. and Elizabeth Edwards giving bond for her property.

The date of Mrs. Lincoln's first trial in which she was declared insane was May 19, 1875; the date of her release was June 15, 1876. She was in the sanitarium not quite thirteen months. That she was insane when she was sent there, and that Robert had exhausted all alternatives that appeared to him available, is, I think, ineluctable to any one reading the evidence. That she was sane on June 15, 1876, when the court so declared her, is not by any means so certain. But no harm came of her release.

18.   "LOVE IS ETERNAL"

Again Mary Lincoln went abroad. During at least a portion of her stay in Europe, Mrs. Lincoln and Robert were not in correspondence and he did not know her address. Part of the time she was in Pau, France, and part in Frankfort, Germany. In the former place in December, 1879, she suffered a serious injury. She was living economically and without a servant, and she mounted a step-ladder to adjust a picture hanging over the mantelpiece, when the step-ladder broke with her. She was confined to her bed for some time, afflicted with inflammation of the spinal cord and partial loss of power in the use of her legs.

When she thought she was able to travel she got as far as Nice, and there again was prostrated. At length she got on board ship, and, somewhat improved in health, she sailed for the home land. How she was received in America is related in the *New York Sun*, which tells this story of the home-coming, in October, 1880, of a woman who had been almost a queen:

"When the *Amerique* reached New York a throng was assembled on the dock and a greater throng was in the street outside the gates. During the tedious process of working the ship into her dock, there was a great crush in that part of the vessel where the gangplank was to be swung. Among the passengers who were here gathered was an aged lady; she was dressed plainly; her face was furrowed and her hair was streaked with white—this was the widow of Abraham Lincoln. She was almost unnoticed. She came alone across the ocean, but a nephew met her at quarantine. She had spent the last four years in the south of France. When the gangplank was swung aboard, Madame Bernhardt and her companions, including Madame Columbier, of the troupe, were the first to descend. The fellow voyagers of the actress pressed about her to bid her adieu, and a cheer was raised, which turned her head and provoked an astonished smile as she stepped upon the wharf. The gates were besieged, and there was some difficulty in bringing the carriage, which was to convey the actress to the hotel. She temporarily waited in the freight office at the entrance to the wharf. Mrs. Lincoln, leaning upon the arm of her nephew, walked toward the gate. A policeman touched the aged lady on the shoulder and bade her stand back. She retreated with her nephew into the line of spectators, while Manager Abbey's carriage was slowly brought in. Madame Bernhardt was handed in and the carriage made its way out through a mass of struggling longshoremen and idlers who pressed about it and stared into the open window. After it went out the others, who had been passengers on the *Amerique,* Mrs. Lincoln with the rest."

That simple newspaper story, it seems to me, can hardly be read without tears. Sarah Bernhardt never in all her career upon the stage played so tragic a rôle as Mary Todd Lincoln performed on that day.

Mrs. Lincoln tarried for a time in New York for medical

treatment. Doctor Lewis A. Sayre, to whom she confided her troubles, gained the impression that she still was exceedingly poor.

Mrs. Lincoln returned to Springfield, and to the home of her sister, Mrs. Edwards. It was the home in which she had first met Abraham Lincoln, the home in which they were married. She did not move among her old friends. She shut herself in her room, and hid herself as much as possible from her own kindred. She shut every window, and pulled down every shade, and moved, a pale ghost, among the trunks and boxes of her finery. To the few friends who called on her, she talked of the ingratitude of Congress, of the painful condition of poverty in which she was placed, and of the virtues of Abraham Lincoln.

Especially did she remember and repeat the story of their last ride together in the afternoon of the assassination, of their happy day-dream: their trip to the Pacific Coast to see the mining of the gold that was to pay the national debt, and also of their journey to Europe and the Holy Land. Let us be thankful that she had this memory to brighten the horizon where her sun had gone down.

Robert T. Lincoln did not meet his mother on the pier in New York. He wisely judged that it was safer to avoid the danger of a scene. She had not forgiven him for sending her to the hospital. But after she had returned to Springfield, Mr. and Mrs. Robert T. Lincoln went down from Chicago and visited her in the old Edwards home. She sat in her deep mourning dress as they entered, and they laid in her lap a baby, saying, "We have brought to you your granddaughter and namesake, Mary Lincoln."

She hugged the baby to her heart with maternal joy, and Robert was forgiven.

So, much, at least, it is good to know, that she did not die unreconciled to her eldest and only remaining son.

These days were mercifully shortened; she died of paralysis on July 16, 1882. The attending physician made a post-mortem examination, and issued a statement that for years she had been the victim of a cerebral disease. This ought to be deemed sufficient explanation of much that needed to be explained of her violence of temper and her unfortunate words and doings. When she died, she had six thousand dollars in cash and seventy-five thousand dollars in Government bonds in the top drawer of her bureau, and had innumerable boxes of silks, and shawls, which she had never opened and was destined never to wear.

So ended a sad existence. And yet, life has its strange compensations. Mary Todd had her radiant girlhood, her gay young womanhood, and a married life that brought its deep satisfactions. If she had her sorrows and antagonisms, she had also her warm friendships and her joys. She married the man she wanted to marry, and she had the full joy of motherhood. If she had a hard time in the White House, still she could say, and did say to Mrs. Grant, who thought she did not care to live there, "You better take it if you can get it; it's a pretty nice place!" Even her tragic widowhood had its golden memories, and when her mind was clear, it was in these she lived. Even the sad lives are not utterly sad. With all she suffered, Mary Todd had a reasonable share in life's satisfactions. We need not pretend that hers was not a tragic life, but neither have we occasion to forget that she found now and then a rose that grew among the thorns, and some of her roses were fragrant and bright.

The story of Mary Todd is a sad story, the story of a woman misunderstood and cruelly persecuted. But this much deserves to be remembered to her everlasting credit:

In the day when her heart was torn asunder, and most of her relations were on the opposing side, she was, all charges and rumors to the contrary notwithstanding, unflinchingly loyal to the Government of the United States. While she sometimes made her husband unhappy, and he not infrequently vexed her, she was an affectionate wife and mother, loving her husband with a passionate devotion and never failing in her faith in his character, his ability and his success. And he loved her; she was the only woman to whom he gave a ring, and in that ring were the words, "Love is eternal."

THE END

CHRONOLOGY

CHRONOLOGY

1725   December 29. Birth, in North Farnham Parish, Richmond County, Virginia, of Joseph Hanks, pioneer of Kentucky, and great-grandfather of President Lincoln.

1744   May 13. Birth, in Berks County, Pennsylvania, of Abraham Lincoln, later of Rockingham County, Virginia, pioneer to Kentucky, and grandfather of President Lincoln.

1765   October 9. Birth in Mecklenburg County, Virginia, of Henry Sparrow, who, April 30, 1790, married Lucy Hanks. He served as a soldier in the Revolutionary War, and died in 1840, in Mercer County, Kentucky. In this book the same year is assumed as the date of birth of his wife, Lucy Hanks. She certainly was not born earlier. In the census of 1810, the two were enumerated at some time in the summer or early autumn as both aged over 26 and under 45. Henry was 45 on October 9 of that year. It is possible Lucy was born in the first half of 1766, and that she was only 18 when her daughter Nancy was born.

1770   August 12. Marriage license to Abraham Lincoln, grandfather of President Lincoln. Bride not named in license record, but the name of the only known wife was Bathsheba.

1778   January 5. Birth in Rockingham County, Virginia, of Thomas Lincoln, father of President Lincoln.

1780   February 18. Abraham Lincoln and wife Bathsheba sold their farm in Rockingham County, Virginia; she relinquished her dower rights September 8, 1781. The family removed to Kentucky, apparently in 1782.

1783–4 Birth on Patterson's Creek, Hampshire County, Virginia, now in Mineral County, West Virginia, of Nancy Hanks, mother of President Lincoln.

1784   March 9. Joseph Hanks mortgaged his farm in that part of Hampshire County, Virginia, which is now Mineral County, West Virginia, and with his family, consisting as the census of 1782 shows, of eleven persons, all white (presumably himself, wife, five sons and four daughters) removed to Kentucky.

1786   May. Captain Abraham Lincoln, grandfather of the President, was killed by an Indian on Long Run of Floyd's Fork, in Jefferson County, Kentucky. His widow Bathsheba removed to Washington County where she reared her family. Soon after 1801 she removed with her daughter Nancy to Mill Creek, Hardin County, and died there, about 1836.

1790   April 26. Marriage bond of Henry Sparrow to marry Lucy Hanks; they were married by Rev. John Bailey.

1793   January 8. Will of Joseph Hanks executed; proved at Bardstown, Nelson County, Kentucky, May 14, 1793.

1795   December 10. Jesse Friend and Mary Hanks were married by Rev. Josiah Dodge in Hardin County, Kentucky.

1796   Thomas Sparrow married Elizabeth Hanks, and these became foster parents of Nancy Hanks, President Lincoln's mother.

1806   June 12. Thomas Lincoln and Nancy Hanks, married at Beechland, Washington County, Ky., by Rev. Jesse Head. Thomas Lincoln was born in Virginia January 5, 1778, and died at Goose Nest Prairie near Charleston, Illinois, January 15, 1851. Nancy Hanks was born in Mike's Run of Patterson's Creek, Virginia, in 1783 or 1784, and died near Gentryville, Spencer County, Indiana, October 5, 1818.

1807   February 10. Sarah, daughter of Thomas and Nancy Lincoln, was born at Elizabethtown, Kentucky. Married Aaron Grigsby, August 2, 1826, died January 20, 1828.

1809   Sunday, February 12. Abraham Lincoln, son of Thomas and Nancy Hanks Lincoln, born on Rock Spring Farm or Sinking Spring Farm, now known as Lincoln Farm, near what is now Hodgenville, in Larue, which then was part of Hardin County, Kentucky.

1809   March 1. Territory of Illinois organized.

1816   Autumn. Thomas and Nancy Lincoln, with their son Abraham, then aged seven, and their daughter Sarah, aged nine, migrated from Kentucky to a farm on Pigeon Creek, near what is now Gentryville, Indiana.

1816   December 11. Indiana admitted to the Union.

1818   October 5. Nancy Hanks Lincoln, mother of Abraham, died of milk-sickness, in Spencer County, Indiana.

1818.   November 4. Mary Todd born in Lexington, Kentucky. This is the date given by her sister.

1818   December 3. Illinois admitted to the Union.

1819   December 2. Thomas Lincoln, married at Elizabethtown, Ky., Sarah (Bush), widow of Daniel Johnston, who was born December 13, 1788. Daniel Johnston had died in October, 1818.

1823   June 7. Thomas and Sally Lincoln united with the Little Baptist Church, he by letter and she by experience.

1826   August 2. Sarah Lincoln married Aaron Grigsby.

1828   January 20. Sarah Lincoln Grigsby died and was buried in the Little Pigeon Churchyard.

1828   Abraham Lincoln, aged nineteen, made his first journey to New Orleans on a flatboat.

1830   March 1. The Lincoln family started upon their fifteen days' journey, arriving in the middle of the month at Decatur, Illinois, nine miles west from which town they made their first home in that state. After assisting his father to build the log house which was to be the new home, Abraham

Lincoln, now twenty-one years of age, left home, and thereafter labored as an independent man.

1831   March.   Abraham Lincoln left Macon County, Illinois, in a canoe; and in the employ of Denton Offutt, assisted in the construction of a flatboat on which he made his second voyage to New Orleans.

1831   April 19.   The flatboat stuck on the Rutledge dam at New Salem, Illinois.

1831   July.   Abraham Lincoln returned to New Salem, which was his home until March 15, 1837.

1832   March.   Abraham Lincoln declared himself a candidate for the Legislature.

1832   April 21.   Abraham Lincoln chosen Captain of Company in Black Hawk War. Company disbanded May 27. Lincoln reenlisted as a private in another company, for a period of twenty days; and on June 16 again reenlisted as a private, and was finally mustered out, at Whitewater, Wisconsin, July 10, 1832; returning to New Salem about the end of July.

1833   May 7.   Abraham Lincoln appointed postmaster of New Salem, a position which he held until the post-office was abandoned in 1837.

1834   August.   Abraham Lincoln elected a member of the Legislature, and thereafter reelected in 1836, 1838 and 1840.

1835   August 25.   Ann Rutledge died.

1836   Summer.   Mrs. Bennett Able left New Salem for Kentucky having previously entered into a half-joking agreement with Abraham Lincoln that he should marry her sister, Mary Owens, whom she promised to bring back with her, an agreement with which Lincoln was "confoundedly well pleased." Mary Owens arrived in New Salem, August 1.

1837   March 15.   Lincoln left New Salem and took up his residence in Springfield, rooming with Joshua F. Speed, above the latter's store, and boarding with William Butler.

1837   April 12. Abraham Lincoln and John T. Stuart entered into a partnership which continued until May 14, 1841; the firm name was Stuart and Lincoln.

1838   Spring. Mary Owens returned to Kentucky, and her relations with Lincoln terminated.

1839   Mary Todd came to reside in Springfield with her married sister, Mrs. Ninian W. Edwards.

1840   Abraham Lincoln became engaged to Mary Todd.

1841   January 1. "The fatal first of January" alleged to have been the date fixed for the Todd-Lincoln wedding, from which it is alleged Lincoln absented himself. This and all statements related to it are hotly denied by relatives of Mrs. Lincoln.

1841   Lincoln proposed to Sarah Rickard (she gives the date as of 1840, but appears to be quite certainly in error.)

1841   May 14. Abraham Lincoln and Stephen T. Logan entered upon a partnership under the firm name of Logan and Lincoln, whose notices as a partnership for the practise of law continued to run until March 27, 1845, though the formal partnership may have been dissolved a few weeks earlier.

1842   Friday, November 4. Abraham Lincoln and Mary Todd were married in the home of the bride's sister, Mrs. Ninian W. Edwards.

1843   August 1. Robert Todd Lincoln, son of Abraham and Mary Lincoln, born. Married September 24, 1868, Mary, daughter of James and Ann Eliza Harlan; died in Manchester Vermont, July 26, 1926.

1844   Sometime in the spring, the firm of Logan and Lincoln was dissolved, and Abraham Lincoln took as his third Springfield partner, William H. Herndon; the firm name was Lincoln and Herndon, and it was never formally dissolved.

1846   March 10. Edward Baker Lincoln, son of Abraham and Mary Lincoln, born; died in Springfield, February 1, 1850.

1847-8 Abraham Lincoln served for a single term as a Representative in Congress.

1850   December 21. William Wallace Lincoln, son of Abraham and Mary Lincoln, born; died in the White House, February 20, 1862.

1851   January 17. Thomas Lincoln, father of President Lincoln, died at his home on Goose Nest Prairie, Coles County, Illinois.

1853   April 4. Thomas or "Tad" Lincoln, son of Abraham and Mary Lincoln, born; died in Chicago, July 15, 1871.

1856   Abraham Lincoln became a Republican; on May 29 delivered his "lost speech" at organization of that party in Bloomington, Illinois.

1858   Abraham Lincoln a candidate for the United States Senate; defeated; the Lincoln and Douglas Debates made Lincoln a national figure.

1860   February 27. Abraham Lincoln's Cooper Union Address.

1860   May 9. Abraham Lincoln selected by the State Republican Convention at Decatur, Illinois, as its candidate for the presidency.

1860   May 18. Abraham Lincoln nominated for the presidency of the United States by the National Republican Convention, in Chicago.

1860   November 6. Abraham Lincoln elected President.

1861   Monday, February 11. Mr. and Mrs. Lincoln and family left Springfield for Washington.

1861   Monday, March 4. Abraham Lincoln inaugurated president of the United States.

1864   November 8. Lincoln reelected.

1865   March 4. Abraham Lincoln's Second Inaugural.

1865   April 9. General Robert E. Lee surrendered the main Confederate army to General U. S. Grant.

1865   April 14. Abraham Lincoln shot at Ford's Theater, Washington; and died next morning.

1865   May 4. Abraham Lincoln buried in Springfield.

1866   Sunday, October 14. William H. Herndon's visit to grave of Ann Rutledge; Friday, November 16, his lecture in the old court-house in Springfield on Ann Rutledge.

1869   December 10. Sarah Bush Lincoln, widow of Thomas, and stepmother of the President Lincoln, died at her home, in Goose Nest Prairie, Illinois.

1871   July 15. Death of Thomas ("Tad") Lincoln, in Chicago.

1882   July 16. Mary Todd Lincoln, widow of Abraham Lincoln, died at Springfield, Illinois, and was buried beside her husband.

1926   July 26. Death at Manchester, Vermont, of Robert Todd Lincoln, last surviving son of President Lincoln.

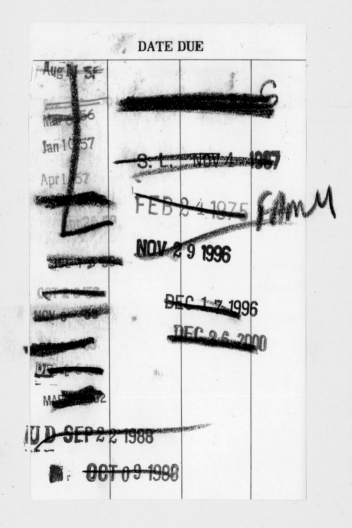